Beyond the UN Charter:

Peace, Security and the Role of Justice

This book is based on the annual Conference

FROM PEACE TO JUSTICE

"Beyond the UN Charter:
Peace, Security and the Role of Justice"

held on 5 and 6 April 2007 in The Hague, The Netherlands

organized by

THE HAGUE
ACADEMIC COALITION

FROM PEACE TO JUSTICE SERIES

BEYOND THE UN CHARTER:
Peace, Security and the Role of Justice

Edited by

Olivier Ribbelink

Hague Academic Press
An Imprint of T·M·C·ASSER PRESS

Published by Hague Academic Press, an imprint of T·M·C·Asser Press
P.O.Box 16163, 2500 BD The Hague, The Netherlands

<www.asserpress.nl>

T·M·C·Asser Press' English language books are distributed exclusively by:

Cambridge University Press, The Edinburgh Building, Shaftesbury Road,
Cambridge CB2 2RU, UK,
or
for customers in the USA, Canada and Mexico:
Cambridge University Press, 100 Brook Hill Drive, West Nyack, NY 10994-2133, USA

<www.cambridge.org>

ISBN: 978-90-6704-282-6

Cover photograph: ANP Photo © AFP

FOREWORD

I am pleased to introduce *Beyond the UN Charter: Peace, Security and the Role of Justice*, the fruitful result of the Third Conference of the Hague Academic Coalition (HAC)* entitled *From Peace to Justice.*

As the theme of the Conference, which was held in The Hague in April 2006, we chose to focus on a problem of a real and pressing nature: contemporary threats to international peace and security and whether or not we can address and resolve them within existing legal and political structures. This is a very relevant and timely topic. We find ourselves at a pivotal moment in history, when the peace and security of the world seems to be under threat from many different directions, and many accepted wisdoms are being questioned and challenged.

Observance of the *jus ad bellum* by states, the rules regulating the use of force, while obviously still necessary, is not in itself a guarantee to ensure our peace or security. Threats to our international peace and security posed by new types of non-state actors, including terrorists, are not the only ones we need to worry about.

International peace and security are challenged by phenomena such as massive violations of human rights or humanitarian law, within states and by both state and non-state actors. They face threats in particular from contingencies such as public health crises, including those posed by, for example, Asian Flu or HIV/AIDS, from the growing deterioration of our environment and the far-reaching consequences this will have, not least in terms of the pressure it will put on ever diminishing natural resources, and thus, possibly, of generating armed conflicts. Thus, we cannot only think of international peace and security as 'just' the absence of aggressive behaviour by states. Its sustainability does not only depend on refraining from certain types of behaviour, but also on taking positive action. We will not escape disaster by remaining inactive. Our health, safety and security depend on taking action now to avert disaster in relation to these threats to our safety and our very existence.

---

* See p. IX.

For the 2006 *From Peace to Justice Conference* choices had to be made. It made sense to focus our attention and efforts on the types of challenges to international peace and security which are at least perceived today as being amongst the most serious, and which are certainly generating the most discussion. And it made even more sense to place our discussion in the context of the larger debate regarding Security Council reform.

We are extremely proud and honoured that Her Royal Highness Princess Margriet of The Netherlands opened the Conference. She is well known for her strong support for and interest in issues of peace and justice, and I specifically want to mention her important work for the International Red Cross and Red Crescent Movement. Until the end of 2004 she shared its Standing Commission. Since November 2005 she has been a Member of the Board of the ICRC Federation. She is also the Vice-chairperson of the Netherlands Red Cross Society. Furthermore, I would like to mention her role as a Member of the Board of Recommendation of the *Yearbook of International Humanitarian Law*, which is published by one of the members of the Academic Coalition, the T.M.C. Asser Institute.

This book, as well as the Conference on which it is based, would not have been possible without the help of the highly motivated staff of the Hague Academic Coalition, of whom there are too many people to mention in this Foreword. However, as the General Director of the lead partner of this Conference, I would like to thank Dr Avril McDonald and Dr Olivier Ribbelink of the T.M.C. Asser Institute, who were responsible for developing the programme for the Conference. Furthermore, I would like to pay tribute to Dr Olivier Ribbelink for his work as the editor of the book that lies before you.

Last but not least, I would like to thank the Province of South Holland, the Municipality of The Hague and the French Embassy for their support.

Prof. Dr Frans A. NELISSEN
General Director T.M.C. Asser Institute
Chairman Hague Academic Coalition

PREFACE

The world today is a very different place than it was when the UN Charter was adopted in 1945. In the intervening years, the main threat to international peace and security foreseen by the drafters of the Charter – attacks on states by other states – has receded, but the world can hardly be said to have become more peaceful or secure. Instead, new threats and potential threats to international peace and security have emerged, which, while no less serious, are not easy or possible to address within the existing legal framework or existing institutions.

These new threats include, but are not limited to, attacks on states by states, including the possibility of rogue states using weapons of mass destruction (WMD), the changing nature of warfare and methods and means of warfare, new types of armed conflict and chaotic situations which cannot easily be accommodated within the traditional framework of the law of armed conflict, new actors, including armed opposition groups, terrorists, and suicide bombers, who present challenges to the established system of international peace and security, which were not envisaged by the drafters of the UN Charter.

We can think, for example, of the challenges to states from *non-state actors*, such as multinational corporations, which cannot be controlled by one state. Their growing power represents challenges to the security of small states in particular, and to human rights norms.

Then, of course, there is *terrorism*, including the possibility of the use of WMD by terrorists, counter-terrorism, including in the context of the 'Global War on Terror', and related to this, the expansive new interpretations of traditional concepts such as self-defence (including anticipatory or pre-emptive self-defence), and a re-embracing of old ideas, such as unilateral self-help. We should not forget about the challenges to *human rights* in the post-September 11 environment, including the perceived conflict between human rights and state (and even international) security, or about global warming and other types of environmental degradation and destruction, as well as public health crises and their impact on peace and security.

The Third Annual *From Peace to Justice Conference* of the Hague Academic Coalition (HAC)*, held in April 2006 in The Hague, with the general theme 'Be-

* See p. IX.

yond the UN Charter: Peace, Security and the Role of Justice', focused on current and emerging threats to international peace and security, which cannot easily or at all be addressed within the framework of the Charter. It aimed to identify some of the most urgent new non-traditional threats to international peace and security; and to examine whether, and to what extent, these can be addressed within the Charter framework, to discuss how the UN Organization could reform in order to address these threats that are no less serious than traditional ones, and finally to analyse the role of new international organizations in contributing to international peace, security and justice and their relationship with the United Nations, particularly the Security Council.

As usual, the Conference started with a plenary session, followed by workshops dealing with specific topics, the results of the workshop discussions being reverted to the plenary closing session.

In the three parts of this book the opinions and conclusions of the Conference concerning the main theme and the two sub-themes are brought together, each contributor addressing the subject-matter from his or her own angle.

Part One combines the four contributions from the plenary session, under the general theme of the conference. The keynote speech on the main theme of the Conference, delivered by Philippe Sands, University of London, is followed by chapters on the response to new threats to peace and security within the framework of the UN Charter, the role of the ICC in the emerging system of international justice, and on the reform of the Security Council.

The other two parts group together articles that deal with more specific topics. In Part Two, there are contributions on military intervention as a legitimate means in international law and international politics. They range from a discussion of the Comprehensive Nuclear-Test-Ban Treaty, international negotiations, multinational peace-support operations, the link between UN reform and the transformation of NATO, and the legitimation of military operations. The articles in Part Three deal with the re-establishment of peace and security after the genocide in Rwanda, and discuss topics as diverse as the role of the ICTR, the role of women, and the importance of Truth and Reconciliation Commissions.

As always, most contributions are in English, the others are in French.

The Hague, March 2008 Olivier RIBBELINK

THE HAGUE ACADEMIC COALITION

The Hague Academic Coalition (HAC) is a consortium of academic institutions in the fields of international relations, international law and international development. It was established to promote collaborative efforts between these six institutions. Specifically, the HAC intends to promote research, education and public debate in support of the development of international policy, law, governance and international negotiations towards justice, peace and sustainable development.

As part of this broad objective, the HAC in particular seeks to support the work of the various international courts, tribunals and other international organisations based in The Hague. Joint HAC activities in support of this mission include:

- annual conferences on topics of relevance given the mission statement, organised by members of the consortium;
- the provision of postgraduate and post-academic courses relevant to students and practitioners in the fields indicated above;
- scholarly and policy-orientated research as well as consultancy activities;
- publications;
- public events targeted at the international community in The Hague, aiming at practitioners and students of international law, diplomacy and development;
- management of the Hague Justice Portal.

Within the HAC's present membership, the Carnegie Foundation (more specifically the Peace Palace Library), the Grotius Centre (Leiden University, Campus The Hague), The Hague Institute for the Internationalisation of Law (HIIL) and the T.M.C. Asser Instituut work in the field of international (and European) law, whereas the Netherlands Institute for International relations 'Clingendael' and the Institute of Social Studies (ISS) focus on international relations, international political economy and development studies. For further information, you may consult <http://www.haguejusticeportal.net>.

TABLE OF CONTENTS

LIST OF ABBREVIATIONS

ANA	Afghan National Army
ATA	Afghan Transitional Authority
AU	African Union
AWACS	Airborne Warning and Control Station
C.I.J. Recueil	Cour internationale de justice, *Recueil des arrêts, avis consultatifs et ordonnances*
CDI	Commission du Droit International (see also ILC)
CEDEAO	Communauté économique des États de l'Afrique de l'Ouest (see also ECOWAS)
CFE	Conventional Forces in Europe
CIJ	Cour Internationale de Justice (see also ICJ)
CIRGL	Conférence Internationale sur la Paix, la Sécurité et le Développement sur la Région des Grands Lacs
CSCE	Conference on Security and Cooperation in Europe
CTBT	Comprehensive Nuclear Test-Ban Treaty
DDR	Disarmament, Demobilization and Reintegration
DPRK	Democratic Peoples Republic of Korea
DRC	Democratic Republic of Congo
EC	European Communities
ECOWAS	Economic Community of Western African States (see also CEDEAO)
ESDP	European Security and Defence
FERFAP	la Fédération des Réseaux des Femmes Africaines pour la Paix
FIDH	Fédération Internationale des Ligues des Droits de l'Homme
FMI	Fonds monétaire international (see also IMF)
FMN	Firme MultiNational/Multinational Corporation

GATT	General Agreement on Tariffs and Trade
HAC	The Hague Academic Coalition
HIV/AIDS	VIH/SIDA
IAEA	International Atomic Energy Agency
ICC	International Criminal Court
ICCPR	International Convention on Civil and Political Rights
ICJ	International Court of Justice (see also CIJ)
ICRC	International Committee of the Red Cross
ICTR	International Criminal Tribunal for Rwanda (see also TPIR)
ICTY	International Tribunal for the former Yugoslavia
ILC	International Law Commission (see also CDI)
IMF	International Monetary Fund (see also FMI)
ISAF	International Security Assistance Force
KFOR	Kosovo Force
MBS	Mutual Beneficial Stalemate
MDR	Mouvement Démocratique Républicain
MEO	Mutual Enticing Opportunity
MHS	Mutual Hurting Stalemate
MONUC	UN Organization Mission in the Democratic Republic of the Congo / Mission des Nations Unies en République démocratique du Congo
NATO	North Atlantic Treaty Organisation
NGO	non-governmental organisation (see also ONG)
NOVIB	Nederlandse Organisatie Voor Internationale Bijstand (OXFAM Novib)
NPT	Nuclear Non-Proliferation Treaty
NRF	NATO Response Force
NWS	Nuclear Weapons States
OEF	Operation Enduring Freedom
OMP	Opération de maintien de la paix / Peacekeeping operation
ONG	Organisation non-gouvernementel (see also NGO)
ONU	Organisation des Nations Unies (see also UN)
OPLAN	operational plan

PEU	peace enforcement unit
POER	programme d'observatoire des élections au Rwanda
POW	prisoner of war
PRT	Provincial Reconstruction Team
ROE	Rules of Engagement
RPA	Rwandan Patriotic Army
RPF	Rwandese Patriotic Front
SACEUR	Supreme Allied Commander Europe
SALT	Strategic Arms Limitations Talks
SC	UN Security Council
SCSL	Special Court for Sierra Leone
SDN	Societé des Nations / League of Nations
SFIR	Stabilization Force in Iraq
SFIR	Stabilization Force
SHIRBRIG	UN Stand-By Forces High Readiness Brigade
SNV	Stichting Nederlandse Vrijwilligers
START	Strategic Arms Reduction Treaty
T.I.G.	travaux d'Intérêt Général
TPIR	Tribunal Pénal International pour le Rwanda (see also ICTR)
UK	United Kingdom
UN	United Nations (see also ONU)
UNAMA	UN Assistance Mission in Afghanistan
UNAMIR	UN Assistance Mission for Rwanda
UNEF	UN peacekeeping force for the Middle East
UNESCO	UN Educational, Scientific and Cultural Organization
UNMEE	UN Mission in Ethiopia and Eritrea
UNSAS	UN System of Standby Arrangements
UNSC	UN Security Council
US	United States
VIH/SIDA	HIV/AIDS
WMD	weapons of mass destruction
WTO	World Trade Organization
WWII	World War II

WELCOME ADDRESS*

H.R.H. Princess Margriet of The Netherlands

As you know, our country is always governed by a coalition. The Hague Academic Coalition, under whose auspices we are meeting here today, is also a coalition, but of a very different kind: not a political body, but a consortium of six academic institutions. They have earned a reputation, individually and as a group, in the disciplines of international law, international relations and international cooperation. It is fitting – and of course by no means a coincidence – that they are all based in this equally international city. A warm welcome to all participants who join us to further explore the cause of peace and justice.

I was delighted to accept the Hague Academic Coalition's invitation to say a few words of welcome today at this annual conference. Not only is the theme, From Peace to Justice, important in itself. I also feel a personal affinity with it, since I serve, and have served for many years, the Red Cross and Red Crescent Movement, an organisation, whose mission is so closely related to today's theme.

Allow me therefore to make my observations from a Red Cross perspective. The Red Cross and Red Crescent Movement, a unique network of National Societies (NS) present in almost every country, is the only network which gains its strength through its combination of local, national and international action. It is a global Movement, yet it works locally and that is where it makes an impact, at grassroots level.

In particular as Chair of the Standing Commission of the International Red Cross, I witnessed the role the Movement plays in the world community's laborious attempts to defend peace and justice, especially in countries where

O. Ribbelink (ed.), Beyond the UN Charter: Peace, Security and the Role of Justice

violence and injustice have taken root. I am not talking only about the assistance and protection the Red Cross provides, but also about the fundamental principles on which it operates: humanity, impartiality (or non-discrimination), neutrality, independence, voluntary service, unity and universality. Acting upon these principles contributes in itself to bringing countries and people closer together and advancing the cause of peace.

World-wide more than 100 million volunteers and 125,000 professional staff are responsible for immediate response in conflict and disaster situations, for community mobilisation, social work and health services. The Red Cross and Red Crescent can build bridges where racial, religious, ethnic, political and social tensions may divide people.

The Red Cross carries weight in many areas and arenas. Thanks to its observer status at the United Nations it can put its concerns on the international community's agenda. It also plays an important role in promoting and developing humanitarian law, both nationally and internationally. Since the early 1990s, humanitarian law has gained visibility as the international community has created instruments for its implementation. It is no more the paper tiger some cynically may have called it some years ago.

Institutions have now been put in place, like the special tribunals and the International Criminal Court whose decisions are further developing and implementing international humanitarian law.

In doing so these institutions contribute to the fundamental values enshrined in it. The fact that all this is occurring in The Hague can only reinforce our feeling that the conference we are opening today belongs here.

Ladies and gentlemen,

On your way to this World Forum Convention Centre you may have noticed the major construction work that is going on here. We might see a certain symbolism in that. We still need some equally major construction work if we are to bring worldwide peace and justice closer to completion.

I wish you every success in taking us a step further. Humanity will benefit from it.

Part I
Beyond the UN Charter: Peace, Security and the Role of Justice

Chapter 1
PEACE, SECURITY AND THE ROLE OF JUSTICE

Philippe Sands*

Issues of international legality are very much in the air in Britain. The May 2005 General Election was dominated by Iraq, and in particular the circumstances in which the British Prime Minister took Britain to war. My book *Lawless World* was published shortly before the election, and describes the way in which the British Government misled Parliament and the public on the intelligence relating to weapons of mass destruction and on the presentation of the British Attorney General's legal advice on the legality of the Iraq war. Earlier this week the British Secretary of Defence – Mr. Reid – gave a lecture in which he asked whether the rules of international law were adequate to deal with new threats.

Last week I was in the United States (US), and the issue of the circumstances in which President Bush took his country to war, and the reasonableness of his Administration's belief that Saddam Hussein's Iraq had weapons of mass destruction, is now firmly on the agenda. The door is open to a comprehensive examination of that issue. I believe that the road to war in Iraq is one that is tainted with international illegality. The conduct of the so-called – and in my view wholly misconceived – 'war on terror' has caused the Bush Administration to abandon the rules of international law. It has done so deliberately and systematically. It has done so in its efforts to create a legal black whole at Guantanamo and to deny the applicability of the Geneva Conventions on the treatment of prisoners of war to Taleban and Al-Qaeda detainees. It has done so in a deliberate policy of detainee interrogations that has sought to avoid the constraints of the 1984 Convention on the prohibition of torture. It has done so in waging an illegal war against Iraq which was

* Professor at University College London, and QC Matrix Chambers.

O. Ribbelink (ed.), Beyond the UN Charter: Peace, Security and the Role of Justice

not authorized by the UN Security Council and was not justified – or even claimed to be justified – as self-defence. And it has done so in its failure to meet its international obligations in pursuing a policy of extraordinary rendition from Iraq and elsewhere.

All of this undermines peace, justice and security. We expect more from the country that has done so much to create the modern system of international rules. Facing a real threat, the systematic dismemberment of international rules has undermined the morale of American troops and others involved in promoting American security, undermined relations with allies and friends, and exposed a great number of individuals to criminal liability. How has this happened, and what is to be done?

Before turning to those issues, let me provide some background. This story begins in August 1941, on a warship off the coast of Newfoundland, at a meeting between US President Franklin Delano Roosevelt and British Prime Minister Winston Churchill. It is a time of great challenge for Britain and the US, yet these two men decide that what they need to do is draw up a blueprint for the new international order once the Nazis have been vanquished. What is needed is a new rules-based system, to replace the then-existing arrangements that allowed a state to do whatever was not expressly prohibited by international law. And since not much was prohibited, there was a great deal states could do. They could wage war without restriction. They could commit genocide against their own populations. They could torture detainees. That was the world of the 1930s.

Roosevelt and Churchill set out to change that. They drafted a one page document – the Atlantic Charter – by which they intended to make known, as they put it, 'certain common principles in the national policies of their respective countries on which they base their hopes for a better future for the world'.[1] The Atlantic Charter was short and visionary and identified eight principles, revolving around three key pillars reflected in the UN Charter: a general obligation on states to refrain from the use of force, except in self-defence or where the UN Security Council or a regional body has authorised them to use force; a commitment to human rights, to maintain the 'inherent dignity' and the 'equal and inalienable rights' of all members of the human

[1] 14 August 1941, reproduced in *Lawless World: America and the making and Breaking of Global Rules* (Allen Lane, 2005), p. 240. The latest edition was published in paperback by Penguin in February 2006.

family; and an undertaking to promote economic liberalisation through the adoption of free trade rules and related international obligations in the fields of foreign investment and intellectual property.

These are the three pillars that have remained in place for the last sixty years. Overarching them was a commitment to the international rule of law. Roosevelt and Churchill committed themselves to recasting the eight principles of the Atlantic Charter into binding legal instruments. And this they did, with later assistance from Truman and Attlee. In a remarkable period between 1941 and 1949 the modern system of international law was put in place through a series of far-reaching treaties which have now received very broad acceptance. In the spring of 1945 51 states agreed on the creation of the United Nations at San Francisco, crystallising in law the modern rules governing the use of force and promoting human rights. That was followed by the UN General Assembly's Universal Declaration of Human Rights – Eleanor Roosevelt's baby which in turn led to the covenants on civil and political rights and on economic and social rights, to regional treaties like the European Convention on Human Rights, and to the Human Rights Act 1998, a singular achievement of the Prime Minister's first government.

The day after the Universal Declaration was adopted, the General Assembly agreed on the world's first human rights treaty, the 1948 Convention on the prohibition of genocide. It was followed by other specialised human rights treaties, such as the 1984 Torture Convention, which obliged its parties to prosecute or extradite torturers and which did away with Senator Pinochet's right to claim immunity before the English courts (also in 1998, it turns out that was a big year for international law). By then also the Allies had agreed on other new rules to stop individuals doing nasty things in the name of the state: the Statute of the Nuremburg Military Tribunal gave birth to the new field of international criminal law. This would eventually lead to the Yugoslav and Rwanda tribunals and then (again in 1998) to the Rome Statute of the International Criminal Court (ICC). There is a direct line from Nuremburg to the indictment and arrest of Charles Taylor, former President of Liberia, and his transfer to the Special Court for Sierra Leone and his trial in The Hague. In the same post-war period, the US and Britain led international efforts to negotiate the four Geneva Conventions on the law of armed conflict, including Geneva Convention III on the treatment of prisoners of war. This is the same instrument that was to become the centre of so much attention in relation to events at Guantanamo, Afghanistan and Abu Ghraib.

Developments in international law were no less far-reaching in the economic field: the Bretton Woods Agreement created the World Bank and the International Monetary Fund, in 1944. And in 1948 agreement was reached on the General Agreement on Tariffs and Trade – the GATT – the world's first global free trade rules and the parent of today's World Trade organisation, the WTO. By *any* standard, these were remarkable achievements in a very short period of time.

The new rules-based system initiated by the Atlantic Charter was not altruism at play. It reflected a view that international rules would promote Anglo-American interests, serve as a bulwark against the Soviet model, and emphasise values to be marshalled against Nazi and fascist threats. But the simple point is that international rules were seen as creating opportunities, not imposing constraints. The Atlantic Charter had an immediate and far-reaching impact. Writing in his autobiography, Nelson Mandela describes the Atlantic Charter as reaffirming his faith in human dignity: 'some in the west saw the Charter as empty promises', he wrote, 'but not those of us in Africa. Inspired by the Atlantic Charter and the fight of the Allies against tyranny and aggression, the ANC created its own charter … which called for full citizenship for all Africans, the right to buy land and the repeal of all discriminating legislation.'

Over the next sixty years the principles set forth in the Atlantic Charter defined a new international order. A great number of international agreements have been adopted since then, touching on issues that affect each and every one of us very directly. Agreements were concluded on trade, investment, commerce, air transport, oceans, boundaries, and human rights. The great majority of these rules are not controversial. They work efficiently and well. They establish the minimum standards necessary for cooperation in an increasingly interdependent world. The emergence of this great body of rules reflects a silent global revolution, and most people are blissfully unaware quite how much international law there is. This does raise serious issues about accountability and legitimacy in international law-making – it is, e.g., a matter of real concern that in the United Kingdom (UK) treaties are generally not debated by Parliament, unless they address an issue of EC law. By all accounts there was for instance no parliamentary debate about the WTO agreements.

I would not leave you with the impression that I am starry-eyed about international rules, to suggest that global rules can sort out all the wrongs of the world, or create an era of peace and security. Plainly they cannot. Events over the last sixty years demonstrate that. There are a great number of rules which require attention. And certainly the world has changed greatly in the period since the UN was created. The number of states has grown from around fifty to around twohundred, a result of decolonisation. The range of issues requiring international cooperation – and hence international legislation – has also grown, to include issues like the environment, tourism and consumer safety. New international actors have emerged: the monopoly of states has diminished and international organisations, non-governmental organisations (NGOs), corporations, individuals are demanding a role in ways that present profound challenges for an international legal order constructed on the assumption that the global order revolved around states alone. Failed states, peripatetic travellers, permeable national borders, malign non-governmental actors like Al Qaeda and other terrorist groups, and the proliferation of weapons of mass destruction, are but some of the issues that pose very real challenges to the established international legal order. Do they require us to revisit the basis of the post World War II (WWII) legal settlement? President Bush has made the argument, and so has Prime Minister Blair, most recently at a speech he gave in Sedgefield in March 2004, which some have seen as an endorsement of Bush's call for a right to pre-emptive strike.

Are the existing rules adequate? That question has been asked with increasing frequency since 9/11. It is said by some that the international legal order is no longer up to the task it was designed to address in the period after WWII, in the face of current challenges. It is said that the rules governing terrorism, wars and rogue states are inadequate. And it is said that the international rules threaten American security and sovereignty. To be sure, those who make this claim most frequently and loudly are often associated with the neo-conservative elements that dominated the agenda of George W. Bush's first Administration. In the months before 9/11 it was clear that the Bush Administration was committed to remaking the international rules, to limiting or killing off the rules that were seen to be too constraining. Many members of this group had been in office in the first Bush Presidency, and they regrouped during the Clinton Administration. Plans were set out in various manifestos. I commend to you in particular the Statement of Principles of the Project for a New American Century, to get a flavour of what was being proposed in the late 1990s (although you may also want to take a look at <www.bushcountry.org>). Tapping on a rich vein of American exceptionalism, the key targets include international law and the rules which had allowed the detention of Senator Pinochet, the Statute of the new International Criminal Court, the Kyoto Protocol on global warming (1997), and various arms control treaties. Each of these treaties would, it was argued, constrain America, undermine sovereignty, and threaten US national security.

Within weeks of taking office in January 2001 President Bush had set a new agenda: the Kyoto Protocol and the ICC statute were 'unsigned', a protocol on biological weapons scuppered, and a new policy of 'a la carte multilateralism' put in place: you pick and choose the bits of international law you like and get rid of the rest. John Bolton was appointed as one of President Bush's senior foreign policy advisers as Under Secretary for Arms Control and International Security at the US Department of State. He would oversee Iran's compliance with its nuclear obligations under the Non Proliferation Treaty. This is the same John Bolton who had, a little earlier, declared that treaties were only political and 'not legally binding'. And very early on a small group of neo-con lawyers were parachuted into key positions at the US Justice Department and the Pentagon. Although their views were not widely shared, particularly among career civil servants and the military, they would come to dominate decision-making.

The point I make is a simple one: even before 9/11 the conditions were in place for an assault on Roosevelt's vision of international order based on new rules. From this perspective, 9/11 presented a terrific opportunity to promote the 'anti-international law' project. Little time was lost. Within days of the attacks on the World Trade Centre and the Pentagon, lawyers in the Bush administration had been charged with putting in place the new legal rules which were necessary to prosecute the response. On the key legal issues there was no consultation with allies, not even Britain. An early decision was taken to characterise the response to Al-Qaeda and international terrorism as a 'war on terrorism'. This had the effect of taking it outside the scope of the ordinary criminal law and into the rules of armed conflict. It turned criminals into warriors. But these rules placed limits on what you could do to detainees. Prisoners of war (POWs) could not be questioned. Acting unilaterally in a manner that was wholly inconsistent with the requirements of the Geneva Conventions, the Administration determined that individual detainees would be placed outside the constraints of the law. The Guantanamo detention facility on land, once leased from Cuba, was chosen because Administration lawyers had advised that its location outside US territory would provide a means of redress under US constitutional law and international law. Guantanamo was created as a 'legal black hole', as the English Court of Appeal later described it.

It is striking that those lawyers in the Administration who conjured up this scheme were conscious that international rules placed constraints on what could be done, not least in relation to conditions of detention and interrogation. The legal advices that have come into the public domain recognise the existence of the international rules but not their well-established consequences. The country that had done more than any other to put in place a new rules-based system was using 9/11 to ditch some of those rules. International law was now part of the problem, not the solution. The year 2002 was not a good one for international law, although quite how bad it was did not become clear until much later, when the legal advice started leaking out into the public domain.

The neo-con lawyers who ventured to speak publicly did not pull their punches. White House General Counsel Alberto Gonzales determined that the Geneva Convention on the treatment of POWs simply did not apply to Al-Qaeda or Taliban because their members were unlawful combatants. The International Committee of the Red Cross (ICRC) – guardian of the rules – has consistently refused to accept this claim. The Administration's view is novel and ditches past US practice, generating a sharp response from US military lawyers who saw straight away that abandoning the rules would leave the US military highly exposed. The new US view was based on the belief that international terrorism had created a new paradigm. Gonzales famously declared that this new paradigm 'renders obsolete Geneva's strict limitations on questioning of enemy prisoners and renders quaint some of its provisions'.[2] Over at the Justice Department, Jay Bybee, a political appointee as Assistant Attorney General, was asked to advise on the standards of conduct required by the 1984 Convention against Torture, as implemented by US federal law. His memorandum of 1 October 2002 is probably the very worst piece of legal advice (if it can be called that) that I have ever seen. It was apparently prompted by CIA questions about what to do with captives alleged to be top-ranking al-Qaeda terrorists who had turned 'uncooperative'. Dispensing with all known canons of treaty interpretation, Mr. Bybee concluded that the concept of 'torture' covers only the most extreme acts, limited to severe pain which is difficult for the victim to endure: 'Where the pain is physical', he writes in his legal memorandum, 'it must be of an intensity akin to that which accompanies serious physical injury such as death or

[2] Ibid., p. 154.

organ failure'. Anything less will not be torture. It is therefore allowed. Where the pain is mental, then it 'requires suffering not just at the moment of infliction but it also requires lasting psychological harm, such as seen in mental disorders like posttraumatic stress disorder'.[3] There is no support whatsoever in international law for such an interpretation. John Yoo was a US Deputy Assistant Attorney General to Attorney General John Ashcroft, charged with advising on the effect of rules such as the Geneva Conventions, the 1984 Convention prohibiting torture, and the ICC Statute. He could not have been clearer in May 2002: 'What the Administration is trying to do is create a new legal regime.'[4] But it was doing so unilaterally, without consultation, and without regard to what the treaties required. It goes against the very essence of the collective, rules-based arrangements that the US and Britain wanted to put in place in the 1940s. The period between 9/11 and the summer of 2004 will, I expect, come to be seen as a low-point for America's engagement with international law. Within the US the media went to sleep, so did the Democrats, so did most international lawyers. Anyone who was willing to speak out could not find a platform. Anyone within Government – and there were many – who tried to speak up for the established rules was overridden. The argument that the rules served American interests got short shrift.

Against that background the President also decided very early on to get rid of Saddam Hussein. The indictment of Scooter Libby seems to have opened the door to a proper examination of the road to war in Iraq. Issues that had long been aired in the UK have only now come onto the US agenda. In March this year, the New York Times ran a front page story on the revelation in the new edition of my book, published in the UK several weeks earlier. Why the wait? With time the details will be fleshed out. But enough has already emerged from insider accounts and from leaked documents to allow a clear image.

Within days of 9/11 President Bush had been persuaded to address Iraq as part of a military response to the attacks on America, even if no credible information pointed to any Iraqi link. America needed to be seen to act decisively, and evidence-based decisions went out of the window. The legitimacy of force required an ally or two, since there was never any real probability that the US would actually go it alone. Tony Blair was conve-

---

[3] Ibid., p. 213.
[4] Ibid., p. 153.

nient and he was amenable. By April 2002 he had been persuaded to join in, without even extracting much of a price. In the summer of 2002 evidence of Iraqi weapons of mass destruction (WMD) was 'thin', as the 'Downing Street Memo' confirmed, and the facts were being fixed around the policy of removing Saddam. Blair's price? Since the war could not be sold as regime change (plainly illegal under international law) it would have to be justified on the grounds of the threat posed by Saddam's possession of WMD.

The autumn of 2002 was dedicated to proving the WMD case, and to getting a green light from the UN Security Council. No smoking gun was found. The Security Council adopted resolution 1441, which left ambiguous the question of whether a further Security Council resolution was needed. But 1441 at least confirmed that war would be arguable if it could be shown that Iraq was in material breach of its disarmament obligation. UN inspectors were dispatched to Iraq. January 2003 was a difficult month. Colin Powell told Jack Straw, his British counterpart, that if the case was too weak for a second resolution then there would be no justification for the US to act unilaterally. George W. Bush and Tony Blair worried that Hans Blix would not find a smoking gun, or worse still might even report that Saddam was cooperating. The two leaders discussed ways of provoking a 'material breach' by Saddam. Bush told Blair he would use force without a further resolution. The starting date for the war was 'pencilled in' for 10 March. The note of the meeting of 31 January 2003 is important because it confirms that the decision to go to war was decided before the end of January and because it indicates that the two leaders recognised that they had no real evidence as to Iraq's possession of WMD.

Matters did not improve in February 2003. No smoking gun emerged. Colin Powell's Security Council presentation bombed. The Niger uranium claim was disputed. Blix reported greater Iraqi cooperation. The lesser members of the Security Council proved to be too independent, and could not be bought or budged. And, contrary to claims that now seek to rewrite history, contemporaneous accounts of individuals who had seen the intelligence disputed the claim that Saddam had – or was about to get – WMD. The sceptical reader need look no further than the resignation speech made in the House of Commons on 18 March 2003 by British Cabinet Minister Robin Cook for a devastating rebuttal of the case based on WMD.

We now know that the decision to go to war was taken on the false claim that Saddam had WMD. It has been established beyond any reasonable doubt that there were no WMD. All that is left to the Bush Administration is the plaintive claim that its belief that Saddam had WMD was a reasonable one. With that claim punctured the whole house of cards collapses. Hence the significance of Joseph Wilson, and why he had to be dealt with. Hence the significance of establishing the role played by the White House in undermining Mr. Wilson, his independence, and his credibility. And hence now the indictment of Lewis Libby. This is positive. Many people are looking to the US for a credible strategy to extricate Iraq, the region and the world from the mess that is now unfolding. That requires less hauteur and hubris, more honesty, and more cooperation with other nations. We face a real threat from forces that seek to destabilize America and who will benefit from a long-term Iraqi quagmire that makes America less likely to act when real threats exist. Let us not gloat but rather hope that the indictment allows the Administration a moment of reflection, and permits the nation to return to reason, decency and lawfulness in its foreign policy decision-making.

In the US the tide of media and public interest only began to turn in the spring of 2004, after a diligent group of journalists uncovered pictures of abuse at Abu Ghraib. With those discoveries there emerged into daylight a series of legal opinions – including the Bybee memorandum – which showed how far some of the lawyers in the Administration – at the very highest levels – were willing to go to override US and international rules. A quiescent Congress began a series of hearings, grilling Paul Wolfowitz, who after much dissembling accepted that putting a bag over someone's head for 72 hours was not humane. And later on that summer the US Supreme Court stepped in to open the door to legal rights for the detainees at Guantanamo. Gunatanamo Bay was, wrote Justice Scalia, 'a foolish place to have housed alien wartime detainees'. By the autumn of 2004 it had become apparent that ignoring international law was not a cost-free exercise. US authority had been undermined. Other States were beginning to rely on US arguments. Is the damage irreversible?

Allow me to park that question for a moment, and say something about the effect on Britain of the new American thinking on international law. I say this because it now appears that it was American legal arguments that helped to convince the Attorney General to conclude that a reasonable case could be made to proceed to war in Iraq without an explicit resolution by the Security Council.

Whereas the US media were largely silent about international legal issues in the period between 9/11 and the summer of 2004, the British media had given a great deal of attention to international law issues. As early as January 2002 – as soon as it was known that a number of the Guantanamo detainees were British nationals – media attention focused on the interplay of rights under the Geneva Conventions and human rights law. Further attention was generated by the *Abbassi* case brought by some of the British detainees to the English courts, challenging the failure of the British Government to take sufficient steps to ensure that the US respected the detainees' rights under international law. The English Court of Appeal rejected the Government's argument that these issues were not justiciable. Although the Court was not willing to order the British Government to take any particular steps, its invocation of international law and criticism of the US actions were direct and unambiguous:

> 'What appears to us objectionable is that Mr Abbassi should be subject to indefinite detention in territory over which the United States has exclusive control with no opportunity to challenge the legitimacy of his detention before any court or tribunal.'[5]

The Court concluded that Mr. Abbassi was being detained arbitrarily in a 'legal black hole' in breach of fundamental human rights and basic principles recognised in English law and international law. The judgment added to political pressure. It reaffirmed the central importance of international law. And it gave a green light to those who considered that the British Government should be held to account by reference to the very standards of international law which it had done so much to put in place. Two years later, of course, the House of Lords gave judgment on the Government's derogation from the Human Rights Act, adopted shortly after 9/11. The UK was the only one of 44 Council of Europe members to enter a derogation, a matter for which it has been criticised in some quarters. But at least it did so, unlike the US which simply ignored the requirement of the Inter-American Convention on Human Rights and the ICCPR in relation to Guantanamo and did not bother putting in a derogation. In the Belmarsh case the Law Lords relied on a number of principles of international law in ruling that the indefinite detention without charge of non-UK nationals at Belmarsh was discriminatory

[5] Ibid., p. 166.

and unlawful. And last December the House of Lords gave a similarly powerful judgment in ruling that evidence obtained by torture could never be invoked before the English courts: the common law and Article 15 of the 1984 Torture Convention were the basis for that judgment.

The judicial decision in the Guantanamo and Belmarsh cases signalled the courts' commitment to ensure that Britain respected its international obligations, and a recognition of the central role that the international rule of law plays in responding to new threats. Abandon the law at your peril, the court seemed to be saying. They also reflected a rejection of the threat that Al Qaeda and 9/11 had given rise to a new paradigm.

The British Government did not adopt the position that international law was irrelevant in deciding whether to go to war. In the US, the general view was that if war was legal under the US Constitution then that was good enough. 'International law? … I don't know what you're talking about by international law', President Bush said in December 2003. From the earliest days, however, the British Prime Minister was plainly concerned to ensure that any actions taken against Iraq would have to be consistent with the UK's international obligations. Nevertheless, as was shown in Lawless World, the Attorney General's secret legal advice of 7 March 2003 was rather different from the public answer he gave to a Parliamentary question on 17 March 2003: in the space of just ten days an advice that the war could well be found to be illegal by a court became an unequivocal view as to the legality of the war.

So why does all this matter, and where does it leave us and international law, for now and for the future? It is time to move on, many will say. Others will say that I am a hopeless European overly concerned with legal niceties.

The events of the last three years matter, first and foremost, because they have significant consequences for international governance. We live in a complex, interdependent world in which social, political, economic and religious values and interests collide with increasing frequency over an ever greater set of issues. International law sets minimum standards of behaviour. Outside of bullying and force it is all we have to provide a framework for resolving those differences. Without international law we are back to the law of the jungle, the very world which Roosevelt and Churchill committed to change when they met off the coast of Newfoundland in August 1941. I want Britain and the US batting for international law, not against it.

There will be occasions where the international rules are wholly inadequate, occasions when States may justifiably feel the need to dispense with the rules and go it alone. 9/11 and the threat posed by Al Qaeda is not, for the time being at least, such an occasion. Nor was the situation in Iraq in March 2003 such an occasion. The rules set forth in the Geneva Convention, in human rights treaties and in the UN Charter in relation to the use of force did not need the treatment they have received.

It is dangerous indeed to begin to imagine a system of international governance in which some States – the large and powerful ones – feel that they can pick and choose the international rules they like and discard those which they don't. Yet that has been the approach adopted by the Bush Administration, reflected in the notion of à la carte multilateralism. And it is an approach for which the British Government has provided considerable support, generally maintaining a public silence on the excesses of Guantanamo and buying into a legal argument for war in Iraq which was denuded of any international support.

The approach degrades international law, and it makes it more difficult to rely on rules when others violate them. If you begin to tinker unilaterally with the international rules you don't like – on human rights, on the Geneva Conventions, on the use of force – then others may be begin to tinker with the rules they don't like – on trade, on intellectual property, on the rights of foreign investors. If you send out a message that you consider the rules to be obsolete and incapable of meeting new paradigms, you prevent yourself from challenging others who then act in the same way. That is a serious problem right now in many areas, for example nuclear proliferation. Imagine how easy it is for those in Teheran to respond to allegations from the US and Britain that they are not complying with the requirements of the Non-Proliferation Treaty.

The British and American Governments would do well to bear in mind the words of George Kennan, the great American diplomat (and not known for a strong attachment to international rules), in his famous telegram from Moscow in 1947, anonymously signed X. He ended his warning of the Soviet threat with these words:

> '[W]e must have courage and self-confidence to cling to our own methods and conceptions of human society. [T]he greatest danger that can befall us in coping with this problem of Soviet communism, is that we shall allow ourselves to become like those with whom we are coping.'

This brings me to my concluding remarks. It may be thought that you might divine that I would be pessimistic about what is to come as well as about the future of international law. But I do not feel that way. Why not? Because the rules of international law which have been the subject of so unremitting an assault in the aftermath of 9/11 have shown themselves to be remarkably robust. They have not crumbled or been washed away. They have their detractors, but in far larger numbers they have their supporters. It is right that governments should re-examine the adequacy of rules. But they are not in need of change. The Geneva Conventions are adequate. The UN Charter is adequate (as the outcome document of the UN Summit in September 2005 confirmed). The Torture Convention is adequate. Iraq has caused untold damage to those who support an expanded concept of humanitarian intervention.

In the US, there remains much which is of serious concern. But it is striking that the Bush Administration has not succeeded in killing off Kyoto or the ICC, or rewriting the Geneva Conventions or the Torture Convention, or building any sort of consensus to support its revised approach to the international rules governing the use of force. Quite the contrary: There are signs that the Bush Administration is rethinking its strategies and its policies. It has reversed its position and dropped its outright opposition to the ICC, deciding not to veto a Security Council resolution referring the situation in Darfur to the ICC. Senator McCain has caused new legislation to be adopted which will commit the US to its obligations under the Convention Against Torture. And privately, a number of senior Administration officials have recognised that the Administration may have made serious mistakes in its so-called 'war on terrorism': Guantanamo is a terrible stain on America's reputation and has undermined the right arguments it makes to promote the rule of law. A more consensual and rules-based approach is needed if necessary cooperation from other states is going to be engaged. There is a broader recognition that peace, justice and security require cooperation, and cooperation requires rules.

Chapter 2
LES RÉACTIONS AUX NOUVELLES MENACES À LA PAIX ET À LA SÉCURITÉ DANS LE CADRE DE LA CHARTE DES NATIONS UNIES

Yves Daudet*

Toute réflexion sur les nouvelles menaces contre la paix et sur l'aptitude des Nations Unies à y répondre doit commencer par un rappel du Préambule de la Charte. Celui-ci, exprimant les préoccupations dominantes de ses auteurs s'ouvre par la formule célèbre « Nous, peuples des Nations Unies, résolus à préserver les générations futures du fléau de la guerre qui deux fois en l'espace d'une vie humaine a infligé à l'humanité d'indicibles souffrances…. ». De fait, si l'on songe que le même homme, a pu à l'aube de sa vie d'adulte, connaître l'enfer de la première guerre mondiale et être encore appelé à combattre ensuite les atrocités de la deuxième, on mesure le sacrifice inouï accompli par cette seule génération. On comprend à la fois la détermination à ce que ces drames ne se répètent plus, et la méfiance à l'égard de la « bête immonde » de Bertolt Brecht. Et, comme il est normal dans un contexte tel que celui de 1945, lorsque le souvenir de ce qu'on a vécu est si proche et les blessures encore ouvertes, la conception que l'on se fait de la paix est très largement la conception première et la plus évidente : la paix c'est l'absence de guerre.

On ne peut dire cependant des auteurs de la Charte qu'ils ont entendu se limiter à cet aspect, même si il est prééminent et si les autres buts de la Charte convergent et se rattachent au maintien de la paix. Comme on le sait, et on y reviendra, la Charte est un instrument d'une grande plasticité et faisant preuve d'une grande faculté d'adaptation aux évolutions du monde. C'est

* Professeur à l'Université Paris 1 Panthéon Sorbonne, Secrétaire général de l'Académie de droit international de La Haye.

O. Ribbelink (ed.), Beyond the UN Charter: Peace, Security and the Role of Justice

pourquoi, pour peu que l'on veuille bien s'en servir en ayant recours aux Nations Unies et au multilatéralisme plutôt qu'à l'unilatéralisme, elle peut répondre à la plupart des situations qui se présentent. Et ce n'est pas le moindre mérite de ses rédacteurs que d'avoir fait témoigné de grandes qualités d'anticipation en concevant un texte qui a permis de répondre à des situations variées et évolutives. Certes, il mérite aujourd'hui quelques révisions. Mais seule la question de la composition du Conseil de Sécurité, certes capitale et, pour cette raison si difficile, nécessite d'être résolue. Pour le reste, le texte permet de faire face à l'essentiel.

Quel est cet essentiel et, plus particulièrement, selon la question qui est posée ici, la Charte permet-elle de réagir aux nouvelles menaces contre la paix et la sécurité internationales ? Ce vaste sujet nécessite d'en définir au préalable les contours exacts.

Que sont ces « nouvelles menaces » contre la paix et la paix elle-même a-t-elle changé de visage ? Au fond, soixante ans plus tard, écrirait-on le préambule de la Charte de la même manière et selon les mêmes termes. A l'évidence non. Très certainement, la conception que l'on se fait de la paix et des menaces qui pèsent sur elle est beaucoup plus large qu'en 1945 même si les auteurs de la Charte en avaient fait une notion « pivot » autour de laquelle s'ordonnent d'autres éléments faisant de la paix une notion marqué par un réel polymorphisme.

La paix est une notion contingente et évolutive, dépendant directement, comme on l'a dit, des situations existantes mais dépendant aussi des mentalités et des aspirations, variables selon ces situations et les moments envisagés. Et, à la vérité, la Charte prend en compte ces fluctuations.

Dans l'énoncé des buts des Nations Unies par l'article 1 paragraphe 1 de la Charte de San Francisco du 26 juin 1945, la priorité est donnée au « maintien de la paix et de la sécurité internationales ». La Charte se situe ainsi dans le fil des Conférences de la paix de La Haye de 1899 et 1907 ainsi que dans celui du Pacte de la Societé des Nations (SDN), tous documents qui, avec des moyens autres que ceux qui seront dévolus aux Nations Unies, cherchaient à établir des relations internationales pacifiques, but fondamental de l'action diplomatique affirmé au cours du XIX° siècle.

Encore faut-il prendre en compte le contexte dans lequel cette recherche de la paix est affirmée. Sans doute les effets en seront-ils différents selon que l'on se trouve dans un système international qui n'interdit pas le recours à la guerre, dans un système où le recours à la force est interdit (ou au moins réglementé) mais les armements acceptés et, enfin, dans celui qui vise le désarmement. Les évolutions à cet égard sont marquées et fondamentales. De même qu'est essentiel le contenu donné à la notion de paix elle-même qui semble devoir se diversifier et se raffiner au fur et à mesure que les armes reculent. Tant que la guerre est présente ou aux portes, la paix est simplement perçue comme le temps où les armes finiront par se taire. Que la menace strictement militaire vienne à s'éloigner et l'on s'avisera que la paix peut alors recevoir d'autres contenus. De fait, l'homme se sent-il plus ou moins en paix selon qu'il risque de mourir de faim ou de périr de la balle de l'ennemi ? D'une attaque d'un pays étranger ou des tortures du dictateur de son propre pays ? D'une pollution majeure ou d'une arme de destruction massive ?

Ainsi, sécurité, développement, droits de l'homme, peut-être même environnement entretiennent-ils d'étroites relations en constituant diverses approches d'une même notion : la paix qui reçoit ainsi constamment et aux diverses périodes de « nouveaux noms » pour reprendre la formule célèbre employée par le Pape Paul VI à propos des rapports entre la paix et le développement. La paix devient alors une notion aux multiples visages en raison des liens qui se tissent entre ses divers fondements. Cela ne va pas sans poser problème, comme toujours lorsque, à force d'en accroître le contenu, une notion risque de perdre sa précision originelle. D'autant que, dans le cadre des Nations Unies, des conséquences institutionnelles précises s'attachent aux questions de maintien de la paix qui relèvent de la responsabilité principale du Conseil de sécurité. Pour définir la compétence de l'organe, il convient donc d'être au clair sur l'objet de son action.

A vrai dire, certains liens entre les notions ont été délibérément voulus dès l'origine par les auteurs de la Charte eux-mêmes qui ont eu d'emblée une vision assez large et englobante de la paix. C'est ainsi que, s'agissant du lien entre la paix et le développement, il est établi à la Conférence de San Francisco, sous une forme hiérarchique, reflétée d'abord par l'énumération de l'article 1 de la Charte: la paix (en premier lieu), les relations amicales entre Etats (ensuite et qui consolident la paix), le développement et les droits de l'homme (enfin et qui permettent de réaliser la coopération internationale). La Cour internationale de Justice confirme la hiérarchie voulue par l'article 1 de la Charte lorsqu'elle estime « qu'il est naturel d'accorder le premier rang à la paix car les autres buts ne peuvent être atteints que si cette condition fondamentale est acquise ».[1]

---

[1] C.I.J., Avis Consultatif du 20 juillet 1962, « Certaines dépenses des Nations Unies », *C.I.J. Recueil*, p. 168.

La hiérarchie apparaît aussi en ce que tout ce qui touche à la paix, largement développé dans la Charte, est confié au Conseil de sécurité investi des pouvoirs d'action et, le cas échéant, de contrainte tandis que le développement sera davantage traité sur la base de normes émanant d'organes tels que l'Assemblée générale ou le Conseil économique et social, donc d'une valeur juridique incertaine et d'une portée souvent illusoire.

Mais cet aménagement de la Charte doit s'apprécier dans le contexte de 1945 où le sous-développement ne revêt pas encore l'importance quantitative qui est aujourd'hui la sienne, non plus qu'il n'est qualitativement conçu de la même façon. En tout cas, le risque qu'il fait peser sur la sécurité n'est perçu que de manière diffuse, lointaine et abstraite. Risque pressenti cependant à travers l'article 65 de la Charte relatif aux liens entre le Conseil économique et social et le Conseil de sécurité. Il est vrai que cette disposition est restée lettre morte, les Etats n'ayant pas su lui donner la portée souhaitable. La menace que le sous-développement fait peser sur la sécurité est aujourd'hui bien connue, à défaut d'être toujours suffisamment prise en compte: si paix et développement sont liés, c'est parce que la préoccupation dominante est la paix au service de laquelle se place le développement; le développement est recherché parce qu'il sert la paix. Enfin, la proposition selon laquelle développer est le moyen d'assurer la paix se renverse. La paix devient alors la source (ou la condition) du développement. Une grande partie de cette nouvelle menace que constituent les migrations illégales se rattache à ces considérations. Or, l'effet déstabilisateur de grands courants migratoires non-contrôlés a été reconnu comme une menace à la paix par le Conseil de Sécurité, dès lors qu'il se produit dans certaines circonstances politiques données. Telle fut la position adoptée à l'égard des Kurdes d'Irak dans la résolution 688 de 1991 ou des boat people haïtiens dans la résolution 940 de 1994. Une communication étant consacrée à la question des réfugiés et des personnes déplacées et à leur impact sur la paix et la sécurité, la question ne sera pas davantage évoquée ici.

Il convient d'ajouter que certaines actions des Nations Unies peuvent permettre de mettre fin aux conflits internes dans des Etats où la démocratie n'est pas assurée et où les droits de l'homme sont bafoués. Ces facteurs d'insécurité interne sont susceptibles d'engendrer à leur tour l'insécurité internationale. Ainsi, la paix n'est-elle pas davantage séparable des droits de l'homme, non plus que de la démocratie et de l'Etat de droit qui sont une manifestation de ceux-ci et une condition de leur mise en oeuvre. Ici encore, les positions prises par le Conseil de Sécurité dans la question d'Haïti sont très significatives.

L'analyse des questions relatives à l'environnement conduirait aux mêmes approches globales. Si on en vient à évoquer l'équilibre d'ensemble du monde, les questions d'environnement rejoignent les préoccupations relatives à la sécurité de la planète, en sorte que la recherche de la paix se fait aussi par la sauvegarde de l'environnement. C'est une donnée qui apparaîtra probablement de plus en plus clairement dans le futur au fur et à mesure que seront tangibles les risques consécutifs aux atteintes à l'environnement, en matière climatique par exemple. Et très certainement, ces risques doivent-ils être désormais classés au nombre des « nouvelles menaces » qui pèsent sur la sécurité du monde.

Les « nouvelles menaces » sont parfois de même nature que les menaces anciennes qui se poursuivent sous des formes différentes: les armes de destruction massive, nucléaires, chimiques ou bactériologiques sont un avatar de la menace des armes tout court, le génocide est l'hyperbole de la violation des droits de l'homme, les « Rogue States », une réalité tristement récurrente de la vie internationale. Mais on rencontre aussi aujourd'hui des menaces à la paix et à la sécurité qui sont nouvelles également dans leur forme et leur contenu. Certaines d'entre elles ont prospéré sur le terreau de la mondialisation dont elles sont une conséquence malheureuse mais inévitable. La globalisation qui favorise l'échange, l'ouverture et la circulation des hommes, des marchandises et des idées favorise aussi la circulation du crime, de la drogue ou de l'argent sale et permet le développement de grands fléaux de société. Et puis, bien sûr et au premier rang des nouvelles menaces, on trouve aujourd'hui le terrorisme à grande échelle. La menace terroriste est omniprésente (par nature, le terrorisme est un ennemi dont on craint qu'il frappe n'importe qui, n'importe où, n'importe quand et avec n'importe quel moyen) et constitue certainement la menace à la paix la plus diffuse et la plus générale de notre début de siècle, même si elle n'est pas un phénomène récent et inédit. Mais la nouveauté d'aujourd'hui est son caractère massif, tapi, embusqué, constitutif d'un risque de chaque instant dont nul n'est à l'abri. Ce n'est plus un assassinat isolé et signé comme ce fut souvent le cas dans le passé, ce sont des dizaines, des centaines, voire des milliers de morts et de blessés à la vie à jamais brisée dans des lieux hautement fréquentés : les Tours de Manhattan, la gare de Madrid, le métro de Londres ou celui de Paris antérieurement, à Nairobi, à Dar-es-Salam, à Bali, ailleurs, encore et toujours. Autant d'actes dont les auteurs ne sont pas toujours identifiés, pas davantage que les exécutants bien souvent sont des kamikazes. A juste titre, le Conseil de Sécurité, dans sa résolution 1377 du 12 septembre 2001 a qualifié ces actes terroristes de « l'une des menaces les plus graves à la paix et à la sécurité au XXI° siècle ... (qui) constituent un défi à tous les Etats et à l'humanité tout entière ».

Quelle réaction imaginer alors contre ces fléaux en demeurant dans le cadre qui m'a été assigné, celui de la Charte des Nations Unies ? Ce qui exclut ainsi deux situations, celle d'une action qui serait contraire à la Charte et conduirait donc à une violation du droit international et celle d'une action qui serait entreprise par un autre canal que celui des Nations Unies, sans constituer pour autant une violation de la Charte.

La réaction aux nouvelles menaces, bien entendu, relève de la compétence de l'Organisation. Dans le Préambule de la Charte, les « Peuples des Nations Unies » ne sont-ils pas « résolus à (...) favoriser le progrès social et instaurer de meilleures conditions de vie dans une liberté plus grande » ? Et ces nouvelles menaces ne font-elles pas, en tous points, obstacle à la réalisation de ce dessein ? Comme à l'égard de toute autre situation qui menace la paix et la sécurité quelque part dans le monde, les Nations Unies, organisation universelle et organisation politique ont donc bien un titre de compétence pour agir et se sont dotées à cette fin d'un organe délibérant, l'Assemblée générale et d'un organe de décision – sous certaines conditions – le Conseil de Sécurité.

Néanmoins, l'appareil institutionnel et les principes établis en 1945 s'inscrivaient dans une société internationale qui, depuis, a été profondément bouleversée. Non pas par l'accroissement du nombre des Etats : ils sont plus nombreux et posent des problèmes plus diversifiés, mais la société internationale, du point de vue de la Charte, reste une société interétatique et les acteurs sont essentiellement les Etats (au sein ou en dehors d'une organisation internationale, elle-même sujet de droit international). Or, depuis le début du siècle et plus précisément le 11 septembre, ces situations sont largement bouleversées par le jeu, à tout instant possible et d'un extrême danger, d'acteurs non étatiques responsables des « nouvelles » atteintes à la paix. La moindre de ces difficultés n'étant pas celle de ne savoir où et comment les saisir. Selon le système de la Charte, le responsable de l'atteinte à la paix est identifiable : un Etat ou un groupe d'Etats pour une action de force. En cas d'attaque terroriste, quel est l'auteur, quelle arme employer contre lui, comment le saisir ? En cas d'attaque kamikaze à quoi sert-il de disposer de procédures d'extradition et de jugement des auteurs de l'acte ? Et comment geler les avoirs de commanditaires souvent mal définis ? La violence consécutive à la grande criminalité et l'instabilité engendrée par les trafics de tous ordres posent des problèmes du même ordre face auxquels la Charte est assez démunie car elle n'était pas faite pour régir cette société là avec ces désordres là.

Les moyens sont ainsi mal adaptés pour des effets, en conséquence et presque mécaniquement, largement insuffisants. On examinera donc successivement 1. les moyens de réaction aux nouvelles menaces, et 2. les effets de ces réactions.

1. Des moyens de réaction mal adaptés aux nouvelles menaces

On sait que la révision de la Charte fait partie d'un ordre du jour permanent mais finalement jamais conduit à son terme. Il paraît au demeurant fort douteux que la réforme du Conseil de Sécurité, qui en est le point le plus essentiel, permette à elle seule de résoudre la question des moyens utilisables pour anéantir les nouvelles menaces. La question est plus large, les enjeux plus vastes. Ce qui est sûr c'est que les moyens offerts par la Charte des Nations Unies ne permettent pas de faire face à ces menaces. Mais à vrai dire, l'ont-ils jamais permis ?

1.1 Les moyens de la Charte comme chacun sait, tiennent en trois chapitres et s'appuient essentiellement sur un organe, le Conseil de Sécurité dont le maintien de la paix est la responsabilité première, grâce à un pouvoir et un devoir d'action, exercé au nom des membres de l'Organisation (ce qui, du point de vue juridique apaise les controverses sur la composition et la représentativité du Conseil). Pouvoir jusqu'à un certain point – et dans les limites de l'article 12 de la Charte pour autant qu'il soit respecté – partagé avec l'Assemblée générale.

Le *Chapitre VI* de la Charte vient préciser le détail de la mise en oeuvre du principe général de règlement des différends par un moyen pacifique. C'est à dire tous les moyens connus dans le droit international et la pratique diplomatique et donne aux parties une liberté de choix et la possibilité d'adapter le mode de règlement aux particularités du différend. L'essentiel étant, ainsi que l'a rappelé la Cour internationale de Justice, « que les parties à un différend... s'efforcent d'y trouver une solution par des moyens pacifiques ».[2]

[2] C.I.J., « Affaire des activités militaires et paramilitaires au Nicaragua et contre celui-ci », 27 juin 1986, *C.I.J. Recueil* (1986) p. 145.

C'est là un principe du droit international complémentaire des principes d'interdiction de la menace ou de l'emploi de la force.

Le *Chapitre VII* de la Charte obéit à une logique différente. La situation est toute autre puisqu'on se trouve en présence de l'une des trois hypothèses suivantes : menace contre la paix, rupture de la paix, acte d'agression. Le danger est donc présent. Il n'est plus seulement hypothétique comme dans le cas du Chapitre VI. On ne peut pour autant prétendre, en prenant en considération la détérioration de la situation, qu'il y ait une gradation au sein de ce qui serait un *continuum* allant du Chapitre VI au Chapitre VII. En effet, sur la base de ce dernier, le fondement de ce qui devient une action des Nations Unies est totalement différent. Il repose sur la notion de « sécurité collective » supposant que la collectivité se ligue contre celui qui menace ou rompt la paix qui doit régner en son sein. Dans cette technique, chaque État participant au maintien de la paix agit non dans son intérêt direct mais en tant que garant d'un ordre international qu'il approuve et dont le respect ne peut être assuré que collectivement avec tout ce que cette situation suppose du point de vue de la nécessité d'une homogénéité de la société internationale et de la force du lien social existant entre ses membres. En ce sens, la sécurité collective est une création aussi noble qu'ambitieuse mais difficile à mettre en oeuvre.

Le Conseil de sécurité qui « constate l'existence » de l'une des trois hypothèses peut alors agir d'une manière adaptée à la situation en procédant par voie de recommandation ou de décision. L'article 39 l'autorise à prendre des mesures de sécurité collective « conformément aux articles 41 (mesures de contrainte non armées) et 42 (mesures de contrainte armées). Sur la base de l'article 41 ont ainsi été décrétées les sanctions économiques mais cet article a été également invoqué lors de la création du Tribunal pénal international pour l'ex-Yougoslavie décidée par la résolution 808 du Conseil de sécurité du 22 février 1993 fondée sur la Chapitre VII de la Charte. Quant à l'article 42, il n'a pas permis d'utiliser une armée des Nations Unies qui n'a pu être constituée faute d'accord sur l'article 43, ce qui a obligé à recourir à des mécanismes de substitution d'une autre nature

Le *Chapitre VIII* de la Charte aménage les relations entre les Nations Unies et les organismes et accords régionaux susceptibles d'intervenir dans un processus de maintien de la paix. Mécanisme au demeurant fortement encadré par la Charte de façon à ne pas entamer le monopole de l'utilisation de la force par les Nations Unies.

L'ensemble de cet édifice normatif va cependant très tôt se révéler inadapté aux circonstances politiques dans lequel il doit déployer ses effets et, rapidement, la pratique suivie requiert des aménagements plus ou moins profonds du système de la Charte. Cette observation est importante et le rappel de ces éléments connus de tous était pourtant nécessaire pour mieux souligner que l'interrogation sur l'aptitude des Nations Unies à régler les situations n'est pas récente, qu'il s'agisse de la résolution Acheson, de la création des Opération de maintien de la paix (OMP) ou de l'institution du chapitre virtuel connu sous le nom de chapitre VI bis, ces initiatives sont tôt apparues et ont constitué des compléments de la Charte répondant à une vision téléologique de celle-ci. Vision qui sera d'une certaine manière homologuée par la Cour internationale de Justice lorsqu'elle considèrera que les dépenses engagées sur la base de la résolution Acheson sont bien des dépenses de l'Organisation.

On peut évidemment être troublé par le fait que, finalement, la Charte, dès ses débuts, n'est pas pleinement ou n'est pas correctement appliquée. Mais en même temps, il faut dire que la Charte a ainsi démontré sa plasticité, sa faculté d'adaptation aux situations variées, voire son aptitude à contourner les obstacles dressés à son application. Les moyens de la Charte n'étant pas bien adaptés, la pratique du système a suppléé à ses imperfections.

1.2 Pourquoi alors ne pas continuer à innover sur la base du texte face aux nouvelles menaces ? La difficulté majeure que l'on rencontre alors ici est qu'on se trouve aujourd'hui en présence d'une transformation profonde de la société internationale. Notre société internationale n'est plus aujourd'hui une société exclusivement composée d'Etats souverains et lorsqu'il s'agit des Etats souverains, leur souveraineté ne s'exerce plus sans contrôle ni partage.

S'agissant de ce dernier élément, on sait aujourd'hui que la souveraineté de l'Etat connaît ses limites. Sans aller jusqu'au devoir d'ingérence sur lequel il convient d'être prudent, il est clair que toute méthode de gouvernement n'est plus nécessairement justifiée au nom de la souveraineté qui voudrait que chacun soit maître chez soi : Dans l'affaire Pinochet, les Lords britanniques rappellent que l'utilisation de la torture ne compte pas au nombre des formes normales d'exercice du pouvoir. De manière plus générale, les atteintes aux droits fondamentaux et aux principes de base de la démocratie obligent à rendre des comptes ; les droits de l'homme quittent le champ interne pour accéder largement à l'échelle internationale et même la lutte contre le terrorisme ne dispense pas du respect des droits de l'homme ainsi que le

Conseil de Sécurité l'a rappelé à plusieurs reprises, en particulier en termes particulièrement nets dans la résolution 1624 du 14 septembre 2005, pour prendre un texte récent « les Etats doivent veiller à ce que toutes les mesures qu'ils prennent pour lutter contre le terrorisme respectent toutes les obligations qui leur incombent en vertu du droit international, et que ces mesures doivent être conformes au droit international, en particulier aux instruments relatifs aux droits de l'homme, au droit des réfugiés et au droit humanitaire ».

Quant au fait que la société internationale n'est plus composée seulement d'Etats souverains et d'organisations intergouvernementales, c'est là probablement la cause la plus grave et la plus profonde des insuffisances de la Charte. Certes, cette situation ne date pas d'aujourd'hui : il y a longtemps que l'on connaît l'existence de Fonds monétaire international (FMN) plus puissantes que les Etats, d'Organisation non-gouvernementel (ONG) fort actives dans certains domaines et, dans l'entre deux guerres, Georges Scelle plaidait déjà pour la reconnaissance au profit des individus de la qualité de sujets du droit international. Ce qui est nouveau aujourd'hui c'est une meilleure prise en compte du rôle actif que peuvent jouer ces acteurs, du fait qu'ils sont souvent officiellement reconnus comme investis d'une certaine légitimité. C'est par exemple la prise en compte de manière très officielle de la place de la « Société civile » par le Secrétaire général des Nations Unies. C'est donc largement une question d'image, de représentation et d'aspiration à la reconnaissance de certains acteurs.

Or, la Charte a été conçue pour régir une société d'Etats et on lui demande de régir aujourd'hui une société aux acteurs multiples et que certaines branches du droit international telles que le droit humanitaire ou le droit international des droits de l'homme rangent au nombre des sujets de ces droits. Une difficulté considérable supplémentaire tient au fait que, parmi ces acteurs, figurent des groupes terroristes souvent ramifiés, faisant peser sur la paix une menace d'une extrême gravité. Par rapport aux périodes précédentes, nous vivons dans la période actuelle une situation beaucoup plus complexe et beaucoup plus difficile à appréhender en présence de laquelle la règle de droit est décalée par rapport à cette réalité qui ne constituait pas la menace principale lorsque la règle a été conçue. Or on sait combien ce type de décalage est dangereux et porteur d'instabilité et, dans ce contexte, on doit se demander quels peuvent être les effets des réactions aux nouvelles menaces.

2. Les effets des réactions aux nouvelles menaces

Comme on l'a vu, les moyens de défense disponibles sont essentiellement des moyens classiques conçus pour faire face à des menaces classiques, ce qui a pour conséquence que les effets des réactions sont assez limités (2.1). Mais il est vrai aussi que les Nations Unies ont tenté de définir des voies nouvelles ou de nouvelles approches, pour faire face à ces fléaux nouveaux ou dont la nouveauté tient à une augmentation démesurée de leur intensité. (2.2)

2.1 **Des effets limités**

Un exemple caractéristique des doutes qui surgissent quant à l'efficacité du système de la Charte sur les situations qu'elle entend régler est donné par la résolution 1368 du 12 septembre 2001, adoptée le lendemain des attentats terroristes aux Etats-Unis. Dans cette résolution, le Conseil de Sécurité, qui considère que les actes terroristes constituent des atteintes à la paix et à la sécurité internationales, commence par reconnaître le « droit inhérent de légitime défense individuelle ou collective ». Mais, comme il a été bien souvent souligné, que signifie ce droit dans le contexte des actes terroristes ? L'article 51 de la Charte est adapté au cas d'une attaque d'un Etat contre un autre Etat par des moyens conventionnels conduisant à une riposte proportionnée et à une saisine du Conseil de Sécurité invité à exercer ses responsabilités. L'article 51, tel qu'il a été conçu, n'est à l'évidence pas adapté à la défense contre l'acte terroriste émanant d'un acteur insaisissable, fuyant et tentaculaire quand il n'est pas non identifié. Le 11 septembre 2001, on a des forts soupçons mais pas des certitudes absolues fondées sur des preuves quant à l'identité des auteurs de l'attentat. Ce ne sont pas des militaires en uniforme qui ont attaqué les tours. Pourtant, comment ne pas réagir ? Et comment ne pas penser à se prémunir contre le renouvellement d'événement du même type et à tenter de les prévenir, sans attendre que l'attaque ait eu lieu. D'où la renaissance du débat sur la légitime défense « préventive » avec tous les risques qu'elle comporte quant à la substitution de l'unilatéralisme au multilatéralisme et, en définitive, à la contradiction interne de cette notion : peut-on encore parler de légitime défense en cas d'action préventive et comment répondre alors à une exigence de proportionnalité ? Chacun a en mémoire les décisions de la Cour Internationale de Justice dans les Affaires des activités militaires et paramilitaires au Nicaragua de 1986 et des plates-formes pétrolières de 2003 selon lesquelles « l'exercice du droit de légitime défense ... suppose tout d'abord qu'une agression ait lieu ». Mais on sait que le terrorisme a un effet polluant sur le droit car il risque d'engendrer des réactions elles-mêmes non conformes au droit. Ce fut le cas, par exemple lors de l'affaire de l'Achile Lauro.

Et si l'on demeure dans la sphère de la légalité, dans l'état actuel du droit international et selon les principes de la Charte, comment faire autrement pour tenter d'atteindre le groupe terroriste que d'utiliser la technique du ricochet en s'appuyant sur l'illicéité du comportement d'un Etat qui héberge, protège, soutient un groupe terroriste dont l'action vise à déstabiliser un Etat étranger, ainsi que l'a fait l'Assemblée générale dès 1970 avec sa résolution 2625 (XV) en condamnant les actes de terrorisme sur le territoire d'un autre Etat en tant que manquement aux relations amicales? C'est donc par un mécanisme du droit international le plus classique que l'on peut organiser la riposte ou recourir à la légitime défense. Les Etats-Unis sur cette base interviendront en Afghanistan et, devant le Conseil de Sécurité, déclarent le 7 octobre 2001, comme le Royaume uni, que les mesures prises contre l'Afghanistan relèvent de la légitime défense.[3] Mais certains Etats ont émis des réserves au regard de cette position qui aboutissait à imputer aux Talibans une responsabilité dans l'attentat du 11 septembre. Puis, la résolution 1378 du Conseil de Sécurité du 14 novembre 2001 condamne

> « les Taliban pour avoir permis que l'Afghanistan soit utilisé comme base d'exportation du terrorisme par le réseau Al-Qaeda et autres groupes terroristes et pour avoir accordé l'asile à Oussama Ben Laden, Al-Qaeda et autres éléments associés, et *appuyant* dans ce contexte les efforts que fait le peuple afghan pour remplacer le régime des Taliban, »

On voit bien ici le Conseil de Sécurité tout à la fois rappeler la règle du droit international qui interdit à un Etat (ici un régime au pouvoir) de servir de base à une activité illicite à l'égard des autres Etats (ici l'exportation du terrorisme) et appeler au remplacement d'un régime politique par un autre dès lors que le premier viole gravement les droits de l'homme et la règle de droit.

---

[3] E. David, dans *La Charte des Nations Unies : commentaire article par article*, J.-P. Cot, A. Pellet & M. Forteau (Éds.), Vol. 1, 2005, Paris, Economica, p. 196.

De manière plus nette encore, dans sa résolution 1383 du 6 décembre 2001 le Conseil de Sécurité mêle ces deux éléments en se déclarant

> « *Déterminé* à aider les Afghans à mettre fin aux conflits tragiques en Afghanistan et à promouvoir la réconciliation nationale, une paix durable, la stabilité et le respect des droits de l'homme, ainsi qu'à coopérer avec la communauté internationale pour mettre fin à l'utilisation de l'Afghanistan comme base pour le terrorisme. »

Ces deux résolutions sont fondées sur le Chapitre VII de la Charte et maintiennent un régime de sanctions établi par des résolutions antérieures dès 1999.

2.2 De nouvelles approches ?

La société internationale et le droit international étant ce qu'ils sont, la marge de manœuvre des Nations Unies est nécessairement étroite. La présence, en tant qu'acteurs de la scène internationale, d'entités qui n'ont pas la qualité de sujets de droit international et qui ne peuvent donc pas toujours être directement atteints, sans crever l'écran de la souveraineté étatique a conduit les Nations Unies à tirer le meilleur parti possible dans plusieurs directions. On en retiendra deux, plus particulièrement significatives, en les décrivant à grands traits faute de temps : celle d'un important développement normatif et institutionnel en matière de lutte contre le terrorisme d'une part, celle du développement de la justice pénale internationale d'autre part.

2.2.1 *Le développement de l'activité normative et institutionnelle en matière de lutte directe contre le terrorisme*

Des nombreux textes ont été adoptés depuis de longues années avant les attentats du 11 septembre 2001, mais c'est à partir de cette date et de la dramatisation de la situation qui en découle que la machine normative va s'emballer sans qu'on soit d'ailleurs certain de l'effet positif de cette surchauffe. En particulier, le Conseil de Sécurité crée un Comité du Conseil de Sécurité chargé de favoriser la participation des Etats à l'arsenal conventionnel existant et à suivre l'application des mesures décidées par la résolution 1373 du 28 septembre 2001, prise en application du chapitre VII de la Charte. Sur cette base sont prises un certain nombre de mesures destinées à empêcher que les Etats apportent un appui matériel, financier ou autre aux activités terroristes, à favoriser la coopération entre Etats, à organiser le gel des avoirs, etc. Cette résolution, applicable à tous les Etats, a par ailleurs une portée normative générale, ce qui a pu du reste être discuté par certains auteurs[4] et sert de socle à toutes les autres résolutions qui seront adoptées par la suite au fil des divers attentats commis ultérieurement.

L'empilement des conventions et résolutions permet de dégager, sinon une définition qui fait toujours défaut, mais au moins des axes de définition, en considérant que l'acte terroriste se définit moins par les moyens utilisés (tous sont bons en quelle que sorte) que par les effets recherchés : intimider une population, contraindre un gouvernement par un acte illicite et entraînant la mort, des blessures graves, sans tenir compte de la qualité de civil ou de militaire de la victime, ou entraîner des pertes économiques considérables et tout cela quelle que soit a qualité de l'auteur de l'acte. Mais c'est là bien entendu, une définition trop large.

2.2.2 *Le développement de la justice pénale internationale*

Les crimes de guerre, les crimes contre l'humanité, les actes de génocide ont à nouveau fait leur apparition sur une grande échelle depuis la fin du siècle dernier, si tant est qu'ils aient jamais disparus. Peut être, simplement, la Communauté internationale ouvre-t-elle davantage les yeux que du temps de la guerre froide où bien des conflits ont été « cachés » là où, aujourd'hui on parle plutôt de conflits « oubliés ». Toujours est-il que les conflits en Yougoslavie puis au Rwanda (où ils n'étaient d'ailleurs pas sans précédents) ont conduit à réactiver la question de la justice pénale internationale, tombée en sommeil dans les travaux de la Commission du droit international, avec la constitution des tribunaux spéciaux puis sera constituée la Cour pénale internationale. On sait que les questions qui ont pu être posées quant à la légalité de la création du Tribunal pour l'ex-Yougoslavie ont été tranchées en faveur de l'affirmative. Ils relèvent tout à la fois de la compétence du Conseil de Sécurité pour créer des organes subsidiaires, de son pouvoir de prendre des mesures diverses sur la base de l'article 41 de la Charte et de sa mission générale de rétablissement de la paix à laquelle concourt la justice, même si sa mission première vise à punir les auteurs de crimes.

---

[4] Voir E. David, op. cit., p. 181.

Il est intéressant de souligner pour terminer qu'au-delà des vicissitudes qui peuvent toujours affecter une institution à la suite de la survenance de tel ou tel événement, il reste qu'un fort mouvement s'est amorcé en faveur d'une généralisation de la justice pénale internationale, pas seulement avec la création de la Cour pénale qui présente un caractère permanent, même si sa compétence connaît des limites, mais aussi avec la constitution de multiples juridictions chargées, avec le concours des Nations Unies, de la sanction de crimes spécifiés. Qu'il s'agisse du Cambodge, du Sierra Leone, du Liban, le recours à la justice pénale internationale, ou mixte fait aujourd'hui figure de procédé normal, naturel. Les Nations Unies sont aujourd'hui fortement impliquées dans ces procédures qui connaissent un raffinement croissant. Notamment lorsqu'il s'agit d'associer des juges nationaux qui satisfont de légitimes considérations nationales et de souveraineté à des juges internationaux qui contribuent à l'impartialité de la justice, une justice qu'on peut vouloir éloigner cependant du lieu de commission des actes, afin de la rendre plus sereine et de la protéger. C'est ainsi que, dans l'actualité la plus récente, par la résolution 1664 du 29 mars 2006 relative aux poursuites contre les auteurs de l'attentat terroriste qui a coûté la vie à l'ancien Premier ministre libanais Rafik Hariri, le Conseil de Sécurité s'appuie sur la solution préconisée par le Conseiller juridique consistant à créer une juridiction mixte en la délocalisant en dehors du Liban pour les raisons que l'on vient d'exprimer. On peut souhaiter que le choix de La Haye soit possible, de même que devrait intervenir la délocalisation à la Haye de la Cour spéciale pour le Sierra Leone afin d'éviter que le jugement de Charles Taylor ne conduise à déstabiliser la région. La Haye capitale du droit international où nous avons la chance d'être réunis aujourd'hui.

Chapter 3
THE ROLE OF THE INTERNATIONAL CRIMINAL COURT IN AN EMERGING SYSTEM OF INTERNATIONAL JUSTICE

Navi Pillay*

1. Introduction

Each chapter in this book is focusing on different elements of the closely interrelated themes of peace, security and justice. I would like to focus mine on the emerging system of international justice and more specifically on the role of the International Criminal Court (ICC) within this system.

2. The emergence of international criminal justice

The first concrete efforts towards the establishment of international criminal courts were the military tribunals of Nuremberg and Tokyo, set up following the Second World War. In the context of this conference, I would note that the creation of the Nuremberg Tribunal was closely linked to the establishment of the United Nations (UN) as a means to ensure international peace and security. Indeed, the Charter of the Nuremberg Tribunal was discussed during meetings of the San Francisco conference that established the UN. For many involved in the Nuremberg and Tokyo tribunals, their primary purposes were to restore international peace and security and to prevent future breaches of the peace. This feeling was shared among the prosecutors and judges who saw the legacy of the tribunals in outlawing aggressive war and

* Judge International Criminal Court.

O. Ribbelink (ed.), Beyond the UN Charter: Peace, Security and the Role of Justice

building a new era of peace.[1] Bill Jackson, the son of the American Chief Prosecutor and himself a member of the prosecution team further elaborated on the close connections between Nuremberg and the UN in protecting the peace. He wrote that '... the principles of Nuremberg ... go hand in hand with the organization of the United Nations as the twin foundations of an international society ordered by law'.[2]

3. The need for accountability

One of the earliest initiatives of the United Nations was an attempt to establish a permanent international criminal court. However, the onset of the Cold War made this effort unworkable for half a century. In the meantime, massive crimes were committed around the world. National courts all too often were either unwilling or unable to prosecute the perpetrators. Without an international tribunal, the perpetrators were protected with impunity. This had negative consequences not only for the immediate victims but also for the international community more broadly.

With the end of the Cold War, things began to change. The last ten years or so in particular have seen more rapid growth in the international rule of law than in any time since the inception of the Nuremberg Tribunal. There is currently a heightened awareness of the importance of establishing the rule of law in securing justice and international peace and stability. In his 2004 report on the rule of law, the United Nations Secretary-General observed,

> '[the United Nations'] experience in the past decade has demonstrated clearly that the consolidation of peace in the immediate post-conflict period, as well as the maintenance of peace in the long term, cannot be achieved unless the population is confident that redress for grievances can be obtained through legitimate structures for the peaceful settlement of disputes and the fair administration of justice'.[3]

---

[1] See, e.g., Telford Taylor, *The Anatomy of the Nuremberg Trials* 226 (1993); opening statement of Robert Jackson, 2 *Trial of the Major War Criminals Before the International Military Tribunal* 153 (21 November 1945).

[2] As quoted in Telford Taylor, *The Anatomy of the Nuremberg Trials* 42 (1993).

[3] 'Report of the Secretary-General, Rule of Law and Transitional Justice in Conflict and Post-Conflict Societies', Para. 2, U.N. Doc. S/2004/616 (23 August 2004).

The dramatic developments of the last decade began with the creation of the United Nations *ad hoc* tribunals for the former Yugoslavia and Rwanda (the ICTY and ICTR), followed by the hybrid courts for Kosovo, East Timor, Sierra Leone and Cambodia, and the permanent International Criminal Court. The emergence of these tribunals grew out of the original purpose behind Nuremberg of contributing to peace and security. Both the ICTY and the ICTR were established by the UN Security Council under its mandate to restore and maintain international peace and security. The connection between international peace and justice is also expressed in the preamble to the ICC Statute. Moreover, the Security Council may refer situations to the ICC in order to maintain or restore peace and security. The Security Council has already done so once in the regard to the situation in Darfur, Sudan.

Peace and security is only one purpose of international criminal courts. Their immediate function is to conduct fair criminal trials of the most serious international crimes, namely genocide, crimes against humanity and war crimes. In doing so, they help ensure that perpetrators of serious crimes are not effectively granted impunity. Through an effective system of punishment, these courts are also intended to contribute over time to the deterrence of these crimes.

Justice is not only about punishing perpetrators and deterring crimes. Justice is also about restoring the dignity of victims. This involves two elements: reparations and participation in trials.

In the case of the ICTR, Rwandans called for a boycott of the Tribunal, giving as one of their reasons the injustice of no compensation for victims. They were particularly aggrieved that the Tribunal was providing HIV antiretroviral medication to detainees whereas victims of sexual crimes during the genocide had none. The judges of both the ICTY and ICTR recognized the importance of creating a special mechanism for reparations that would function alongside the tribunals.[4] One of the major advantages of the ICC is that the Court is empowered to order reparations to victims. In addition, a Trust Fund has also been established for the benefit of victims and their families.

---

[4] Letter dated 12 October 2000 from the President of the International Tribunal for the Former Yugoslavia addressed to the Secretary-General, U.N. Doc. S/2000/1063, Annex (3 November 2000); Letter dated 9 November 2000 from the President of the International Criminal Tribunal for Rwanda addressed to the Secretary-General, U.N. Doc. S/2000/1198, Annex (15 December 2000).

Another significant innovation of the ICC is that for the first time victims have the right to participate in international criminal proceedings as victims, not only as witnesses called by the prosecution or defence. This allows victims, subject to the needs of guaranteeing a fair trial, an opportunity to tell their story directly. The UN Secretary-General has noted that such forms of participation 'can also help victims to reclaim their dignity'.[5]

4. The role of international courts

There are many different modes of ensuring accountability for perpetrators and delivering justice for victims. I have spoken about international and hybrid courts. However, we must remember that the first responsibility to prevent and punish crimes belongs to States. National courts are also better placed to handle international crimes in light of their access to evidence and witnesses and their closeness to victims and affected populations. If national courts always adequately fulfilled this role, there would be no need for international courts. However, history has shown that this has not always been the case.

International mechanisms are needed to act where national courts are unwilling or unable to genuinely investigate or prosecute the most serious international crimes. In the context of the International Criminal Court, this is made explicit in the 'principle of complementarity'. Under this principle, the Court will ordinarily defer to national proceedings. The Court will only act where a State is unwilling or unable genuinely to carry out an investigation or prosecution. Furthermore, a case must be of sufficient gravity to justify action by the Court. The ICC is thus a court of last resort.

The principle of complementarity throws into focus the need to assist in strengthening domestic jurisdictions' ability to combat impunity for serious crimes through fair and impartial trials. In an ideal world, all states would incorporate the crimes within the ICC's jurisdiction in their domestic laws and investigate and prosecute the perpetrators of these crimes. Indeed, one of the benefits of the creation of the ICC since before the beginning of its operations has been the reinforcement by a number of States of their domes-

---

[5] 'Report of the Secretary-General, Rule of Law and Transitional Justice in Conflict and Post-Conflict Societies', Para. 39, U.N. Doc. S/2004/616 (23 August 2004).

tic legislation relating to international crimes. Nonetheless there still remains a need for international courts.

5. The role of the ICC

Of course, not all international courts are alike. The ICTY and ICTR were important pioneers in the field of international justice. They demonstrated that international trials are possible and have made significant contributions to the procedures and jurisprudence of international justice. Some have criticized the cost, delays and small number of cases of these *ad hoc* tribunals. We should hold a critical enquiry so that we can learn from errors made; however, it is also important to note how the tribunals met the new challenges they faced and the long-term significance of the jurisprudence they produced. The tribunals were groundbreaking new institutions and they overcame many difficulties related to inadequate administrative support and resources, bureaucratic and logistical impediments to holding trials expeditiously in areas remote from the scene of the crime, and a lack of full and consistent cooperation of States. I recall how, in November 1995, I confirmed the first indictment of the ICTR in a hotel room using a borrowed typewriter, as premises for the Tribunal had yet to be negotiated. Despite such challenging circumstances, the tribunals have persevered and have improved their practice over time. They have left a lasting legacy.

At the same time, the inherent limitations of the *ad hoc* tribunals also illustrate why the ICC was needed.

First, the ICC is a standing court, immediately and permanently available for crimes committed within its jurisdiction. This alleviates the political and financial obstacles which have delayed and maybe even prevented the establishment of other *ad hoc* tribunals. Moreover, the *ad hoc* tribunals have only begun to find their stride recently. This inefficiency is addressed by the creation of the permanent ICC.

The second advantage of the ICC is its broader geographical jurisdiction. The *ad hoc* tribunals and subsequent hybrid courts have been limited to specific situations occurring in one country or a few neighbouring countries. The ICC's jurisdiction is not limited to a specific country or countries. I should be clear to address any potential misconceptions: the ICC does not have universal jurisdiction. It may only exercise jurisdiction over nationals of states accepting the Court's jurisdiction or crimes on their territories. These are the two most clearly established bases of jurisdiction under international law and domestic law. In addition, the Security Council may refer situations to the Court independent of the location of the crime or the nationality of the perpetrators. Such a referral could be vetoed by any of the permanent members of the Council.

However, aside from Security Council referrals, the Court's jurisdiction only applies to States that have accepted the Court's jurisdiction. Therefore, the Court's potential impact depends on the number of States joining the Court. To date a hundred States have become Parties to the Court's Statute and one other State has also accepted the Court's jurisdiction. This broad geographical reach, combined with the Court's permanent nature, increase it potential deterrent effect.

The third advantage of the ICC is that it is an independent institution, established by a treaty. Its jurisdiction only applies to events that occur after a State joins the treaty. This means that States are free to choose to join the ICC or not. Some have questioned the legitimacy of the *ad hoc* tribunals as imposed after the fact by outside actors. Those criticisms are not well-founded. However, the ICC goes further in eliminating the possibility of such criticisms. It is a Court set up by States to judge actions on their own territories or by their own nationals if they become unwilling or unable to do so.

Notwithstanding these differences, the ICC is very much a continuation of the work begun by the *ad hoc* tribunals. The experiences of the ICTY and ICTR provided the background for the establishment of the substantive and procedural law of the ICC. One common challenge of all three courts was to reconcile different legal systems in a manner which guarantees a fair trial. In the case of the ICC, I would highlight four ways in which this has been achieved.

First, the Court is premised on the need for an independent, yet accountable judiciary. The judges of the ICC are bound by the Rome Statute and Rules and are accountable to the Assembly of States Parties which has the statutory power to remove a judge upon recommendation of a two-thirds majority of other judges. The required qualifications for election as a judge are also scrupulously set out in the Statute.

Second, the rights of the accused are fully protected at all stages of proceedings. To highlight a few rights, the Statute guarantees: the presumption of innocence, the right to counsel, the right to examine witnesses, and the prohibition on *in absentia* trials. The Statute also provides clear protections for rights of persons during investigations including: the right to counsel, the right to remain silent, and the right not to be arbitrarily arrested or detained.

Third, the Statute recognizes that a fair trial involves more than protecting the rights of the accused and suspects. The Statute and Rules also protect victims and witnesses. Special focus is paid throughout to the particular needs of victims of violence against women and children.

The fourth aspect I would highlight is an innovation – the Pre-Trial Chamber. The Pre-Trial Chamber must authorize investigations undertaken by the Prosecutor *proprio motu*. It also acts during the investigation and pre-trial stages to safeguard the rights of persons, in particular victims, witnesses and accused. By addressing preliminary issues that would otherwise take up the time of the Trial Chamber, the Pre-Trial Chamber may also increase the efficiency of trial proceedings.

6. The effectiveness of international justice

How effective have international courts been? We are only now beginning to receive the first indications of their effectiveness. Discussions of the impact of the Court increasingly appear in newspaper articles and other media reports from areas where investigations are ongoing. These often express hope or appreciation about the role of the Court. In his Report on the Rule of Law, the Secretary-General credited the ICC, through its mere existence, with

> 'having an important impact by putting would-be violators on notice that impunity is not assured and serving as a catalyst for enacting national laws against the gravest international crimes'.[6]

[6] 'Report of the Secretary-General, Rule of Law and Transitional Justice in Conflict and Post-Conflict Societies', Para. 49, U.N. Doc. S/2004/616 (23 August 2004).

The Court is a new institution. Its judges and Prosecutor took office in 2003. The first arrest warrants were unsealed in October 2005, and the first accused was surrendered to the Court in March 2006. As the Court continues to develop its practice, its potential impact will be strengthened, and we will learn more about its role in the system of international justice.

It must be acknowledged that judicial tribunals alone cannot achieve the goals of peace or justice. Many actors from governments to civil society organizations have a role in a comprehensive and integrated process to foster peace, democratic governance and access to justice.

To be effective, international justice must be a collaborative effort. International courts can only fulfil their important functions with sufficient State cooperation. International courts do not have police forces or enforcement mechanisms and are wholly dependant on the cooperation of States to carry out arrest and enforce sentences. With State cooperation, which was particularly good for the ICTR in Africa, the *ad hoc* tribunals were able to secure arrests, conduct investigations inside countries, and hear live testimony of thousands of witnesses. Such cooperation was not always forthcoming. For instance, Rwanda withheld witnesses from time to time in protest against the prosecutor's investigations of supporters of the pro-Rwandese Patriotic Front (RPF) government; and in the former Yugoslavia, suspects indicted by the ICTY over ten years ago, namely Karadzic and Mladic have not been arrested. The only solution available to the tribunals has been to complain to the Security Council as the body that could command compliance with UN obligations.

The ICC is also dependant on the cooperation of States. In addition to immediate support in arrest and surrender of persons, such cooperation could include for example the sharing of evidence, logistical support to Court activities in the field, or providing access to witnesses within a State's territory. In ratifying the Statute, States Parties accept a general obligation to cooperate with the Court as well as to provide specific instances of cooperation. Such cooperation must then be turned into action. In addition, the Court may negotiate additional agreements with States when necessary to facilitate cooperation. For example, the Court concludes agreements with States regarding the relocation of witnesses and the enforcement of sentences. And it is not only States Parties that support the Court. Any State in a position to assist the Court may also provide cooperation. International organizations also provide critical support to the Court. The Court has a Relationship Agreement with the UN[7] as well as subsidiary agreements with specific UN bodies. Cooperation with the UN is essential as the Court may often operate in areas where there is a UN peacekeeping or other presence. The Court is also in the process of negotiating agreements with the African Union and the European Union.[8]

Finally, civil society can provide important forms of support to international courts. Civil society has been particularly involved in urging ratifications of the Rome Statute. Non-governmental organizations also play important roles in the field in assisting victims to apply for participation or reparations and in increasing awareness and understanding of the ICC.

7. Conclusion

At the United Nations 2005 World Summit, Heads of State and Government from around the world accepted the responsibility of their States to protect their populations from genocide, war crimes, ethnic cleansing and crimes against humanity.[9] This expression of commitment to preventing these serious crimes is an important statement that must be translated into effective action.

If we are to continue to make progress in the fight against impunity and the search for peace, we must build on the past decade's efforts to strengthen the rule of international law. To quote the UN Secretary-General one last time,

> 'We all have a duty to do whatever we can to restore [respect for the rule of law]. To do so, we must start from the principle that no one is above the law, and no one should be denied its protection. ... And it is by rigorously upholding international law that we can, and must, fulfil our responsibility to protect innocent civilians from genocide, crimes against humanity and war crimes.'[10]

---

[7] 'Negotiated Relationship Agreement between the International Criminal Court and the United Nations', 4 October 2004, ICC-ASP/3/25.

[8] The 'Agreement between the International Criminal Court and the European Union on Cooperation and Assistance' was concluded on 10 April 2006, and entered into force on 1 May 2006, ICC-Pres/01-01-06.

[9] '2005 World Summit Outcome', Para. 138, U.N. Doc. A/Res/60/1 (24 October 2005).

[10] 'Address to the General Assembly', 21 September 2004, U.N. Doc. A/59/PV.3.

Chapter 4
REPENSER LA RÉFORME DU CONSEIL DE SÉCURITÉ : REPRÉSENTATIVITÉ, TRANSPARENCE, PERFORMANCE

Linos-Alexandre Sicilianos*

1. Introduction

Dans la Déclaration du Millénaire, les chefs d'État et de gouvernement des États membres de l'Organisation des Nations Unies (ONU) avaient proclamé leur intention de redoubler d'efforts « pour réformer les procédures du Conseil de sécurité sous tous leurs aspects ».[1] Rappelant cette décision, le Secrétaire général, M. Kofi Annan, estimait dans son rapport « Dans une liberté plus grande : développement, sécurité et droits de l'homme pour tous » qu'« aucune réforme de l'Organisation des Nations Unies ne serait complète sans une réforme du Conseil de sécurité ».[2] Pourtant, cinq ans après la déclaration solennelle précitée et en dépit des efforts et des propositions circonstanciées du Secrétaire général, le Document final du Sommet mondial de 2005[3] a été plutôt maigre sur la réforme du Conseil de sécurité. On sait que la pierre d'achoppement de cette réforme a été l'élargissement du Conseil de sécurité et plus particulièrement les réticences quant à la création de nouveaux sièges permanents. Devant cette impasse, les chefs d'État et de gouvernement ont préféré renvoyer la question à l'Assemblée générale.[4] Il est vrai que le Document final réaffirme la « responsabilité principale » du Conseil dans le domaine du maintien de la paix et de la sécurité internationales, ce qui n'est

* Professeur agrégé à l'Université d'Athènes, Membre du Comité des NU pour l'élimination de la discrimination raciale.

[1] A/RES/55/2, 8 septembre 2000, par. 30.

[2] A/59/2005, 24 mars 2005, par. 169.

[3] A/RES/60/1, 16 septembre 2005.

[4] Ibid., par. 153.

O. Ribbelink (ed.), Beyond the UN Charter: Peace, Security and the Role of Justice

pas dénué d'importance à une époque caractérisée par la résurgence de l'unilatéralisme. Les chefs d'État expriment également leur conviction que la réforme du Conseil de sécurité est « un élément central » de la réforme générale de l'Organisation.[5] Il n'empêche que, pour cette raison précisément, l'impossibilité d'aboutir à un accord sur l'élargissement et, partant, sur l'accroissement de la représentativité du Conseil a été perçue comme un échec majeur du Sommet.

Cependant, bien que la question de l'élargissement occupe, pour des raisons politiques évidentes, une place d'élection dans les débats relatifs à la réforme du Conseil de sécurité, il ne faudrait pas y voir le seul aspect de cette réforme. Par « réforme » on n'entend pas seulement celle qui implique un amendement de la Charte des Nations Unies, comme le changement de la composition du Conseil. Le terme en question revêt une portée plus large qui englobe des modifications relatives au mode de fonctionnement du Conseil. Il est significatif, en effet, que le Document final du Sommet mondial de 2005 recommande

> « que le Conseil de sécurité continue à adapter ses méthodes de travail de façon à ce que les États qui n'en sont pas membres participent davantage, le cas échéant, à ses travaux, à ce qu'il réponde mieux de son action devant l'ensemble des États membres et à ce qu'il fonctionne dans une plus grande transparence ».[6]

La transparence des travaux du Conseil constitue une préoccupation importante de la communauté internationale depuis un certain nombre d'années, tant il est vrai que la plupart de ses décisions sont prises à huis clos, sans la participation substantielle des acteurs impliqués, et que les moyens de communication de ce « club fermé » avec le monde extérieur, y compris le rapport annuel à l'Assemblée générale, sont réduits au strict minimum.

Le troisième aspect de la réforme du Conseil de sécurité, évoqué lui aussi dans le Document final du Sommet mondial de 2005, est peut-être le plus substantiel puisqu'il concerne la « performance » de cet organe, c'est-à-dire l'accroissement de son efficacité, et surtout « la qualité de [la] mise en œuvre » de ses décisions.[7] Il est vrai que depuis le début des années 1990 le Conseil

---

[5] Ibid., par. 152-153.
[6] Ibid., par. 154.
[7] Ibid., par. 153.

de sécurité a été présent, d'une façon ou d'une autre, dans pratiquement toutes les grandes crises internationales. Les critiques d'antan relatives à la carence du Conseil et à son blocage presque systématique à cause de l'exercice répété du droit de veto – critiques qui tendaient, en réalité, à légitimer toutes sortes de mesures unilatérales – se justifient difficilement dans la conjoncture actuelle. Il n'empêche que la multiplication spectaculaire des résolutions du Conseil de sécurité et l'extension de la portée de ses activités – élargissement parallèle à celui de la notion de « menace contre la paix » – posent inévitablement la question de l'efficacité et de l'effectivité de ses décisions.

Représentativité, transparence, performance : voilà les trois thèmes qui résument les débats, surtout les plus récents, autour de la réforme du Conseil de sécurité, et qui sont liés entre eux dans une large mesure. Il est évident, en effet, que plus le Conseil sera représentatif et transparent, plus ses décisions seront susceptibles d'être correctement et promptement mises en œuvre par les États membres.

2. L'ÉLARGISSEMENT DU CONSEIL : UN « NŒUD GORDIEN » ?

L'élargissement du Conseil de sécurité de onze à quinze membres a été effectué en pleine période de décolonisation. Plus de quarante ans après, la composition du Conseil ne reflète plus les changements cataclysmiques survenus entre-temps. Ainsi que le constatait le « Groupe de personnalités de haut niveau sur les menaces, les défis et le changement »,

> « [s]i les menaces et les défis qui guettent la paix et la sécurité internationales, de même que les rapports de force entre ses membres, ont changé de physionomie depuis sa création, le Conseil n'a quant à lui guère évolué ».[8]

Or, ce décalage entre les réalités du monde contemporain et la composition figée du Conseil ne va pas sans affecter sa légitimité et, partant, l'adhésion à ses décisions. L'élargissement du Conseil constituerait une nouvelle donne, qui devrait avoir des effets bénéfiques sur sa capacité de mobilisation de la communauté internationale. On sait, en effet, que plusieurs opérations de

[8] Cf. le rapport du Groupe de personnalités de haut niveau sur les menaces, les défis et le changement, « Un monde plus sûr : notre affaire à tous », doc. A/59/565, 2 décembre 2004, par. 245.

paix, par exemple, n'arrivent pas à se mettre en place rapidement ou à s'acquitter pleinement de leur mandat faute de ressources humaines et de contributions financières suffisantes. D'un autre côté, toutefois, un élargissement exponentiel du Conseil risquerait de nuire à sa flexibilité. Il en irait probablement de même en cas de création de nouveaux sièges permanents avec droit de veto. Trouver la solution idéale pour accroître la représentativité et la légitimité du Conseil de sécurité – ou, si l'on veut, pour « démocratiser et responsabiliser le Conseil »[9] – sans remettre en cause sa flexibilité, en créant de nouveaux blocages, constitue un véritable défi que la communauté internationale n'a pas su relever depuis plus de dix ans.

On sait, en effet, que les débats autour de ce problème ne sont pas nouveaux et que dès 1993 l'Assemblée générale a créé un

> « Groupe de travail à composition non limitée chargé d'examiner la question de la représentation équitable au Conseil de sécurité et de l'augmentation du nombre de ses membres, ainsi que d'autres questions ayant trait au Conseil de sécurité » (dorénavant Groupe de travail).[10]

Vouloir dresser l'historique de ces débats dépasserait de loin les limites de la présente étude.[11] Notre intention est de nous focaliser sur la situation telle qu'elle se dégage des travaux récents de l'Assemblée générale, et d'essayer de déceler les tendances dominantes.

2.1 **Les propositions récentes**

On relèvera ainsi qu'au cours des préparatifs du Sommet mondial de 2005, le « groupe des quatre » – c'est-à-dire l'Allemagne, le Brésil, l'Inde et le

---

[9] Selon l'expression du Groupe de personnalités de haut niveau, ibid., par. 249 *in fine*. On rappellera à cet égard que la « démocratisation » du système des Nations Unies, à commencer par le Conseil de sécurité, a été l'un des thèmes chers à l'ancien Secrétaire général, B. Boutros-Ghali, ainsi qu'en témoigne notamment son « Agenda pour la démocratisation », doc. A/51/761, 17 janvier 1997. Cf. également à ce sujet R. Mehdi (dir.), *La démocratisation du système des Nations Unies* (Paris : Pedone 2001).

[10] Cf. notamment les récents rapports de ce Groupe, doc. A/58/47, A/59/47.

[11] Pour une telle rétrospective, cf. O. Fleurence, *La réforme du Conseil de sécurité. L'état du débat depuis la fin de la guerre froide* (Bruxelles : Bruylant 2000), notamment pp. 56 s. Cf. également les rapports cités à la note précédente ; le rapport du Groupe de personnalités de haut niveau (précité, note 8), par. 244 s., ainsi que le rapport du Secrétaire général, « Dans une liberté plus large… » (précité, note 2), par. 168 s.

Japon – a pris l'initiative de présenter un projet de résolution, appuyé par plusieurs autres États,[12] selon lequel le nombre des membres du Conseil augmenterait de 15 à 25. Plus particulièrement, ce projet prévoyait l'ajout de six membres permanents : deux États africains, deux États asiatiques, un État du groupe de l'Amérique latine et des Caraïbes et encore un provenant du groupe d'Europe occidentale et autres États. Les quatre nouveaux membres non permanents seraient élus selon le schéma suivant : un État africain, un État asiatique, un autre de la part du groupe des États de l'Europe de l'Est et le dernier en provenance du groupe de l'Amérique latine et des Caraïbes. Contrairement aux propositions du Secrétaire général qui tentaient une recomposition des groupes régionaux en fonction de critères purement géographiques – Afrique, Asie et Pacifique, Europe, Amériques[13] –, le projet du « groupe des quatre » s'en tenait aux cinq groupes géopolitiques actuels, reflétant les divisions d'antan, tout en rééquilibrant la composition du Conseil en faveur des groupes africain et asiatique. Par ailleurs, le projet en question excluait l'exercice du droit de veto de la part des nouveaux membres permanents pour une période de quinze ans au moins, jusqu'à ce que la situation créée par les amendements de la Charte soit réexaminée.[14] De plus, le projet du « groupe des quatre » contenait des dispositions détaillées sur la procédure d'élection des nouveaux membres permanents, sur le contenu des amendements à apporter à la Charte, ainsi que sur la révision des méthodes de travail du Conseil, question sur laquelle on reviendra plus loin. Bref, ce projet présentait un schéma complet et, à notre sens, équilibré. Cependant, l'attitude négative de la Chine à l'entrée du Japon au Conseil de sécurité en tant que membre permanent,[15] les réserves des États-Unis concernant notamment le nombre des nouveaux sièges, ainsi que les demandes plutôt maximalistes des États africains ont constitué, semble-t-il, les facteurs principaux qui n'ont pas permis à ce projet d'aboutir lors du Sommet mondial de 2005.

---

[12] Doc. A/59/L.64, 6 juillet 2005.

[13] Cf. les « formules A et B », contenues dans le rapport précité, note 2, par. 170. Malgré cette différence de perception des enjeux géopolitiques, le projet du « groupe des quatre » s'inspirait largement de la « formule A » proposée par le Secrétaire général.

[14] Doc. A/59/L.64, par. 5 b) et 7.

[15] Le projet du « groupe des quatre » offrait effectivement cette possibilité puisqu'il prévoyait, on l'a vu, la création de deux sièges permanents revenant aux États asiatiques, l'un réservé apparemment à l'Inde, l'autre au Japon, même si aucun État n'était cité.

La position du groupe africain s'est reflétée, en substance, dans un autre projet, présenté par le Ghana, le Nigeria, le Sénégal et l'Afrique du Sud en décembre 2005.[16] Moins détaillé que celui du « groupe des quatre », le projet en question visait plus particulièrement à renforcer drastiquement le poids des États africains au sein du Conseil. C'est ainsi qu'au lieu de trois sièges supplémentaires revenant au groupe africain – deux sièges permanents, un siège non permanent –, le projet en question en prévoyait quatre, dont deux sièges non permanents. Le nombre total des États membres du Conseil serait porté à 26, au lieu de 25, les autres sièges supplémentaires étant distribués de la même manière que dans le projet du « groupe des quatre ». Par ailleurs, les nouveaux membres permanents auraient les mêmes prérogatives et privilèges que les membres permanents actuels, y compris le droit de veto. Les États africains disposeraient ainsi de sept sièges au total (au lieu des trois sièges non permanents dont ils bénéficient actuellement), dont deux sièges permanents avec droit de veto.

Ainsi qu'il a été abondamment souligné lors des débats de l'Assemblée générale au cours de sa soixantième session,[17] le groupe africain est manifestement sous-représenté dans la composition actuelle du Conseil de sécurité. La nécessité de renforcer sa participation ne fait pas de doute, d'autant plus que bon nombre de crises sur l'agenda du Conseil concernent l'Afrique. Cependant, le projet susmentionné ne semble pas avoir d'écho en dehors des États africains, y compris parce qu'il prévoit le droit de veto au profit des nouveaux membres permanents, ce qui est largement perçu comme source de blocage.

Le troisième projet, émanant du groupe d'États « unis pour le consensus » (Italie, Espagne, Pakistan, Argentine, Canada, Turquie, etc.), s'inspire de la « formule B » proposée par le Secrétaire général dans son rapport « Dans une liberté plus grande »,[18] en ce qu'il ne prévoit pas la création de nouveaux sièges permanents. Selon cette proposition, le Conseil de sécurité serait composé de 25 membres, dont les cinq membres permanents actuels. L'Assemblée générale élirait 20 membres non permanents en fonction de leur contribution au maintien de la paix et de la sécurité internationales et du critère de la répartition géographique équitable. Parmi les membres non permanents, six seraient élus au titre du groupe africain – qui doublerait ainsi sa

[16] Doc. A/60/L.41, 14 décembre 2005.

[17] Cf. A/60/PV.47-50, 10-11 novembre 2005.

[18] Op. cit., par. 170.

participation actuelle –, cinq autres proviendraient de l'Asie, quatre de l'Amérique latine et des Caraïbes, trois de l'Europe occidentale et des autres États et deux de l'Europe de l'Est. Les membres non permanents seraient élus pour une période de deux ans. Ils seraient rééligibles immédiatement. En effet, chacun des cinq groupes géopolitiques existants déciderait de la réélection ou de l'alternance de ses propres membres au Conseil. Il s'agit là d'un élément intéressant qui permettrait la prolongation du mandat des États ayant un poids particulier au sein des différents groupes et qui pourrait aboutir à la création *de facto* de sièges semi- ou quasi permanents. Tout en ayant le mérite de la flexibilité, ce schéma conférerait un pouvoir important aux groupes géopolitiques.

2.2 Les débats au sein de l'Assemblée générale

Les débats au sein de l'Assemblée générale au cours de la soixantième session[19] ont tourné autour de ces propositions sans aboutir à un résultat concret, comme le souhaitaient les chefs d'État et de gouvernement.[20] On peut néanmoins en dégager certaines tendances. La première constatation est que l'idée de l'élargissement du Conseil de sécurité bénéficie d'un très large appui, sinon d'un consensus. Cependant, même si les trois projets susmentionnés convergent ou presque sur le nombre des sièges supplémentaires à créer (dix, ou onze selon le projet africain), les États-Unis restent sceptiques, exprimant leur préférence pour une augmentation moins forte des membres du Conseil afin de ne pas entamer son efficacité. Les États-Unis insistent, par ailleurs, sur la nécessité de prévoir des critères pour l'élection au Conseil de sécurité, tels que le PIB et la population des pays concernés, leur possibilité de contribuer aux opérations de maintien de la paix de l'ONU, le respect des principes démocratiques et des droits de l'homme, la contribution au budget de l'Organisation, l'attachement à la lutte contre le terrorisme et à la non-prolifération des armes de destruction massive et la répartition géographique équitable.[21]

---

[19] *Supra*, note 17.

[20] Cf. le Document final du Sommet mondial de 2005, précité, par. 153.

[21] On rappellera à cet égard que l'article 23, par. 1, de la Charte énonce deux critères seulement pour l'élection au Conseil de sécurité, à savoir « la contribution des Membres de l'organisation au maintien de la paix et de la sécurité internationales et aux autres fins de l'Organisation » et la « répartition géographique équitable ». (Pour un commentaire de cette disposition, cf. R. Geiger, « Article 23 », dans B. Simma (gen. ed.), *The Charter of the United*

Au sujet de ce dernier critère, les débats au sein de l'Assemblée générale indiquent que le problème de la représentativité du Conseil, tel que celui-ci est composé actuellement, concerne principalement la participation des pays en développement et notamment des pays asiatiques et africains. Le fait que plusieurs foyers de crises sur l'agenda du Conseil se situent dans ces deux continents est un argument fort qui milite en faveur d'une représentation accrue de ces groupes d'États au sein du Conseil, d'autant plus que le phénomène ne semble pas circonstanciel, notamment pour ce qui est de la situation en Afrique.[22]

Toutefois, le dilemme le plus important concerne la création ou pas de nouveaux sièges permanents. Parmi les « cinq grands », seule la Chine semble clairement opposée à l'adjonction de nouveaux membres permanents. Il ne faut pas oublier, cependant, que selon l'article 109, paragraphe 2, de la Charte, toute modification de celle-ci présuppose l'assentiment de tous les membres permanents du Conseil de sécurité. Par ailleurs, la création de nouveaux sièges permanents suscite des réserves plus ou moins fortes auprès d'un certain

---

Nations. A Commentary, 2nd ed. (Oxford : Oxford University Press 2002), vol. I, pp. 437 ss. ; M. Benchikh, « Article 23 », dans J.-P. Cot, A. Pellet, M. Forteau, *La Charte des Nations Unies. Commentaire article par article*, 3e éd. (Paris : Economica 2005) vol. I, pp. 867 ss.). Lors des débats au sein du Groupe de travail, certaines délégations ont souligné que ces deux critères devraient être appliqués conjointement et non pas séparément, de façon à accroître les chances pour les États plus petits d'être élus au Conseil de sécurité. Dans le même ordre d'idées, il a été avancé que la population d'un État et sa puissance économique ne devraient pas entrer en ligne de compte, puisque tous les États membres devraient être traités de manière égale, en conformité avec le principe de l'égalité souveraine des États (A/58/47, annexe IV, par. 34). On relèvera également que le critère relatif à la contribution au maintien de la paix et aux autres buts de l'ONU se prête à des interprétations diverses. Se limiter à la contribution financière constituerait une interprétation restrictive du critère en question. D'autres formes de « contribution » sont tout aussi importantes, y compris les efforts de médiation, la promotion du respect du droit international en général et du principe du règlement pacifique des différends en particulier, les initiatives dans les domaines du développement, du respect des droits de l'homme, de l'assistance humanitaire, etc. En d'autres termes, le libellé du premier critère de l'article 23, par. 1, de la Charte est suffisamment large pour permettre la prise en compte d'une série d'éléments. Vouloir introduire *expressis verbis* de nouveaux critères risquerait ne pas pouvoir faire l'objet d'un consensus, ainsi qu'il a été remarqué par plusieurs délégations au sein du Groupe de travail (A/58/47, annexe IV, par. 39).

[22] Cf. le rapport du Secrétaire général sur « Les causes des conflits et la promotion d'une paix et d'un développement durables en Afrique », doc. S/1998/318, 13 avril 1998. Cf. également l'analyse de G. CAHIN, « Les Nations Unies et la construction d'une paix durable en Afrique », dans R. Mehdi, *La contribution des Nations Unies à la démocratisation de l'État* (Paris : Pedone 2002), pp. 133-159.

nombre d'autres États, à commencer par les auteurs du troisième projet mentionné précédemment.

Cette situation pose la question de la procédure à suivre pour aboutir à une solution. Pour certains, il faudrait éviter le vote et chercher un « consensus de qualité » pour ne pas créer des fractures au sein de l'Organisation sur un sujet aussi important que la composition du Conseil de sécurité.[23] Pour d'autres, en revanche, le vote ne devrait pas être exclu.[24] Au vu de ces approches contrastées, il a été décidé de renvoyer le problème de l'élargissement au Groupe de travail susmentionné chargé d'examiner la question de la représentation équitable au Conseil de sécurité et de l'augmentation du nombre de ses membres.

Faut-il y voir un renvoi de la question aux « calendes grecques » ? Personne ne saurait répondre avec certitude. Force est de constater, cependant, que la solution du « nœud gordien » qu'est devenu l'élargissement du Conseil de sécurité demande imagination et volonté de compromis de tous les côtés. Persister à formuler des propositions non réalistes aboutit en fait au maintien du *statu quo*, situation qui va à l'encontre du but recherché – garantir la représentativité et la légitimité du Conseil – et des intérêts de ceux qui soumettent de tels projets. S'il est vrai que l'augmentation des membres du Conseil est particulièrement délicate à la fois politiquement et juridiquement, puisqu'elle implique un amendement de la Charte, il ne faudrait pas oublier que les difficultés importantes auxquelles s'est heurtée pendant des mois la création du Conseil des droits de l'homme ont pu être dépassées et que la résolution y relative de l'Assemblée générale[25] a été finalement adoptée à une majorité écrasante.

3. Le renouveau des méthodes de travail du Conseil : en quête d'ouverture

Cela dit, on ne soulignera jamais assez que la réforme du Conseil de sécurité ne se résume pas à son élargissement. Qui dit réforme dit aussi révision des méthodes de travail du Conseil dans le sens d'une plus grande transparence. Contrairement à la question de sa composition, le renouveau des méthodes

[23] Cf. en ce sens le plaidoyer du représentant de l'Italie, A/60/PV.50, p. 19.
[24] Cf. en ce sens la déclaration du représentant du Brésil, A/60/PV.49, p. 18.
[25] A/RES/60/251, 15 mars 2006.

de travail du Conseil n'implique aucun amendement de la Charte. Même si certaines ouvertures peuvent être observées ces dernières années, la nécessité d'une plus grande transparence des travaux du Conseil a été soulignée par le Groupe de travail,[26] par le Groupe de personnalités de haut niveau[27] et par le Secrétaire général.[28] Dans le Document final du Sommet mondial de 2005, les chefs d'État et de gouvernement ont repris cette recommandation.[29] Les travaux de l'Assemblée générale lors de sa soixantième session s'inscrivent dans le même ordre d'idées, d'autant plus que le projet de résolution du « groupe des quatre » contient un paragraphe substantiel sur le renouveau des méthodes de travail du Conseil de sécurité[30] et qu'en novembre 2005 le groupe des « cinq petits pays » a présenté une autre proposition consacrée à cette même question.[31] Plusieurs idées se dégagent de l'ensemble de ces éléments.

3.1 Information et communication

On rappellera, tout d'abord, que le Document final du Sommet mondial de 2005 recommande que le Conseil de sécurité « réponde mieux de son action devant l'ensemble des États membres »,[32] recommandation qui concerne manifestement les rapports annuels du Conseil à l'Assemblée générale. Qualifiés de « descriptifs et routiniers » par le représentant du Guatemala,[33] ces rapports contiennent, certes, plusieurs informations d'ordre procédural mais peu d'éléments permettant de se faire une idée claire des enjeux en cause devant le Conseil de sécurité et de l'impact de son action. Or, la Charte des Nations Unies accorde une importance certaine aux rapports annuels du Conseil à l'Assemblée puisqu'elle s'y réfère à deux reprises dans les articles 15, paragraphe 1, et 24, paragraphe 3. Ces rapports devraient être la liaison

---

[26] Cf. A/58/47, annexe IV, par. 43 s. ; A/59/47, annexe II.

[27] Cf. A/59/565, rapport précité, par. 258.

[28] Cf. A/59/2005, par. 168.

[29] Cf. *supra*, note 6 et le texte y relatif.

[30] A/59/L.64, par. 8.

[31] Il s'agit d'un projet de résolution distribué officieusement le 4 novembre 2005 par le Costa Rica, la Jordanie, le Liechtenstein, Singapour et la Suisse. Cf. à ce sujet les déclarations de ces pays à l'Assemblée générale et notamment celle du représentant de la Suisse, A/60/PV.48, p. 8.

[32] Document précité, par. 154.

[33] A/60/PV.49, p. 23.

principale entre ces deux organes, en constituant un moyen de coordination et de complémentarité indispensables entre les activités du Conseil de sécurité et de l'Assemblée générale dans le domaine du maintien de la paix et de la sécurité internationales. C'est la raison pour laquelle un certain nombre de délégations au Groupe de travail ont estimé que les rapports annuels du Conseil devraient être

> « factuels, complets, approfondis et analytiques et comporter une évaluation des activités et de l'efficacité de l'action du Conseil ainsi que des informations concernant les demandes que le Conseil a reçues en vertu de l'Article 50 de la Charte des Nations Unies et la suite qu'il leur a réservée ».[34]

S'il est vrai que l'inclusion d'une importante partie analytique pourrait exiger des négociations plus ou moins longues au sein du Conseil, l'idée que les rapports annuels soient plus complets et plus approfondis a été largement partagée au sein du Groupe de travail. On y a souligné également que l'examen du rapport du Conseil de sécurité par l'Assemblée générale devrait être plus substantiel et interactif, avec la participation active des membres du Conseil et la possibilité pour les non-membres de leur poser des questions.[35] Encore faut-il relever que les articles 15, paragraphe 1, et 24, paragraphe 3, de la Charte prévoient également la soumission de rapports spéciaux à l'Assemblée générale, possibilité qui mériterait d'être exploitée par le Conseil de sécurité.

Dans le même ordre d'idées, on mentionnera la problématique relative au caractère public ou non des séances du Conseil. Pour plusieurs délégations, il faudrait limiter autant que possible les séances privées et les consultations officieuses et leur réserver un caractère exceptionnel, tout en multipliant les séances publiques et en les annonçant suffisamment à l'avance pour permettre aux États intéressés d'y participer. Par ailleurs et afin d'assurer une meilleure information sur les travaux du Conseil, il serait important que les exposés de celui-ci aux non-membres soient plus fréquents et plus approfondis, et qu'ils portent sur les questions débattues au sein du Conseil lui-même et de ses organes subsidiaires, y compris sur les missions *ad hoc*. Il faudrait également

---

[34] A/59/47, annexe II, par. 5. L'article 50 concerne les « effets secondaires » des mesures préventives ou coercitives prises par le Conseil de sécurité au titre du chapitre VII à l'égard des États non visés par ces mesures. Pour une analyse approfondie de ce sujet, cf. D. L. Tehindrazanarivelo, *Les sanctions des Nations Unies et leurs effets secondaires* (Paris : PUF 2005) pp. 70 ss.

[35] Ibid.

que les projets de résolution, les déclarations présidentielles ainsi que les rapports du Secrétaire général au Conseil soient mis à la disposition de tous les États membres de l'Organisation le plus tôt possible, que les séances de récapitulation de la présidence du Conseil soient rétablies de façon systématique et que les évaluations mensuelles de la présidence soient plus complètes et analytiques.[36] Bref, il est nécessaire de renforcer la communication entre les membres du Conseil et les autres États membres de l'ONU en réduisant l'opacité qui semble entourer souvent les travaux du Conseil.

3.2 Consultation et concertation

La transparence dans le fonctionnement du Conseil présuppose également que celui-ci implique davantage dans ses travaux les États particulièrement concernés par ses décisions. Il en va ainsi notamment des États qui fournissent des contingents aux opérations de maintien de la paix ou qui participent aux forces multinationales mises sur pied sur l'autorisation du Conseil. On rappellera à cet égard que selon l'article 44 de la Charte

> « [l]orsque le Conseil de Sécurité a décidé de recourir à la force, il doit, avant d'inviter un membre non représenté au Conseil à fournir des forces armées en exécution des obligations contractées en vertu de l'article 43, convier ledit membre, si celui-ci le désire, à participer aux décisions du Conseil de Sécurité touchant l'emploi de contingents des forces armées de ce membre ».

Il est vrai que cette disposition était censée s'appliquer dans le contexte de la mise en œuvre des « accords spéciaux » de l'article 43, accords qui n'ont jamais été conclus. Cependant, la *ratio* de l'article 44 était d'offrir la possibilité aux États participant à des opérations militaires en vertu du chapitre VII d'être représentés et de se faire entendre au sein du Conseil. Pour reprendre la formule percutante du délégué des Pays-Bas lors de la Conférence de San Francisco : « *No military action without representation* ».[37]

Dans cet ordre d'idées, il est important que le Conseil organise des consultations régulières avec les États qui fournissent ou qui seraient prêts à fournir des contingents militaires et des forces de police, notamment aux premières étapes de la planification des missions, mais aussi pendant la mise

---

[36] Ibid., par. 6-7 ; A/59/L.64, projet précité, par. 8, al. a), d) et e).

[37] *United Nations Conference on International Organization*, vol. XII, p. 316.

en place, le déroulement, le suivi et le démantèlement des opérations de maintien de la paix ou des opérations autorisées, menées par des forces multinationales, y compris en cas de prorogation ou de modification du mandat de telles opérations, ainsi que sur des questions opérationnelles spécifiques. Des consultations appropriées devraient avoir lieu également avec les États qui participent aux opérations de maintien de la paix sur les plans financier ou politique ou qui sont directement concernés ou affectés par une telle opération.[38] Plus généralement, le Conseil de sécurité devrait exploiter davantage les articles 31 et 32 de la Charte en consultant les États non-membres sur une base régulière, notamment ceux qui ont un intérêt particulier pour la question inscrite chaque fois à l'ordre du jour du Conseil.

Des considérations analogues s'appliquent au sujet de l'accès des États non-membres du Conseil de sécurité aux organes subsidiaires de celui-ci. Pour certaines délégations au sein du Groupe de travail, il y aurait un manque de transparence des réunions des organes subsidiaires. Il faudrait, par conséquent, que ces réunions soient ouvertes, autant que de besoin, aux États non représentés au Conseil. On a pu proposer également que la composition des organes subsidiaires soit élargie à des États non-membres du Conseil,[39] proposition plutôt insolite du point de vue institutionnel. En effet, permettre à des États non représentés au Conseil de participer au cas par cas, à titre d'observateur, à des réunions qui les concernent est une chose, élargir la composition des organes subsidiaires pour y inclure d'autres États – selon des procédures et en fonction de critères qui restent imprécis – en est certainement une autre. Quoi qu'il en soit, le besoin d'ouverture des organes subsidiaires du Conseil de sécurité, et notamment des comités de sanctions, aux États non-membres du Conseil se fait sentir. Il importe notamment que les États tout particulièrement affectés par les régimes de sanctions puissent s'adresser plus aisément aux comités des sanctions afin d'expliquer les difficultés qu'ils affrontent et de chercher une solution selon les termes de l'article 50 de la Charte.[40]

---

[38] Cf. A/59/L.64, projet précité, par. 8, al. f).

[39] A/59/47, annexe II, par. 18.

[40] Cf. sur ce point les recommandations de l'Assemblée générale dans l'annexe II de la résolution 51/242 en date du 15 septembre 1997, intitulée « Question des sanctions imposées par l'Organisation des Nations Unies ». Tout autre est la question des procédures qui permettraient aux comités des sanctions d'examiner les plaintes éventuelles de ceux qui estiment avoir été indûment inscrits sur la liste des particuliers ou entités visés par les sanctions (cf. à ce sujet le rapport précité du Groupe de personnalités de haut niveau, doc. A/59/565, par. 182).

Au-delà de l'ouverture du Conseil de sécurité aux États membres, on mentionnera également la question des rapports de celui-ci avec les autres organes principaux de l'ONU. Il est évident que cette question touche au problème plus vaste des équilibres institutionnels au sein de l'Organisation. Sans vouloir entrer dans les méandres de ce débat, on insistera notamment sur la nécessité d'une synergie plus poussée entre le Conseil de sécurité, l'Assemblée générale et le Conseil économique et social. Dans cet ordre d'idées, on a évoqué à diverses reprises l'importance d'organiser des consultations régulières entre les présidents de ces trois organes.[41] Loin d'y voir une simple formalité, il faudrait au contraire exploiter les potentialités d'une telle proposition, tant il est vrai que le maintien et surtout la consolidation de la paix après la fin des conflits[42] dépassent souvent les compétences, voire les capacités d'action du Conseil de sécurité. La création de la Commission de consolidation de la paix par l'Assemblée générale[43] et par le Conseil de sécurité,[44] agissant de concert – processus qui constitue une véritable nouveauté du point de vue institutionnel – offre de nouvelles perspectives, tout en soulignant la nécessité d'une coopération plus étroite entre les organes principaux de l'Organisation.

Des considérations analogues valent *mutatis mutandis* pour ce qui est de l'ouverture du Conseil de sécurité à d'autres acteurs en dehors du système onusien, à commencer par les organisations régionales et sous-régionales. Malgré les déclarations de bonnes intentions, y compris lors du Sommet mondial de 2005,[45] et en dépit des efforts entrepris ces dernières années, il reste un fait que les potentialités du chapitre VIII de la Charte sont aujourd'hui encore largement sous-exploitées, particulièrement pour ce qui est de la coopération avec l'Unité africaine. Ainsi que le constatait le Groupe de personnalités de haut niveau, « [l]es activités de concertation et de coopération entre l'ONU et les organisations régionales devraient être élargies ». Et le Groupe de proposer que de telles activités concertées puissent être consignées officiellement dans un accord qui porterait notamment sur des réunions entre chefs de secrétariat, sur l'intensification des échanges d'informations et de

---

[41] Cf. A/59/47, annexe II, par. 8 ; A/59/L.64, par. 8 g).

[42] Sur cette question, cf. l'analyse approfondie de P. Daillier, « Les opérations multinationales consécutives à des conflits armés en vue du rétablissement de la paix », t. 314 *Recueil des cours* (2005) pp. 233-431.

[43] A/RES/60/180, 20 décembre 2005.

[44] S/RES/1645 (2005), 20 décembre 2005.

[45] Cf. A/RES/60/1, par. 170.

données d'alerte rapide ainsi que sur des activités communes d'information de civils et de militaires et des échanges de personnel dans le cadre des opérations de paix.[46]

La concertation avec les institutions financières devrait, elle aussi, être renforcée, ainsi qu'il résulte clairement des résolutions portant création de la Commission de consolidation de la paix.[47] On mentionnera, enfin, l'ouverture du Conseil de sécurité aux ONG, voire plus généralement à la société civile, sujet presque tabou il y a encore quelques années. Aujourd'hui il est presque inutile d'insister sur l'importance de la contribution d'un nombre important d'ONG à l'œuvre du Conseil, notamment sous forme de sous-traitance, que ce soit dans le domaine humanitaire ou dans le contexte de la consolidation de la paix.

S'ouvrir à l'ensemble des acteurs susmentionnés va dans le sens d'une plus grande transparence des travaux du Conseil, tout en étant susceptible d'accroître ses moyens d'action et donc sa performance.

4. Le renforcement des moyens d'action du Conseil : en quête d'efficacité

Aborder la question de la performance du Conseil de sécurité ne signifie aucunement que l'on adhère aux opinions de ceux qui l'accusent d'immobilisme. Parler de la carence du Conseil pour tenter de justifier une série de mesures unilatérales était un argument invoqué à satiété durant la période de la guerre froide.[48] Exhumer cette argumentation ne répond plus aux circonstances actuelles, tant il est vrai que depuis 1990 le Conseil a pu se prononcer et édicter des mesures dans presque toutes les crises ayant pris des dimensions internationales. Pendant la même période, le Conseil a fait preuve d'une inventivité certaine en adaptant continuellement ses moyens d'action. On rappellera ainsi la transformation profonde des opérations de maintien, voire de rétablissement ou d'imposition de la paix ; les autorisations répétées de recourir à la force ; le déploiement successif ou simultané de « casques bleus » et de forces multinationales ; la diversification des sanctions non

[46] Cf. A/59/565, rapport précité, par. 272.

[47] Cf. A/RES/60/180, par. 7 e) et par. 9 ; S/RES/1645 (2005), par. 7 e) et par. 9.

[48] Pour une réfutation de cette argumentation, cf. L.-A. Sicilianos, *Les réactions décentralisées à l'illicite : des contre-mesures à la légitime défense* (Paris : LGDJ 1990) pp. 413 ss.

militaires, y compris l'édiction de « sanctions intelligentes » contre des entités non étatiques ou des individus ; le couplage des sanctions non militaires avec des opérations de maintien de la paix ou des opérations autorisées ; la mise en place de tribunaux pénaux *ad hoc* ; l'adoption de résolutions à caractère « législatif » en matière antiterroriste[49] ou dans le domaine des armes de destruction massive ;[50] ou encore l'administration provisoire de territoires. Bref, en exploitant la théorie des pouvoirs implicites et en interprétant et en appliquant de manière large la notion de menace contre la paix, contenue dans l'article 39 de la Charte, le Conseil a su élargir son champ d'activités et diversifier ses moyens d'action.[51]

4.1 Créer et exploiter des synergies nouvelles

Cependant, repenser et rénover continuellement les moyens d'action du Conseil pour répondre aux nouvelles menaces contre la paix et la sécurité internationales sont une nécessité absolue. Dans cet ordre d'idées, il serait essentiel que le Conseil exploite davantage les potentialités du chapitre VIII de la Charte en intensifiant sa coopération avec les organismes régionaux. Les propositions du Groupe de personnalités de haut niveau,[52] reprises en grande partie par le Secrétaire général,[53] devraient enfin devenir une réalité. Le Document final du Sommet mondial de 2005 insiste, lui aussi, sur l'expansion de la consultation et de la coopération entre les Nations Unies et les organisations régionales et sous-régionales à travers des accords formels entre leurs secrétariats respectifs, ainsi que sur l'implication de telles organisations dans les travaux du Conseil de sécurité, lorsque cela s'avère approprié. Par ailleurs, les organisations régionales qui disposent de capacités de prévention des conflits ou de maintien de la paix devraient être encouragées à placer ces moyens dans le cadre du Système de forces et moyens en attente des Nations Unies.[54]

---

[49] Cf. S/RES/1373 (2001), 28 septembre 2001.

[50] Cf. S/RES/1540 (2004), 28 avril 2004.

[51] Pour une appréciation d'ensemble de l'adaptation continue des pouvoirs du Conseil de sécurité, cf. L.-A. Sicilianos, « Après l'Irak : vers une redéfinition des pouvoirs du Conseil de sécurité ? », dans K. Bannelier, Th. Christakis, O. Corten, P. Klein, *L'intervention en Irak et le droit international* (Paris : Pedone 2004) pp. 59-82, notamment pp. 69 ss.

[52] A/59/565, par. 272.

[53] A/59/2005, par. 231 s.

[54] A/RES/60/1, par. 170 ; dans le même sens cf. A/59/2005, par. 213.

Toutefois, le Document final reste silencieux sur la proposition la plus audacieuse du Secrétaire général, tendant à modifier les règles régissant les budgets des opérations onusiennes de maintien de la paix de façon à permettre à l'Organisation de financer, ne serait-ce qu'exceptionnellement,

> « au moyen de contributions obligatoires des opérations régionales autorisées par le Conseil de sécurité, ou d'autoriser des organisations régionales à participer à des opérations de paix à composantes multiples, sous la tutelle de l'ONU ».[55]

Le Document final ne reprend pas non plus une proposition du Groupe de personnalités de haut niveau, concernant la possibilité pour l'ONU d'offrir aux opérations régionales un appui sur le plan matériel, en puisant dans ses propres stocks.[56] Or, il est bien connu que certaines organisations régionales et sous-régionales, telles que l'Union africaine ou la Communauté économique des États de l'Afrique de l'Ouest (CEDEAO), ne disposent pas toujours des moyens nécessaires pour s'engager efficacement sur le terrain. Un soutien financier et matériel à certaines organisations régionales pour mener à bien des opérations « sous la tutelle » de l'Organisation mondiale constituerait un important pas en avant dans le domaine du maintien de la paix et de la sécurité internationales. Dans le même ordre d'idées se situait également une autre proposition du Groupe de personnalités de haut niveau, concernant les capacités régionales et sous-régionales de l'Afrique et faisant appel aux pays donateurs de s'engager à mener à bien, sur une période de dix ans, « une campagne d'appui continu aux activités de renforcement des capacités s'inscrivant dans la stratégie globale de l'Union africaine ».[57] Aucun engagement explicite en ce sens ne figure dans le Document final du Sommet mondial de 2005. On ne peut donc que constater que les avancées entérinées par les chefs d'État et de gouvernement en matière de coopération effective avec les organisations régionales restent plutôt maigres et que le Sommet mondial a perdu une occasion historique de changer la donne en cette matière.

Il est à espérer, en revanche, que la Commission de consolidation de la paix, nouvellement créée, puisse combler la « faille énorme dans la structure institutionnelle des Nations Unies »,[58] à savoir l'inexistence d'un élément

---

[55] A/59/2005, par. 215.

[56] A/59/565, par. 272.

[57] Ibid.

[58] Selon l'expression du Secrétaire général dans sa note explicative sur la Commission de consolidation de la paix, doc. A/59/2005/Add.2, par. 2.

du système en mesure d'aider les pays à réussir à passer de la guerre à une paix durable. Cette lacune a conduit à diverses reprises à l'anéantissement des efforts du Conseil de sécurité en matière de rétablissement de la paix. Ainsi que le notait le Secrétaire général, « [e]nviron la moitié des pays qui sortent d'un conflit retombent dans la violence dans les cinq années qui suivent ».[59] Il s'agit là d'une constatation dramatique pour la crédibilité de l'Organisation mondiale. La mise en place de la Commission de consolidation de la paix devrait constituer le « chaînon manquant » entre l'action du Conseil de sécurité et celle du Conseil économique et social et d'autres acteurs du système dans le domaine de la reconstruction et du développement durable.

Les résolutions « fondatrices » de la Commission lui confient des fonctions plutôt larges, telles que la mobilisation de ressources, la proposition de stratégies intégrées aux fins de la consolidation de la paix et du relèvement après les conflits, l'amélioration de la coordination entre tous les intéressés au sein du système des Nations Unies et en dehors en vue de la reconstruction et du développement durable des pays concernés, etc.[60] La Commission fonctionnera de façon ouverte en associant à ses travaux une série d'acteurs et notamment les autorités du pays concerné, des représentants des pays de la région qui participent aux activités d'après conflit, des représentants des pays qui participent à l'entreprise de relèvement, le principal représentant de l'ONU sur place, des représentants des institutions financières régionales et internationales, tout particulièrement la Banque mondiale, le Fonds monétaire international (FMI) et d'autres bailleurs de fonds. Par ailleurs, la Commission mènera ses travaux « en étroite consultation » avec les organisations régionales et sous-régionales dans le but de les associer aux efforts de consolidation de la paix conformément au chapitre VIII de la Charte.[61] Autrement dit, les résolutions portant création de la Commission concrétisent plusieurs idées avancées, on l'a vu, pour le renouveau des méthodes de travail du Conseil de sécurité lui-même. Cependant, la Commission de consolidation de la paix aura un rôle purement consultatif et prendra toutes ses décisions par consensus,[62] éléments qui pourraient être de nature à affaiblir l'efficacité de son action.

---

[59] Ibid., par. 1

[60] A/RES/60/180, par. 2 ; S/RES/1645 (2005), par. 2.

[61] A/RES/60/180, par. 7-11 ; S/RES/1645 (2005), par. 7-11.

[62] A/RES/60/180, par. 18 ; S/RES/1645 (2005), par. 18.

Une autre évolution qui mérite d'être mentionnée à cet endroit est la création du Conseil des droits de l'homme,[63] organe qui a commencé à fonctionner le 19 juin 2006. Il est vrai que le Conseil en question est un organe subsidiaire de l'Assemblée générale[64] et non pas du Conseil de sécurité. Il n'empêche que d'après son mandat, le Conseil des droits de l'homme contribuera à la prévention des violations des droits de l'homme. Il devrait réagir promptement en cas d'urgence et formuler des recommandations en relation avec des violations graves et systématiques des droits de l'homme.[65] Étant donné que de telles violations ont souvent été qualifiées de menaces contre la paix et la sécurité internationales en donnant lieu à des mesures prises par le Conseil de sécurité,[66] il est évident que les travaux de celui-ci pourraient bénéficier des activités du Conseil des droits de l'homme. On sait que, par le passé, il y avait peu de synergie entre la Commission des droits de l'homme et le Conseil de sécurité. Il est donc essentiel que la création du Conseil des droits de l'homme constitue un nouveau départ dans ce domaine.

4.2 **Limiter l'utilisation du veto**

Une autre question qui a été amplement débattue dans le processus de réforme des Nations Unies et du Conseil de sécurité en particulier concerne l'utilisation du droit de veto. S'il est vrai que l'usage de ce droit est devenu relativement rare depuis la fin de la guerre froide, il est tout aussi certain qu'il s'agit là d'un élément ayant « un côté anachronique qui sied mal à l'institution, étant donné l'avancée de la démocratie ».[67] Cependant, toute proposition tendant à abolir ce droit[68] s'avère irréaliste à l'heure actuelle. La question est de savoir si l'on peut limiter son utilisation en vue d'éviter le blocage du Conseil.

Dans cet ordre d'idées, le Groupe de personnalités de haut niveau a proposé d'instituer un système de « vote indicatif » qui permettrait à tout membre du Conseil de demander que chacun prenne position sur un projet de décision.

---

[63] A/RES/60/251, 15 mars 2006.

[64] Ibid., par. 1.

[65] Ibid., par. 3 et 5 f).

[66] Cf. G. Cohen-Jonathan, « Le Conseil de sécurité et les droits de l'homme », dans *Le droit des organisations internationales. Recueil à la mémoire de Jacques Schwob* (Bruxelles : Bruylant 1997) pp. 19-70.

[67] Selon les termes du Groupe de personnalités de haut niveau, doc. A/59/565, par. 256.

[68] Cette proposition a été avancée au sein du Groupe de travail, A/59/47, par. 20.

Dans une telle hypothèse, les « non » n'auraient pas force de veto et le résultat du scrutin n'aurait pas force exécutoire. La mise aux voix officielle d'un projet de résolution serait régie, elle, par les procédures actuelles du Conseil. Une telle formule contribuerait à « responsabiliser » les membres permanents qui usent de leur droit de veto.[69] Sans être dénuée d'intérêt, une telle procédure conduirait difficilement l'État membre intéressé à modifier son vote. Elle pourrait néanmoins provoquer la renégociation du projet de résolution sous examen.

Une autre idée serait d'encourager les membres permanents à s'auto-limiter en s'engageant solennellement à n'utiliser leur droit de veto que lorsque des intérêts vitaux sont véritablement en cause et à renoncer à faire usage de ce droit en cas de génocide ou de violation massive des droits de l'homme.[70] Reprise en substance par certaines délégations – comme celle du Canada – lors de la soixantième session de l'Assemblée générale,[71] cette dernière idée semble avoir été inspirée par le cas du Kosovo. En tout état de cause, renoncer au droit de veto en cas de génocide, de nettoyage ethnique, de crimes de guerre ou de crimes contre l'humanité découlerait du « devoir de protéger », entériné par le Document final du Sommet mondial de 2005.[72] Une telle renonciation serait conforme également au devoir des États de coopérer pour mettre fin à toute violation grave de normes du *jus cogens*, obligation énoncée par la Commission du droit international (CDI) lors de la codification de la responsabilité de l'État pour fait internationalement illicite.[73]

5. Remarques finales

La réforme du Conseil de sécurité constitue un aspect essentiel de la revitalisation des Nations Unies. Partant de l'analyse précédente, on souligne que cette réforme est un processus continu qui a commencé depuis quelques années déjà, du moins si l'on tient compte de l'évolution significative des moyens d'action du Conseil, telle qu'elle apparaît à travers les nombreuses

[69] A/59/565, par. 257.

[70] Ibid., par. 256.

[71] Cf. notamment les déclarations des représentants du Canada (A/60/PV.49, p. 11) et du Chili (ibid., p. 13).

[72] A/RES/60/1, par. 138 s.

[73] Cf. l'article 41, par. 1 du texte de la CDI sur ce thème, dans le Rapport de la CDI à l'Assemblée générale, doc. A/56/10, p. 55.

résolutions que celui-ci a adoptées depuis 1990. En effet, par « réforme » du Conseil il ne faudrait pas entendre uniquement l'élargissement de celui-ci, tendant à lui assurer une représentativité plus grande et donc une légitimité accrue. D'autres aspects de cette réforme sont tout aussi significatifs puisqu'ils concernent la transparence de ses travaux ainsi que l'accroissement de la performance du Conseil. L'objectif de la présente contribution a été de mettre en évidence cette vision plus large de la réforme du Conseil et de souligner que ses aspects principaux sont liés et qu'ils se renforcent mutuellement.

Il est vrai que la question de l'élargissement du Conseil a souvent monopolisé les débats non seulement parce qu'elle implique un amendement de la Charte, mais aussi et surtout parce qu'elle recèle des enjeux extrêmement importants. Les récents débats au sein de l'Assemblée générale montrent que tous les États ou presque s'accordent sur la nécessité d'augmenter les membres du Conseil de sécurité pour que la composition de celui-ci reflète les réalités contemporaines. Toutefois, aussi bien le nombre de sièges à créer que le statut des membres supplémentaires continuent à soulever des difficultés, la question clef étant de savoir si l'on crée de nouveaux sièges permanents ou non. Il faudra certainement de l'imagination et un certain sens du compromis pour résoudre le « nœud gordien » qu'est devenu au fil des ans l'élargissement du Conseil de sécurité. À défaut, on perpétuera une situation insatisfaisante qui nuit à la crédibilité du Conseil et à sa possibilité de mobiliser la communauté internationale.

La légitimité du Conseil de sécurité est liée aussi à celle de la transparence de ses travaux. Dans cet ordre d'idées, il est important que le rapport annuel du Conseil devienne plus substantiel et qu'il soit débattu au sein de l'Assemblée générale. Plus généralement, il importe de renforcer la communication entre le Conseil et les États membres de l'ONU qui n'en font pas partie de façon à réduire l'image d'opacité qui entoure souvent les travaux de cet organe. Outre cet effort d'information et de communication, il est tout aussi nécessaire que le Conseil consulte davantage les États qui sont particulièrement intéressés par les questions inscrites à son ordre du jour et notamment les États qui fournissent des contingents à des opérations de maintien de la paix, qui y contribuent financièrement ou qui subissent les effets secondaires des sanctions non militaires. Des observations analogues valent *mutatis mutandis* pour ce qui est de la concertation institutionnelle avec l'Assemblée générale et le Conseil économique et social, ainsi que pour l'exploitation des potentialités qu'offre le chapitre VIII de la Charte. Il faudrait par ailleurs que le Conseil s'ouvre davantage aux institutions financières internationales qui accompagnent le processus de paix, ainsi qu'à la société civile et notamment aux ONG qui sont particulièrement actives dans le domaine de l'aide humanitaire.

Créer et exploiter des synergies nouvelles devrait accroître également la performance du Conseil de sécurité. Soutenir activement les organisations régionales et sous-régionales, et notamment les organisations africaines, est une mesure vivement recommandée à la fois par le Groupe de personnalités de haut niveau et par le Secrétaire général. Ce soutien financier et matériel contribuerait à renforcer les capacités de ces organisations en s'inscrivant à terme dans la logique de la « division du travail », prônée dans le temps par M. Boutros-Ghali.[74] La création de la Commission de consolidation de la paix ouvre, elle, de nouvelles perspectives qui devraient permettre de combler la « faille énorme » dans la structure institutionnelle des Nations Unies, à savoir l'inexistence d'un élément du système en mesure d'encadrer efficacement la transition de la guerre à la paix et d'éviter que plusieurs pays ne retombent dans le chaos peu après le départ des forces onusiennes. Il ne faudrait pas méconnaître, par ailleurs, les potentialités qu'offre la création du Conseil des droits de l'homme, notamment dans le domaine de la prévention des violations graves et systématiques des droits de l'homme qui constituent en même temps des menaces contre la paix et la sécurité internationales. Enfin, renoncer au droit de veto en cas de génocide, de nettoyage ethnique, de crimes de guerre ou de crimes contre l'humanité découlerait du « devoir de protéger », notion entérinée par le Document final du Sommet mondial de 2005.

En dehors de l'élargissement du Conseil de sécurité, aucune des mesures et des idées mentionnées précédemment ne présuppose un amendement de la Charte. Leur réalisation, au moins en partie, contribuerait à renforcer la légitimité et l'impact du Conseil de sécurité. Réaffirmer au plus haut niveau politique que cet organe a la « responsabilité principale » du maintien de la paix et de la sécurité internationales[75] ne suffit pas. Encore faut-il fournir au Conseil de sécurité les moyens nécessaires pour qu'il puisse s'acquitter efficacement de cette responsabilité.

---

[74] Cf. l' « Agenda pour la paix », doc. A/47/277-S/24111, 17 juin 1992, par. 60 ss.
[75] Cf. le Document final du Sommet mondial de 2005, précité, par. 152.

Part II
International Politics and International Law: Military Intervention as a Legitimate Means

Chapter 5
THE COMPREHENSIVE NUCLEAR-TEST-BAN TREATY; FROM POLITICAL WILL TO A LEGALLY BINDING INSTRUMENT AND BEYOND – A CASE STUDY

Jaap Ramaker*

1. Negotiations

For negotiations to be successful basic preconditions have to exist

The road leading from a *general political will* to solve a particular issue to the regulation thereof in a legally binding instrument is long, winding and full of hurdles most of the time. This is particularly true in the case of international legal instruments let alone in the field of international security issues. The existence of such a political will in itself presupposes that the subject at hand is *topical* at a particular point in time: the issue has to 'live' in the minds of governments and politicians, in the media and in public opinion at large.

Also, certain *basic conditions* have to be met before one can start the entire negotiating process leading up to a legally binding instrument with a reasonable expectation of success. Relevant for us is that the end of the Cold War and the resulting transition from a bipolar to a multipolar world – a process still very much going on – did create such basic conditions for the conclusion of international instruments in the field of weapons of mass destruction.

---

* Ambassador, Member of the Netherlands Advisory Council on International Affairs, Special Representative to promote the ratification of the Comprehensive Nuclear-Test-Ban Treaty (CTBT).

O.M. Ribbelink (ed.), Beyond the UN Charter: Peace, Security and the Role of Justice

During the Cold War, in particular the Northern Hemisphere had lived too long under the threat of a nuclear exchange with all its devastating consequences. Once the Cold War was over the elimination of the threat posed by the existence of huge arsenals of weapons of mass destruction, notably chemical and nuclear weapons and their means of delivery became highly topical.

The type of negotiating forum determines its outcome

What one needs – quite apart from the preconditions I just mentioned – in order to tackle issues like these is a proper negotiating forum. Various formulas have been used in this respect, sometimes with success, sometimes without. I mention:

- Bilateral fora as used during the Strategic Arms Limitations Talks (SALT) and Strategic Arms Reduction Treaty (START) negotiations between the Soviet Union and the United States;
- Regional fora, for instance the CSCE that negotiated the Conventional Forces in Europe (CFE) agreement in the early 1990s;
- Multilateral (i.e., global) fora notably the Geneva-based Conference on Disarmament and its predecessors that negotiated, for instance, the NPT, the Chemical Weapons Treaty and most recently in 1996 the CTBT;
- *Ad hoc* diplomatic conferences, open-ended or not, such as the Ottawa Conference at which the Convention on the Prohibition of Anti-Personnel Mines was concluded in the mid-1990s.

In this context it is particularly important to distinguish between open-ended diplomatic conferences, on the one hand, and a permanent body like the Conference on Disarmament on the other. In the latter case states had become members of the Conference on Disarmament on a permanent basis. As members they were free to decide whether or not the Conference would start negotiations on this subject or that. In the former case, a diplomatic conference of an *ad hoc* character, states decided to participate in that conference because they wanted to negotiate a treaty on the subject for which the conference had been convened. In other words, if a particular country is not willing to negotiate on this or that particular subject it will simply not participate in that conference.

The choice of an appropriate forum poses a dilemma

The dilemma which the choice of the right forum may pose can be formidable. To give an example: the Ottawa Convention on Anti-Personnel Mines, a subject highly topical in the sense I just described some ten years ago, was negotiated in an *ad-hoc* conference of those countries already converted so to speak. The main producers, exporters and users of anti-personnel landmines chose to remain away from the conference in question. They therefore stayed out of the negotiations on the prohibition of that most lethal of conventional weapons. As a result the Ottawa Convention now in place is certainly legally binding for its State Parties. It does not, however, apply to those most relevant countries because these did not participate in the negotiations. As a result, for those who stayed outside the Convention regime the Convention at the moment can have normative value at best.

In the case of the Test Ban negotiations, on the other hand, the negotiating body, the Conference on Disarmament in Geneva, was an existing body with a fixed list of Member States. Very relevant for the substance to be negotiated, namely a prohibition of nuclear weapons testing, was the fact that all five recognised nuclear weapons states: China, France, Russia, the United Kingdom and the United States were (and still are) members of that Conference. The three nuclear capable states at the time which did not adhere to the 1968 Nuclear Non-Proliferation Treaty (NPT) also participated in the Test Ban negotiations: India and Pakistan as members of the Conference, and Israel by virtue of its observer status. If, therefore, negotiators could at the end of the negotiating process agree on a legally binding instrument prohibiting nuclear weapons testing, then all relevant countries would be covered automatically. The outcome of the negotiations in that case would be highly relevant. The bad news, however, is the fact that while the CTBT envisions covering all relevant states, this not only complicated the negotiations but also accounts for the fact that ten years after its conclusion the Treaty has not yet entered into force.

Obviously – and this is another way of illustrating the dilemma in choosing the proper negotiating forum – the 'Ottawa process' with its like-minded participants could relatively easily reach an agreement. Even though the result of the negotiations was reached without binding major players and its concrete contribution to disarmament therefore being debatable, it nevertheless exists and functions. In the 'Geneva process', on the other hand, all the major players participated but as a result the actual negotiations were much more difficult. And at the end of the day some could not accept the outcome of the negotiations, the actual treaty text. So while in principle all relevant players are covered, no binding legal instrument on the prohibition of nuclear weapon test explosions is in place. Major obstacles still have to be removed before the Test Ban can take effect.

Negotiators will first have to negotiate what they want to negotiate

Whatever the forum chosen, however, *ad hoc* or permanent, negotiators must reach a basic agreement on what it actually is that they will negotiate on before actually starting the negotiating process itself. They have to agree on what will be part of the negotiations and what will be clearly outside the scope of the negotiations. In other words, they will have to negotiate a mandate. If the objective of the negotiations is clear-cut these negotiations on what to negotiate will not take up much time. In the case of the Nuclear Test Ban the nuclear weapons states wanted to have a very clear prior agreement on what was and what was not going to be part of the negotiations. After all, the future of their nuclear arsenals could be heavily influenced by the treaty text to be elaborated.

One way or another, negotiators need some rules for the road

No matter how clearly delineated the substance of the negotiations may be, negotiators need rules for the road too. What they also need, therefore, are clearly formulated rules of procedure. These rules should help solve disagreements between negotiators that might arise during the negotiations. These rules should also stipulate – most importantly – how to reach decisions. While *ad-hoc* diplomatic conferences may often decide by majority on matters of substance, multilateral bodies are usually governed by the consensus rule. In this latter case, therefore, each of the participants wields the power of veto (at least formally) with all the complications that entails.

Once negotiations are over, there is still a long way to go

Negotiating a treaty text is only the first step on the road towards an international legally binding instrument. A draft treaty on an issue of worldwide relevance once completed will have to be sent to the United Nations General Assembly. After adoption by the General Assembly it will be opened for signature. By virtue of international treaty law State Signatories will henceforth have to refrain from acting against the object and purpose of the international instrument in question even though the treaty has not yet entered into force.

State Signatories will subsequently have to ratify the treaty in question, each one according to its own constitutional requirements. Once these constitutional requirements have been fulfilled a State Signatory will deposit its Instrument of Ratification with the Depository mentioned in the Treaty. In most worldwide treaties the Secretary-General of the United Nations acts in that capacity.

A treaty enters into force once the conditions stipulated in its entry into force clause have been met. Generally, a specified minimum number of Ratifying States that deposit their instruments of ratification with the Depository will allow the treaty in question to take effect. Thus the long road from political will to codification into an international legally binding instrument has almost come to an end.

Parties, for instance, must have confidence that a treaty will be complied with

What remains is to make sure that the parties to the treaty, once it has entered into force, will comply with its provisions. In treaties on arms control, disarmament and non-proliferation rigorous verification and compliance clauses are usually in place. Confidence-building measures can help prevent non-compliance. Monitoring can detect cheating. In cases of non-compliance States Parties can invoke procedures as described in the treaty in question. They can either try and solve issues between themselves through 'Consultation and Clarification' or by deciding to conduct inspections on-site, or they can resort to an outside body, e.g., the United Nations Security Council.

2. A CLOSER LOOK AT THE COMPREHENSIVE TEST-BAN TREATY (CTBT)

Let us now take a closer look at the Comprehensive Test-Ban Treaty. Where did the idea come from? What does the Treaty prohibit? What are its concrete effects? What is its relation to the Nuclear Non-Proliferation Treaty? What is the present state of affairs? Where do we go from here? What conclusions can be drawn from this case study on the CTBT?

The idea of banning nuclear weapons test explosions is over half a century old

The ambition to ban nuclear weapons test explosions is over half a century old by now. The first to come up with the idea to prohibit these tests and thereby prevent the further development of nuclear weapons was the then Prime Minister of India Nehru back in 1954. If his proposal would have been accepted at the time the world would have been spared from the nuclear arms race that defined the Cold War era. Precisely the dynamics of that Cold War however prevented negotiations to ban nuclear weapons testing completely for many decades. This does not mean that during the Cold War no milestones were reached when it came to nuclear arms control, disarmament and non-proliferation. To mention a few: in 1963 an agreement was reached on a partial test-ban treaty banning all nuclear weapon test explosions other than those underground. As test explosions remained permitted, however, nuclear weapons development could simply continue. The 1968 NPT was remarkably successful in freezing the overall number of nuclear weapon states to the five which existed in 1968. But the NPT did not stand in the way of further increases in the nuclear weapons arsenals of the five NWS recognised as such by the NPT.

Not until the end of the Cold War it was possible to start working towards a *comprehensive* ban on nuclear weapons test explosions, a ban on *all* nuclear weapon test or other nuclear explosions in *all* environments including underground for *all* time. In the early 1990s first Russia, then the United States under the elder President Bush, declared a moratorium on this type of nuclear weapons testing. The moratoria of these two countries at long last laid the basis for an agreement to negotiate a comprehensive ban on nuclear weapon test explosions.

The Test-Ban negotiations

By 1993 all the conditions seemed finally to have been met for the negotiations to begin on a total ban on nuclear weapons testing. The Cold War was over. As the world emerged from the shadows of the Cold War the subject was highly topical. The more so, because China continued testing and France's resumption of nuclear weapon test explosions inflamed public opinion worldwide. And, finally, the Conference on Disarmament provided the necessary mechanism to negotiate a treaty.

The *first* step was to negotiate a mandate that took the better part of 1993. The final text reads as follows:

> '… to negotiate intensively a universal and multilaterally and effectively verifiable comprehensive nuclear-test-ban treaty, which would contribute to the prevention of the proliferation of nuclear weapons in all its aspects, to the process of nuclear disarmament and therefore, to the enhancement of international peace and security'.

I quote this extensively just to hint at the difficulties that may exist even before the start of the actual negotiations. During the 1980s several attempts to agree on a negotiating mandate failed. In the mandate finally agreed on in 1993, each word is a code for a whole world of different meanings. Taken together they reflect both agreement and the glossing over of disagreements for the sake of an early start to the negotiations between the negotiators.

With all the different positions the negotiators had between themselves they nevertheless now shared at least a negotiating mandate which they had all agreed upon.

Moreover, they had agreed on a deadline for the conclusion of the negotiations, namely September 1996. That deadline was to be found in a General Assembly Resolution unanimously adopted the year before and therefore shared by all the negotiators.

It was up to the Chair of the negotiations in 1996 (which I then occupied) to iron out the differences on substance that had been exposed in the first two years of the negotiations and to propose compromise draft treaty texts likely to command consensus. No easy task that in itself deserves another presentation, well beyond the scope of this contribution.

The actual start was at the beginning of 1994. The negotiations ended in the summer of 1996. The CTBT was opened for signature in September 1996 by the then Secretary-General of the United Nations Boutros Ghali.

Thus, a *second* step was taken on the road towards an international legally binding instrument on nuclear weapons testing.

What is it that the CTBT prohibits?

Simply put, the Treaty prohibits *explosive* nuclear weapons testing. The Treaty's scope is thus narrowly defined. It excludes, for instance, sub-critical testing, laboratory testing or computer simulation. This sounds simple, but it was not. The limitations just mentioned were hidden in the formulation of the negotiating mandate I quoted before. For instance, the five Nuclear Weapon States continually negotiated amongst themselves on what constituted a nuclear explosion in parallel to the wider test-ban negotiations.

What effect will such a ban on nuclear weapon test explosions have?

It is important also to understand what effect the test ban will have once it will have entered into force and therefore will have an internationally legally binding character. To answer that question I limit myself to the following comments.

The CTBT, once it will have entered into force, would advance global nuclear non-proliferation and disarmament in a number of ways. Firstly, and most notably, by preventing aspiring nuclear weapon states from moving beyond the manufacturing of a crude nuclear weapon (which would be a major contribution of the CTBT to preventing the spread of nuclear weapons over an ever increasing number of possessors of these weapons). And secondly, by curbing the development of advanced new types of nuclear weapons (which is a major constraint which the CTBT puts on the existing nuclear weapon states), thus reducing nuclear arms competition by nuclear weapon and nuclear-capable states in today's world of new challenges to the global – nuclear – security environment. I mention by way of example India and Pakistan, who at present maintain unilateral moratoria on nuclear testing, but no doubt wish to resume testing, presumably with a view to developing new, e.g., thermonuclear weapons, and China, that equally maintains a nuclear testing moratorium, but apparently is ill at ease as a consequence of recent developments, such as the development by the United States of a ballistic missile defence capability, and perhaps, more recently, by the agreement on nuclear co-operation reached between the United States and India.

The CTBT complements the NPT

From what I have said so far it ought to be clear that the CTBT does not stand by itself. It is important to realise that the NPT does not solve the question of nuclear disarmament and nuclear proliferation completely. The five nuclear weapon states are allowed to possess nuclear weapons under the NPT. India, Israel and Pakistan, which at the time of the test-ban negotiations were considered to be *nuclear-capable states*, choose not to adhere to the Nuclear

Non-Proliferation Treaty. Therefore they are not bound by any international legally binding instrument not to develop nuclear weapons. We know that India and Pakistan possess nuclear weapons, while Israel in all likelihood is – or once it so decides, can be very soon – in the same position.

The CTBT, on the other hand, intends to cover all of these states and by virtue of its entry into force clause will do so as soon as the Treaty will have taken effect. However, it will not do so until and unless a list of 44 States mentioned by name, including all eight countries I have just mentioned, have signed and ratified the CTBT. In this manner the NPT and the CTBT complement each other. In fact they can be seen as the two pillars on which the entire nuclear non-proliferation regime rests or will have to rest.

Conceptually speaking the CTBT and the NPT are closely connected in another way. The 1968 Nuclear Non-Proliferation Treaty was originally concluded for a period of 25 years after its entry into force in 1970. The NPT was given an indefinite extension – against strong opposition from many non-aligned non-nuclear weapon states – in 1995, albeit with a number of conditions. The most important was the condition that the five existing Nuclear Weapon States committed themselves to the conclusion of a CTBT within a year after the decision to indefinitely extend the NPT. The CTBT was indeed concluded in 1996. The commitment to subsequently bring the CTBT into effect was confirmed in the 2000 NPT Review Conference. This commitment and a number of others, regrettably, could not be reconfirmed in the NPT Review Conference in New York in May 2005. This was at the heart of the failure to reach agreement on a number of paragraphs on disarmament and non-proliferation in the Final Document of the World Summit held in New York in September 2005.

What is the present situation with regard to the CTBT?

Since the conclusion of the CTBT in 1996 a *de facto* global moratorium on nuclear weapon test explosions is in place. This moratorium has been – partly – broken only once since the conclusion of the CTBT in 1996, namely by India and Pakistan in 1998. These two states, however, are well aware of the existing norm against the conduct of nuclear weapon test explosions which is now in place even before the entry into force of the CTBT (as I could note during my recent visit to Pakistan).

By increasing the overall numbers of signatures and ratifications this norm against nuclear weapons testing is slowly but surely strengthened. By way of illustration: the following figures represent the status of the Treaty in the spring of 2006.

	Signatures	Ratifications
CTBT as such	176 States	132 States
Of the 44 States whose ratification is required for entry into force	41 States	34 States

Those States which have signed and ratified the CTBT include all 25 Member States of the EU; all NATO members except the United States; and all G-8, once again with the exception of the United States. The ratifiers include three of the five recognised (by the NPT) Nuclear Weapon States, France, Russia and the United Kingdom. Of the three non-NPT nuclear-capable states, Israel, India and Pakistan, Israel has signed the CTBT but not yet ratified it. India and Pakistan choose not to join the CTBT. All of the countries just mentioned are part of the list of 44 States whose ratification is required for the CTBT to take effect.

3. How do we proceed?

From the overview just given it is clear that the formal conditions for the CTBT to enter into force have thus far not been met. Early last month Vietnam deposited its Instrument of Ratification with the Secretary-General of the United Nations in New York. As a result ten countries still have to follow the Vietnamese example before the CTBT can enter into force. Two of these ten countries, Indonesia in South East Asia and Colombia in Latin America, have no particular concerns with the substance of the Treaty. They should have ratified the CTBT a long time ago, were it not for specific reasons related to their domestic situation.

In the case of one of the two missing nuclear weapon states, the United States, a Republican majority in the Senate denied the Treaty the two-thirds of the votes necessary for 'advice and consent' in 1999. This was still during the Clinton Administration. Perhaps for that reason the CTBT often does not appear on the list of international instruments which the United States, in the meantime under President Bush, opposes. China, the fourth of the five recognised nuclear weapon states, still has not seen its way to ratifying the CTBT for reasons that are not entirely clear.

Apart from the countries just mentioned, the remaining 'hold outs' are to be found in three troublesome regions in the world: on the Korean Peninsula the DPRK has neither signed nor ratified; in south Asia the same holds true for India and Pakistan; and in the Middle East Egypt, Iran and Israel have all signed the Treaty, but each one of them, for its own reasons, has thus far not ratified the CTBT.

A shifting paradigm complicates matters further

Apart from these factual considerations that stand in the way of giving the intended prohibition of nuclear weapon test explosions legal effect there are a number of other factors worth considering.

While the end of the Cold War created the conditions under which the negotiation of a comprehensive ban on nuclear weapons testing became possible, in the meantime we have seen a shift in paradigm. In particular under the influence of the current US Administration and its *à la carte* approach to multilateral instruments the international agenda on nuclear arms control, disarmament and non-proliferation has undergone dramatic changes.

In fact the United States sought and to a great extent succeeded in reformulating that agenda. This approach was well under way before September 2001, but gained considerable strength thereafter. Only relatively recently did the second Bush Administration begin to realise, so it seems, that a shift in their policies is needed. In the case of Iran they now seem to realise that they cannot succeed alone. The focus of the United States remains, however, almost exclusively on non-proliferation. Matters of arms control, let alone disarmament, have fallen largely by the wayside.

Moreover, the non-proliferation 'sub-agenda' has itself been redefined. Non-proliferation policies have become 'exclusively' focussed on the 'countries of concern' as they were called not too long ago, or to the remaining 'bad guys' of the axis of evil, as they were called in recent years, Iran and the Democratic Peoples Republic of Korea (DPRK). At the same time the 'inclusive' approach aimed at strengthening the existing multilateral regimes has been abandoned to a large extent. At the very minimum these regimes have been given lip service only, in order to underpin the policies crafted to curb the specific nuclear programmes of Iran and the DPRK. It is that agenda that we see reflected from day to day in the headlines of the newspapers. And it is for that reason that Iran dominates the daily headlines. With all of this, the regime approach is moving to the background and with it for that matter the CTBT.

In addition – and in contrast to the last decade of the twentieth century – we now see international terrorism as the main concern of governments around the world. Terrorist groups, non-state actors, have increasingly become the focus of attention. Not surprisingly much energy has been put into the negotiation of instruments such as the International Convention for the Suppression of Terrorist Bombings and the International Convention for the Suppression of the Financing of Terrorism.

To the extent that these terrorist groups would pose, sooner or later, a nuclear threat, new measures are being devised to counter this as well. The United States Nuclear Threat Initiative aimed at increasing the security of the Russian nuclear arsenal is one example. Various instruments to increase the security of nuclear transportations, and measures to enhance not only the safety, but also the security of nuclear reactors, are other examples. The recent proposals of the Director-General of the International Atomic Energy Agency (IAEA), Mohamed El Baradei, to bring large parts of the nuclear fuel cycle, that can be described as the road from natural uranium to enriched uranium and therefore potentially to highly enriched – weapons grade – uranium and plutonium, under international control, fits that pattern at least partly as well.

It is not a question of 'either/or' but rather of 'and/and'

While many of these new measures and policies are essential, they do not obviate the need for maintaining and strengthening the older regimes and approaches. The regime based on the NPT has served us well over many decades. Undermining that regime as, for instance, many experts think the recent nuclear co-operation agreement between India and the United States does, ought to be avoided at all cost. An early entry into force of the CTBT could only strengthen that regime. With the shift in focus I just described it is all too easily forgotten that precisely in cases like Iran and the DPRK the CTBT is highly relevant at the end of the day. What remains practically totally unmentioned in the media is the fact that both Iran and the DPRK will ultimately need a nuclear weapons testing programme if they are to build a 'usable' nuclear device capable of being delivered on a missile. This does not diminish the importance of the current efforts in the framework of the

IAEA Governing Board in Vienna and the Security Council in New York to try and prevent precisely that. Neither does it on the other hand diminish the continued importance of the Comprehensive Test-Ban Treaty.

In the summer of 2002 the United States National Academy of Sciences published a highly authoritative report on the CTBT entitled: 'Technical Issues related to the Comprehensive Nuclear Test Ban Treaty'. It addressed the three main concerns that had been raised during the debate in the US Senate of October 1999: first, the consequences of a ban on nuclear weapon test explosions on the safety and reliability of the United States nuclear stockpile; second, the capabilities of the international nuclear-test monitoring system currently being set up in Vienna; and third, the additions to their nuclear weapon capabilities that other states (i.e., other than the United States) could achieve through nuclear weapons testing that might escape detection.

The report concluded *inter alia* that:

> 'The worst-case scenario under a non-CTBT regime poses far bigger threats to U.S. security – sophisticated nuclear weapons in the hands of many more adversaries – than the worst-case scenario of clandestine testing in a CTBT regime, within the constraints posed by the monitoring system'.

The hope remains that the United States will revisit the issue of its ratification of the CTBT, realistically speaking on a bipartisan basis, with a view to analysing whether or not, on balance, the United States would not be better off with the CTBT than without it.

What conclusions can we draw?

Today's theme revolves around the question of how to transform existing political will on a particular issue into an international legally binding instrument. The case of the Comprehensive Test-Ban Treaty provides us in this respect with a number of lessons.

Lesson number one: even when essential preconditions to start negotiations are in place and subsequently negotiations will be concluded successfully, all of this in itself is not a sufficient guarantee for ultimate success. To illustrate this: the Cold War is behind us but new security concerns have replaced old ones. As a result, what governments, the media and the general public at large consider to be topical has shifted. Thus the original pressure to solve the issue, in our case nuclear weapons testing, is at least greatly diminished.

Lesson number two: all of this means that once negotiations on an international legal instrument are over the moment has to be seized. Complacency when it comes to swiftly completing the entire process from negotiating and signing a text until its ratification can come at a considerable price.

Lesson number three: the longer the period until the actual entry into force takes, the greater the possibility that the result of painstaking negotiations will have been overtaken by certain events. In fact, in this case study one could argue that the recent nuclear co-operation agreement between India and the United States may force India's neighbour China to react. This could, as a result, slow down the ratification process in China. This in its turn would push back the date of the Treaty's entry into force even further. The current programme which in the United States is known under the name Reliable Replacement Warhead or RRW program (according to press reports this is also under way in the United Kingdom, a CTBT Ratifying State) may well undermine the arms control dimension of the CTBT also. By the same token it risks diminishing its value as an instrument to prevent further nuclear proliferation.

Where to go from here is the question which still remains

All of what I have had to say is also a plea for strengthening multilateralism in nuclear arms control, disarmament and non-proliferation. Strengthening the existing global regimes remains as important as putting in place additional *ad-hoc* measures – including those by limited groups of countries – indispensable as they may also be. As stated above, it is not a question of 'either/or' but of 'and/and'. We should guard against throwing away the baby with the bath water so to speak.

The 1968 Nuclear Non-Proliferation Treaty is generally seen as the proverbial cornerstone of the entire present-day non-proliferation regime. I have argued that the CTBT and the NPT are closely intertwined. In my view promoting the first will strengthen the second. In other words, the CTBT remains as relevant if not topical as it was considered to be at the time of its negotiation. It is for that reason that the Ratifying States (now 132) meet every second year in order to discuss how best to promote the ratification process. They do this both in terms of the overall number of ratifying and signatory states and with a view to increasing the number of signatures and ratifications of those remaining ten states that still have to come on board before the Treaty can actually take effect.

In the Conference of Ratifying States held in Vienna in September 2003, I was appointed as the Special Representative to promote precisely that process. In that capacity I have visited to date Vietnam, Pakistan, China, and Indonesia. As a Special Representative I also attended regional conferences in the Pacific and in the Caribbean. The margins of the UN General Assembly Sessions in New York provided another opportunity for me to discuss with Foreign Ministers, and others, the advantages of adhering to the CTBT. So will other bilateral visits and international and regional fora in the months to come.

President Clinton at the time called the CTBT 'the longest sought, hardest fought prize in arms control'. Negotiations would not have succeeded without the strong support of the United States. The CTBT will not enter into force unless and until the United States resumes the leadership role it traditionally played. In the meantime the Ratifying States will keep up the momentum.

Chapter 6
NEGOTIATING PEACE, SECURITY AND JUSTICE

Paul Meerts*

The thinking about the significance and nature of international negotiation processes started after the Second World War. Before that time one can point to the work of diplomats like François de Callières,[1] and at a later stage Harold Nicholson,[2] who have said many things worthy of consideration about the phenomenon of negotiations between states. In the 1960s scientific interest was being raised more seriously. Thinkers like Fred Iklé[3] and Howard Raiffa[4] tried to find patterns in something as intangible as a process. For this purpose various methods were used, from the description of real negotiations to mathematical models in which the factors of the negotiation process were being objectified. In that way there was common ground between the authors for whom negotiation did not take a central role but who had carried out research into facts and factors which played a major role in the negotiation process. It relates, for instance, to the power factor, the psychological factor,[5] and the game theoretical aspects.[6]

---

* Netherlands Institute of International Relations 'Clingendael', The Hague, The Netherlands.

[1] F. De Callières, *The Art of Diplomacy*, (English translation) (New York: Addison Wesley Longman 1983).

[2] H. Nicholson, *Diplomacy* (London: Oxford University Press 1963).

[3] F. Iklé, *How Nations Negotiate* (New York: HarperBusiness 1987).

[4] H. Raiffa, *The Art and Science of Negotiation* (Cambridge MA: Harvard University Press 1982).

[5] I.W. Zartman and J.Z. Rubin (eds.) *Power and Negotiation* (Ann Arbor: University of Michigan Press 2000).

[6] R. Axelrod, *The Evolution of Cooperation* (New York: Basic Books 1984).

O. Ribbelink (ed.), Beyond the UN Charter: Peace, Security and the Role of Justice

Negotiation is 'just' one way – but if it can be applied it is a very cost-effective one – to create and enhance peace, security and justice. Other tools can be facilitation, mediation, arbitration, adjudication, warfare, etc. We will limit ourselves here to interstate negotiation, asking ourselves about its nature and utility, and relate it on its fringes to warfare and adjudication. Negotiation can be used to avoid wars, and it is nearly always used after wars are over. Negotiation can be used to avoid adjudication, but it is always used to give rise to adjudication. This means: laws are products of negotiation processes, especially on the international level. Negotiation is a cost-effective mechanism in concluding peace, creating a secure environment for that peace to flourish, and establishing sustainability through the implementation of justice. But it is, of course, a question of interrelationship. Peace creates favourable conditions for negotiation processes, because security is needed to protect the negotiators – there have been times where killing the ambassador of the enemy was seen as a way to show strength – and justice secures the implementation of the fruits of the negotiation processes.

In this contribution we will look at a few central issues in negotiating peace, security and justice. First of all, the question is asked: who are dealing with interstate negotiation, who practice the processes, who analyse processes / positions / people, who train the negotiators and how? Secondly, we will take a closer look at the people and their positions, asking ourselves questions about behaviour and the balance between common and diverging interests. Thirdly, the question of processes and the factors influencing those processes (power) will be commented upon, but also the use of negotiation as a tool in international relations: when does it work, and when not? Fourthly, the relationships between negotiation, adjudication and warfare are brought to the fore. Finally, some concluding remarks will be made.

1. Academics and practitioners

From an academic point of view the thinking about – and the research in – international negotiation processes cannot be described as a separate discipline. However, multidisciplinary research programmes can be found within the social sciences in which an increasing number of political scientists, sociologists, psychologists and mathematicians are already involved. This upward trend is shown in the increasing number of books and articles in journals, and the founding of periodicals such as *Negotiation Journal*[7] and *International Negotiation.*[8]

We might expect these academics to use their findings to train practitioners, and we could expect practitioners to help academics with their research, but strangely enough this is not the case. Practitioners, researchers and trainers do not communicate at the same level. Leaving aside the fact that many of the researchers are also lecturers on international negotiation at universities, and that they use their discovery of the 'secrets' of negotiation to enhance the insight of their students, they are not by definition skilled trainers. Teaching is mostly about literature, and although simulation games are used to illustrate theory, teaching is still a far cry from real training. Trainers are – if everything is up to standard – capable of providing participants with experience in negotiation processes. However, contrary to teachers/researchers, trainers are often not aware of the bulk of modern literature. They often copy what others copied from someone who once upon a time developed a practicum on the basis of academic insights. But these trainers can be charismatic people, who may not know as much about negotiation as they do about private sector management, but who have the empathy to influence the thinking and frame of mind of the participants in the course. They radiate strength. Participants will often remember their personality many years thereafter, but they will forget about the things they learned about negotiation.

One would expect 'a natural life cycle': practitioners help researchers to understand the soul of the negotiation process, while trainers would use the insights from research to train effective (future) practitioners. One could expect common understanding to grow, as the sub-discipline of negotiation processes developed over the past twenty years, bringing the three groups together in joint fora. There is indeed some more communality, but on average the cleavages between practitioners, academics and trainers have not been bridged. How come? How can one remedy this?

First of all, we must look at the reasons behind the persons. Many practitioners, especially those in the Interstate Negotiations Arena – first and foremost diplomats – do not really believe that negotiation is a science. To many of them it is an art which is inborn and cannot be learned. This is especially true for the old-fashioned diplomats. One might hope for a change as time goes by, but for the moment these senior diplomats dominate the scene, as

[7] *Negotiation Journal* (New York: Plenum Press).

[8] *International Negotiation* (Leiden/Boston: Martinus Nijhoff Publishers).

they hold the most important diplomatic posts. Apart from their perception – and perception determines reality – they are often handicapped by not fully understanding their own behaviour. They are effective diplomatic negotiators, but they are not really aware of the 'why' questions. What does one do in order to be effective? How do we negotiate? They are so much into their routine, that they do not have the insight of efficacy traits in their own dealings with other states. It is a little like an excellent car driver, who is so good because he does not need to bother about the technicalities of driving, he has his routine, and can therefore develop a helicopter view. The mind and eyes concentrate on the environment and not on the mechanics. In itself this is good – did not Sun Szu say that strategy is to change the context in such a way that it will be ripe for victory? The most effective negotiators have a grip on the context. But it does hamper them in really understanding what they are doing, in order to be effective.

Often practitioners have a certain 'dédain' for academic negotiation research and education. They do not really believe in training as a tool to become a better negotiator. Of course I am stereotyping here, but there is an element of truth in this: many practitioners do not want to lose time by conferring with academics on the issue of international negotiation processes. And there is something else: they do not want negotiation 'experts' to have a look in their kitchen. First of all, because this might harm the 'national' interests of their country (the secrecy of the negotiation in order to keep some room for manoeuvre). Secondly, because they might lose face if consultants observe that mistakes are made and opportunities are lost. We should keep in mind here that even diplomatic negotiators are human beings (sic!). They sometimes show emotions, they show non-verbal leaks (e.g., unconscious body language), and they do not want this to be revealed to the outside world. 'Open Covenants, openly arrived at' – it never worked!

And then there is the problem that practitioners, civil servants, are not by definition effective teachers. Actually, they are often boring, and they often have a problem in conveying their message to the audience. Of course there are notable exceptions, but on the whole it is a bad idea to ask (former) ambassadors to teach negotiation. Their accounts of the past do not necessarily raise awareness, as we need exercises to do that. Ambassadors who work with simulations, or who chair games, often pose problems for the teaching staff because they tend to look too one-sided at the level of reality of the games,[9] and will criticize them for not being correct in detail. This kind of

[9] H.G. Klabbers (ed.), *Simulation-Gaming* (Oxford: Pergamon Press 1988).

realism precludes good simulation games from working smoothly. They will thus create unnecessary complications by hampering the dynamics of the exercise, whereby the participants will miss the plot. After all, good role-play only works well if the simulation exercise is easy to understand concerning substance and procedure but also complicated – and thereby interesting – concerning its process and implementation. Course participants will have problems in experiencing the processes if the game is too close to reality. Balancing reality and fiction is one of the major dilemmas in games designed for learning processes. This is the first 'reality dilemma'. The game must be realistic, but does not – and should not – need to fully mirror reality. Because in that case the game will fail to accomplish what it is aiming at: training the (potential) international negotiator. For academics and trainers this poses a problem. Practitioners sometimes spoil simulation games by openly commenting in a negative way, with the result that academics, trainers and their exercises will lose legitimacy in the eyes of the students.

More serious is the second 'reality dilemma' insofar as practitioners do not allow researchers (and trainers) to observe real-time negotiations. It sometimes happens that negotiation 'experts' are invited to witness bilateral negotiations, but especially in multilateral interstate bargaining the closed session is the rule. The consequence of this is twofold. Firstly, practitioners do not profit from the insights of negotiation research, and indeed serious mistakes are made on matters like timing and trust, strategy and tactics, skills and styles. Indeed, at many conferences we know that obvious mistakes were made, and it would have been probable that process experts would have noticed these, and might have helped in avoiding the process going off-track. Secondly, this attitude by the practitioners hampers academics and trainers in a serious way: not to be able to observe real negotiation processes has as a consequence that alternative means, such as the observation of mock communication, and the study of 'memoirs' and other written accounts, have to be used in order to come as close as possible to the real processes. Interviews and surveys might help somewhat, but interviewees have a tendency to omit the things they did wrong and to stress their glorious moments.

As has been stated, also between academics and trainers we see an abyss. There are several reasons for this. One might be that academics feel that trainers – especially those from private sector companies – do not really deliver something worthwhile. Their knowledge of literature is often scarce, second hand and confined to pieces of 'academic' work long overhauled. Or it is literature given to them by others, who will have often transferred it into applicable exercises. Trainers also have a problem in understanding the more complicated academic findings and even if they do, transformation into practical tools is often precluded by the complexity of the scientific findings. Therefore trainers, like Willem Mastenbroek[10] and Raymond Saner,[11] will have to create their own tools. And as practitioners often do not believe in the value and relevance of the academic findings, so do academics mistrust the added value and correctness of the training devices. Academic programmes on negotiation analysis are on the whole very different from training modules and they are seen by many trainers – and practitioners – as being too theoretical, and therefore not applicable to the education of new practitioners.

Academics go for substance, trainers often go for money. There are many exceptions to this 'rule', but it is true that trainers are often in the service of a company – or themselves – and they train for a living. It is just too costly to invest time in academic conferences and in writing chapters and articles, although there are consultants who try to balance the two. Trainers are in haste and as time is money, training programmes will often be 'routines', formats that will be applied to whatever situation. Tailor-made seminars are quite rare; seminars balancing good content and good exercises are even more of an enigma.

2. Parties and positions

Who conducts the negotiations? In the framework of this article, I will limit the analysis of the phenomenon of international negotiation to negotiations between representatives of governments. These state representatives can be divided into two categories: politicians and diplomats/civil servants. Consequently, negotiations between states can be held either on a political or on a diplomatic/official level. The political level is the highest level and mostly preceded and followed by diplomatic/official consultations. The latter category can also be subdivided, depending on the question whether an ambassador/ director-general, a young diplomat/policy advisor, or someone in between these ranks, is conducting the negotiations.

---

[10] W. Mastenbroek, *Negotiate* (Oxford: Basil Blackwell 1989).

[11] R. Saner, *The Expert Negotiator* (Leiden/Boston: Martinus Nijhoff Publishers 2005).

The actors appear at the negotiation table from different positions. Apart from the interests which they have to consider one can assume that one negotiator will be more skilled than the other, will have a better knowledge of his dossier, is more motivated, better trained and could have more credit within his delegation, ministry or government than the other. Human differences will influence the course of the negotiations, not in the sense that on their own they would be the most influencing factor, but at decisive moments they can tip the balance. In other words, the more the other factors – which influence the negotiation process – are balanced against each other, the greater the margins in which personal characteristics of the negotiator will play a role. Personal influence is a marginal theme, but margins can determine outcomes in the same way as profit margins determine the success of a company.

The readiness of actors to be involved in the process depends on their interests. Negotiations will only take place when the parties, in one way or another, actually need each other. A relationship should exist between (parts of) the interests of the parties. It is for the negotiator very important to know to what extent the interests of both parties run parallel, or whether they largely exclude each other. In the first case a strategy of cooperation will be chosen (integrative negotiating), in the second case a more competing approach (competitive negotiation). The negotiations take place in a situation where interests practically converge with, in addition, reasons to cooperate (the lower limit) or when the interests do not converge but enough reasons exist for consultation (the upper limit). Outside these limits there is no question of negotiating but of conflict or staying aloof.

In most cases the mutual (overlapping) and competing (conflicting) interests will play a mixed role. In addition, there is often a third category of interest, in which matters are important for one's own party, but that do not touch the other (neutral interests). However, one always needs to keep an eye on the latter category. To be neutral concerning interests can be of importance for those parties who are not participating in the consultations, but who will (or can) speed up the ongoing negotiations. In case the Dutch and the Belgians will not reach an agreement, but the Dutch can offer the Germans something in exchange for which the Germans will give something to the Dutch, which is useful for the Belgians, then this can lead towards a positive rounding-up of the Dutch-Belgian negotiations ('expanding the cake').

In other situations, interests can be arranged in such a way that even with the lack of parallel interests, reasons may occur for negotiating. In those cases no agreement will be reached regarding the subject but that is not, in fact, what the parties involved have in mind. For instance: two countries have the intention to enlarge their armaments but public opinion opposes these plans and demands negotiations on weapons control before upgrading their defence is acceptable. Through negotiating both states meet the conditions which will make the enforcement of their defence possible. Not only the stated conditions are met, there is also the opportunity to point out that the other party is unwilling, and obviously has aggressive intentions in mind. Moreover, it is an advantage that both states are in consultations with each other and can exchange information. In some cases the desire to negotiate has only been prompted by the necessity to open up a flow of information. In that way the mutual desire to negotiate has only been prompted by the wish of each party to prevent an agreement from being reached. In such a situation there is an agreement of intentions *not* to come to an agreement. Much more difficult is the situation where one of the parties does want an agreement, and the other does not (Chamberlain versus Hitler). The latter party abuses the former for totally different goals. The negotiation disguises, just as previously mentioned, the idea to use means other than negotiations. The question is whether, in this case, one can speak of genuine negotiations, when not all parties were striving for a negotiated agreement that had to be successfully implemented in the future.

This takes us to the question of Forward and Backward-Looking Outcomes.[12] This issue has to do with Peace and Justice. On the question of Forward and Backward-Looking Outcomes it should be noted that a lasting peace is in need of justice to be done, plus the instalment of institutions guiding future cooperation between the contending parties. In other words: the institutionalisation of the process of cooperation. The European Union is a typical example of such an institutionalised process, the Peace of Westphalia can be seen as a very Forward-Looking Outcome, because it created the very system of sovereign states in which we are living today. However, parties might have reasons for concluding peace, in other words their interests might converge, while they have opposing positions concerning justice being done. The ruling elite might very well be ready to implement a cease-fire, and to quit their posts, but they would not be happy to be prosecuted before the International Criminal Court, or any other tribunal. They will therefore refuse

[12] I.W. Zartman and V. Kremenyuk, *Peace Versus Justice* (Lanham: Rowman & Littlefield 2005).

to conclude a peace, because they want to be protected against prosecution. Contrary to the title of the series of conferences of The Hague Academic Coalition (HAC) 'From Peace to Justice', we are confronted here with the dilemma 'Peace versus Justice'. In some cases peace can therefore not be attained, or when it can be attained, to do justice will be difficult, if not impossible. Institutions might not be created as the parties could not agree on this. And if they would agree, then the institutions might be so weak that peace and justice would be under a constant threat of collapse.

We need to analyse the positions of the countries in order to know if an outcome can be expected. If positions and underlying needs are completely opposed, then we cannot expect a successful negotiation process. As soon as there is an overlap of interest, an outcome can be expected. Even without overlapping minimum and maximum reservation points of contending parties, an outcome could still be constructed. Provided that the parties have included more than one issue in their negotiation process, and that by combining these issues, zones of overlap will come into reach ('package deals'). Depending on the interrelationship between the interests of the participating parties we can expect more or less peace and/or justice, and thereby more or less security and/or stability.

There is one more element at stake here, the question of context. What is the situation we are in? Negotiation is highly situational, what is effective in one context can be disastrous in another. But also the question whether negotiation and bargaining will be effective as a tool in conflict resolution is very much connected to its context. William Zartman[13] postulates that we need a push and a pull in order to start any negotiation process and to create an outcome. The push is the Mutual Hurting Stalemate (MHS). A status quo which is painful for all the involved parties to the extent that they prefer a change (through negotiation) over the situation they are locked into. At the same time there should be a perceived way out of the deadlock: the pull in the form of a Mutual Enticing Opportunity (MEO). We should note here that not everything is negotiable, but in case there are structural problems instead of situational problems to be solved, we might at least hope for mutual respect. Such as the (in)famous Peaceful Coexistence at the time of the Cold War, what the author of this article would call a Mutual Beneficial Stalemate (MBS). Beneficial and satisfactory as it ensures a peaceful situation in such

[13] I.W. Zartman, *Concepts: Mutual Enticing Opportunity (MEO), in PINpoints # 24* (Laxenburg: IIASA 2005).

a way that the major powers can use the stand-off to control their own 'allies'. The MBS is stable, compared to the MHS, but it thereby paradoxically precludes negotiation from being used as a tool in dealing with the underlying conflicts, because the dominant powers have no interest in solving them. Their allies may have such an interest, however, and they will do everything to undermine the MBS in order to open the situation to change. But they will only be successful if there is a regime change in the capitals of the hegemonic powers. In other words, negotiation can only be a successful tool if the context can be changed first. And, additionally, while context determines perception, perception determines reality.[14]

3. Process and power

The way in which parties reach a settlement can also be divided into three categories. In the first place, there is the procedure whereby parties would like to see what are, for them, the all important points included in the settlement: the synthesis of interests. A synthesis is often difficult to reach and even more difficult to implement. Secondly, there is the synergy of interests. In that case one tries to work not from a partial interest, but from a mutual interest. These kinds of results can be very satisfying, and can be well implemented. However, the requirements are a very good atmosphere during the negotiations, and lots of time. Thirdly, there are compromise and compensation. Compromise comes in the form of mutual concessions, in which each party loses some and wins some, or in which parties compensate each other for their losses, by trading concessions ('package deals'). Especially in unequal power situations where one party has to deal with fewer concessions than the other, this formula can lead to 'operation accomplished, patient deceased'. Agreement may be reached, but the loser might end up wishing to sabotage the implementation.

In connection with the aforementioned problems with implementation, experienced negotiators will arrange the agreement in such a way that it can be implemented step by step. If the implementation does not proceed according to plan the damage will be limited. The implementation is, as it were, ingrained in the agreement and still leaves room for negotiations during the process of implementation. A disadvantage of such a course of action is that

[14] B.A. Goodfield, *Insight and Action* (London: University of Westminster Press 1999).

the trust between parties – especially at the beginning – will remain slight. And trust is the basis of every negotiation when an agreement is called for.

A negotiation process means going through various phases: preparation and diagnosis, information, searching for formulations, bargaining, the drafting of all the details. The factors which influence this process are so numerous that a thorough understanding of the actual proceedings is almost impossible. Previously it was pointed out that the negotiators with their own characteristics and circumstances have a certain influence, but that the real determining factor does not rest with them. These are ingrained in the power of the countries they represent, or, in other words, in the power structure, the measure of asymmetry. How 'distorted' is that power structure and which factors determine this 'distortion'?

The question of in which direction the negotiation process is moving is therefore predominantly a question of power. It is interesting to note here that negotiation processes between equal powers are as a rule not very effective. Some power difference is needed in order to get the negotiation process to flow. Power can be distinguished in three components: power which is marginal and originates from the negotiator himself (power of conduct), power of the state which is being represented (structural power) and the power which belongs to the state regarding the issues being negotiated (comparative power).[15]

Structural power involves the total of power factors that are available to a country in relation to that of other nations. This power is determined by issues such as the size and location (e.g., a strategic position) of the territory of the state, the nature of its borders, its inhabitants, the presence of natural resources, its economic structure, the level of technological development, the financial power of the country, the ethnical diversity of the population, the social homogeneity, the stability of the political system (i.e., how legitimate is the government?) and the nature of its people (whatever that may be, and whether it exists at all). The question which then follows is: in which way does a country handle its power? What is its 'national strategy'? Is the country reticent in the use of its power (Germany before 1989), or does it use

[15] W.M. Habeeb, *Power and Tactics in International Negotiation* (Baltimore/London: The Johns Hopkins University Press 1988). Habeeb speaks, respectively, of 'behavioural power', 'aggregate structural power' and 'issue-specific power' Much of the following views about the possibilities which small states have to overcome in negotiations with large states are taken from him.

its power in a self-conscious manner (Germany after 1989)? Structural power is of importance when answering the question of which countries involved in the negotiations will reach the best negotiation results in the end.

It is a necessary, but not a satisfactory, condition for explaining the negotiation results. In other words: it is not correct to more or less assume that in negotiations between a large and a small state the 'stronger' state will acquire the best negotiation results. History provides too many examples to the contrary (United States-Vietnam, Soviet Union-Afghanistan, United Kingdom-Iceland) to be able to come to a simple comparison by predicting the total weight of power of one country or the other. To obtain a better understanding, their comparative power should be drawn into the analysis. With comparative power one means the power structures around the issues being negotiated, that is, the power which is relevant in this particular situation. In practice it is impossible for a country to put forward every power potential in every field. For example: does the Russian Federation, or the Republic of Turkey for that matter, because of its enormous army, have an overweight of power over, e.g., Italy, when negotiations are taking place in the field of economic cooperation? That is very doubtful. The existence of such an army certainly plays a role. But the danger is being neutralised by the politico-military coalitions in which Italy finds itself. From an economic point of view, one could argue that the gigantic economic potential of the Russian Federation could result in it having a strong position in the negotiations. But the time when this potential will be converted into a strong economic position is still a long way off. Italy's comparative power is bigger than the Russian Federation when, e.g., the modernisation of the car industry in Russia is the issue.

Comparative power is built of three components: the internal sources of power, the relation with sources of power of the other states involved, and the relevance for the issues being negotiated. There are, however, famous examples of countries with minimal internal sources of power who, through special circumstances (like playing powerful states, or factions within those powerful states, against each other), can build up a great relevant 'blackmail power'. Take, for example, the Netherlands and Surinam during the negotiations about development aid when the latter country became independent. Comparative power is decisive, and structural power plus the power of conduct will enforce or weaken the relevant factors of power. Surinam has been capable of building up process power, or relational power, because it has been dependent on Dutch resources. Add to this the historical dimension (the

Netherlands as the colonial power and feeling guilty about what it has done to its colonies in the past) and we can expect quite a favourable negotiation process as far as Surinam is concerned, notwithstanding – or better because of – its weaker position.

Comparative power is influenced by three factors. Firstly, the alternatives which might be available for the relevant issue: the fewer alternatives a country has, the weaker its cause. Secondly, to what extent has the country committed itself: how far will the willingness go to make use of its power factors? Is there, for example, a willingness to weaken its economic power in favour of its military power? Thirdly, to what extent does the country have control over the issues under negotiation? A small nation can have a lead position over a bigger one, when it controls, for instance, the dispute in question. See, for example, Iran in connection with the American diplomats who had been taken hostage during the so-called 'Iranian Hostage Crisis'. The hostages were at first in the hands of fanatics who were outside the control of the Iranian government. Only when they were being held by the Iranian government was it possible to negotiate their freedom.

4. Bashing or bargaining

A distinction should be made in negotiating in relation to other interactions between states, such as armed conflict, the use of international courts of law or arbitration, the use of services from third states as honest brokers, diplomatic consultations in which certain issues are being clarified and points of view exchanged, as opposed to the phenomenon of imposed settlements or 'dictates' such as 'Versailles', in which interaction was hardly the case. The following question presents itself: in which cases will states prefer the instrument of negotiation, and when will they choose alternatives in international relations? If war is politics by other means,[16] could we then postulate that negotiation is war by other means? In other words: while the use of force is one way to manage a conflict, negotiation is another, and adjudication is a third road to be followed.

The choice has everything to do with the question whether negotiation in a given situation is more preferable than the use of other international inter-

[16] C. von Clausewitz, *On War*, edited and translated by M. Howard and P. Paret (Princeton: Princeton University Press 1984).

actions. And negotiating will be 'more advantageous' in case the state, through negotiations, would be able to acquire what it has in mind in a 'cheaper' way than in any other way. In short, the question about the limitations of the negotiation process is a matter of cost-benefit analysis. Depending on the situation at that moment the balance will be different each time. When the expected benefit will be considerably higher than the cost, the desire for a stable negotiation process is obviously justified.

The problem remains that cost-benefit can, relatively speaking, hardly be determined, keeping in mind the influence of other states with their own cost-benefit, and given the impossibility, up to the present day, to verify costs. That is the first and biggest obstacle to providing at any one time an instrument for totally getting to the bottom of 'the science of negotiation'. The second obstacle is that the researcher is not allowed to attend really important negotiations, and to carry out research in a systematic manner. Reports by the negotiators themselves are usually too biased, and not systematic enough, to enable a real scientific analysis. And thirdly, should there be a possibility of a good analysis, then the results will be nonetheless so abstract because of the many factors that play a role that a more or less practical application, e.g., through training courses, will be difficult.

Nevertheless, the number of useful explanations about the role and direction of international negotiation processes is increasing. Slowly, but surely, a sense of communal interest can be defined between the various points of view about the way the field of negotiation could be approached. All these contributions are of great value. But one has to be wary of those who think that they have found the stone of wisdom. They may have carried the building stones, maybe even a keystone, but certainly not a cornerstone. Maybe that cornerstone will present itself in the form of sound research, analysing in which cases negotiating can, and in which circumstances negotiating can not, be an instrument of international relations.

It is interesting to observe that the notions of international negotiation processes as a method of bridging opposing interests, views and perceptions, have evolved over time. In the 17th and 18th centuries, negotiations were often used as a tool in warfare. Notably King Louis XIV of France used this constellation in order to break up coalitions formed against him. This resulted in a series of short-lived peace treaties and ongoing warfare on the European continent. Moving into the 19th century, the role of negotiation in interstate relations became more and more substantial, as the costs of war soared through the development of modern weapons technology, which resulted in an enormous toll of human lives. In the 20th century, states tried to strengthen the value, and enhance the stability, of international negotiation processes through institutionalisation. That is, the building of institutions, in order to channel and stabilise negotiation processes and thereby to secure assured outcomes. Thus we witnessed the creation of the League of Nations, the United Nations, the OSCE, NATO, the European Union, etc. With the Second World War as a turning point, we might postulate that nowadays warfare can be a tool in negotiation, whereby negotiation is seen as the main tool in managing interstate and other conflicts. We have come a long way since the 17th century. The institutionalisation of the processes, and the relative ineffectiveness of war (by using military means we can win the war, but not the peace) greatly enhanced the effectiveness, and therefore the role, of negotiation as a tool in conflict resolution.

In the context of the series 'From Peace to Justice'[17] it seems justified to focus for a moment on the developments at the end of the 19th and the beginning of the 20th century. International adjudication was very much seen as a tool with major potential for the resolution of international conflicts. The two Hague Peace Conferences were convened with high hopes for the future. The Peace Palace was opened in 1913, to host the first court on international judicial conflict management and resolution: the Permanent Court of Arbitration. After the misery of the First World War, we saw the creation of the Permanent Court of International Justice, followed after the Second World War by the International Court of Justice. All three in The Hague, and in the Peace Palace. However, notwithstanding the growing role of adjudication as an instrument in interstate conflicts, a certain disappointment with its effectiveness ensued. War and negotiation, or for recent history negotiation and war, did remain the major factors in international conflict management. In view of its relative efficiency and effectiveness, and the growing strength of the building blocks around it, we might hope for negotiation to become the dominant methodology in bargaining for international rules and regulations, and in regulating international conflict situations in order to secure peace and justice. It remains important, therefore, to study the subject and train practitioners in effective behaviour.

---

[17] *From Peace to Justice Series* (The Hague: Hague Academic Press).

5. Concluding remarks

International negotiation processes, in the sense of interstate or diplomatic bargaining, are one of the tools to be used in conflict management – if they can be used at all. Because, as we have seen, the situation should be ripe for negotiation and the negotiation should be ripe for a result. In numerous cases negotiation cannot be expected to work, and other phenomena such as avoidance (neglect) and violence or the threat of violence (domination) arise. The modes of bargaining (collaboration, compromise, and accommodation) cannot be used of one's free will, as one might be forced to apply them. As has been noted before, there is also a third road, not leading to solutions, but at least putting an end to, or to avoid, the use of force – though the threat of force will remain: 'peaceful coexistence'. Furthermore, there is a close interrelationship with other mechanisms, such as adjudication and warfare. These two latter instruments in conflict situations in international relations are both an alternative and a supplement to negotiation processes.

As a supplementary factor to the process of international negotiations, they can be used to enhance assured outcomes in those negotiation processes. International negotiation has by definition a less assured outcome than national negotiations. In national negotiations a third party can force an outcome, when needed. And this is often needed, because a state cannot start negotiations with other states if the internal process does not produce a mandate for the negotiators of that state. Transnational negotiations, e.g., in strong regimes such as the European Union,[18] will produce more assured outcomes than in national negotiations, but less guaranteed results than in international negotiations, such as the World Trade Organisation, the Organisation for Security and Cooperation in Europe, or the Shanghai Cooperation Organisation. In some cases the use of force, as a tool in an ongoing negotiation process, can help to push the opponent to the table. Adjudication might have the same effect: villains might feel so anxious about the threat of a penalty by a court, in or outside The Hague, that they feel inclined to negotiate. But, as we have seen, it can also bring them to non-negotiation as they prefer fighting over peace, in case they might be the 'victim' of justice, the moment peace has been implemented.

---

[18] P.W. Meerts and F. Cede (eds.), *Negotiating European Union* (Basingstoke: Palgrave/Macmillan 2004).

As an alternative to negotiation they can be used in situations where negotiations are not necessary, are not seen as a workable tool, or are not desirable to the states involved in the conflict. There must be something to negotiate about, something to negotiate on, and something to be satisfied with. Adjudication can replace negotiations, as can arbitration or mediation. But so can warfare. At the same time it should be noted that both adjudication and war will, as a rule, be supplemented by negotiation processes: adjudication, because we have to negotiate the (international) laws that judges will or will not apply; and warfare, because we have to negotiate its consequences. Negotiation stands at the beginning and at the end of these phenomena, but it can also be used as a tactical device within adjudication and warfare.

Peace, security and justice can be outcomes, as well as tools, as well as sources of international negotiation processes. They are sources of negotiation because peace, security and justice are seldom decided upon just like that. The moment peace, security and justice are in place, negotiations are needed to create the framework for their effective implementation. The very instance they are established, they need refinement through negotiation or by other means. Post-negotiation is needed in order to clarify perceptions, to decide on details, and to protect the subjects and objects of the negotiation outcomes. Negotiations are furthermore used as tools in unfolding processes of peace, security and justice. Once these are established, bargaining will take place in order to solve tactical issues, to ensure the success of the peace process, the security arrangements to protect it, and the judicial system to ensure it. And last but not least, the negotiation processes are the sources of peace, security and justice, which can be regarded as the outcomes of the processes of international bargaining. To use perhaps the metaphor of a tree: the roots are the needs of the parties involved, the trunks are the processes of negotiation, and the branches are the peace processes – when needed secured by strings attached – while the existence of the tree is justified by the beneficial atmosphere which its leaves help to produce, in the interest of the people, or at least some of them.

Chapter 7
MULTINATIONAL PEACE SUPPORT OPERATIONS: PROBLEMS AND PROSPECTS

Kees Homan*

1. Introduction

Since the fall of the Berlin Wall in 1989 and the subsequent end of the Cold War, there has been a marked increase in the attention paid to multinational peace support operations. Multinational operations refer to integrated operations by the armed forces of at least two nations. In principle, multinationality increases the legitimacy of participation in a military force as well as the solidarity between the participating nations (burden and risk sharing).

The international community has three choices for managing multinational operations: the United Nations (UN), a regional organization, or an *ad hoc* coalition. Whichever arrangement is chosen, it must provide an effective interface between the military commanders and the political leaders, including a mandate that defines the purpose, scope, and, possibly, the time-frame of the military operations.

The formation of European multinational forces is a result of the volume reductions made by most European countries in their armed forces, which have gone hand in hand with the search to optimise available resources, and the formation of multinational units presented itself as one of the best solutions.[1] This development is not, however, synonymous with the integration

* Maj. Gen. (ret.) (RNLMC, MA/LL M). Former director of the Netherlands Defence College and currently researcher at the Netherlands Institute of International Relations Clingendael, The Hague, The Netherlands and regular commentator for Dutch and foreign public news services.

[1] See 'Multinational European forces', Assembly of Western European Union, The interim European security and Defence Assmbly, Document A/1804, 3 December 2005.

O. Ribbelink (ed.), Beyond the UN Charter: Peace, Security and the Role of Justice

of those forces. They remain almost entirely under national command and their assignment is invariably the outcome of a sovereign policy decision, based on a nation's appraisal of the degree to which engagement is appropriate to its interests.

Multinational forces are also a source of difficulties for military planners, and using them for operations is often not an easy matter, not least because states themselves may intervene when it comes to assigning a national unit to one mission or another. It can create difficulties, for example, in a humanitarian or peacekeeping operation, which suddenly becomes a combat operation.

Recent developments have been both organisational, such as the restructuring of the North Atlantic Treaty Organization (NATO) and the development of the EU's European Security and Defence Policy (ESDP), and operational, for example the UN involvement in missions that threaten to escalate beyond peacekeeping into more military-demanding peace enforcement.[2] The two coalesce as the UN seeks to employ the resources of regional organizations, such as NATO and the EU, for these missions.

2. Preconditions

Various preconditions play a key role in the successful conduct of multinational operations. The Netherlands Defence Doctrine, published in October 2005, mentions the following preconditions:

a. *Respect*. Mutual respect for the ideas, culture, religion and customs of partner nations helps to lay the foundations for cooperation and unity of effort. One way to achieve unity of effort is through joint doctrine.
b. *Harmony*. Good personal relations.
c. *Interoperability*. Use by the participating nations of a similar system of command and control and the availability at all command levels of communication systems which are compatible with each other and with those of relevant civil organisations both contribute significantly to the success of the operation.
d. *Allocation of tasks*. A multinational force commander should give each individual international partner tasks which are in keeping with the ca-

[2] See D.A. Leurdijk, 'Robuuste "peacekeeping", VN bereid tot hardere aanpak bij vredesoperaties', Nederlands Instituut voor Internationale Betrekkingen 'Clingendael', February 2005.

pabilities of that nation's units and which do not conflict with national guidelines. He should take account of the views of the various multinational partners in his planning.

e. *Management of assets*. Multinational partners can request help from one another in respect of logistic support. The more similar the logistic systems of the various partners, the greater the opportunity for support of this kind. Arrangements can be made for this prior to the operation and adjusted if necessary as the operation progresses.[3]

These preconditions are easily formulated, but meet substantial obstacles in practice.

3. Mandate

Most multinational peace support operations are based on a mandate from the UN Security Council. The mandate guides the peace operation in terms of tasks, powers and restrictions.[4]

Members of the UN Security Council (SC) – its permanent members in particular – have to agree on the desired outcome of the operation, and ensure that it has a clear mandate. Members of the SC have to ensure that the mandate is achievable. Achievable means that one cannot say that the operation will protect thousands of civilians from slaughter, with only a lightly armed battalion on the ground. Achievable also means that one cannot authorise a mission with tens of thousands of troops if one knows that member states will not come forward with sufficiently trained and equipped troops (or will not agree to pay for them). Achievable also means not mandating a peacekeeping force when the environment requires a peace enforcement force.[5] If there is one lesson that emerges very distinctly from the experiences of the Yugoslav and Somalia operations, it is the imperative need for the SC to carefully deliberate over decisions to set up peace operations. Because both operations were set up without adequate preparations and a frame-

---

[3] *Netherlands Defence Doctrine*, pp. 60-61. Full text available at: <www.mindef.nl/organisatie/beleid/doctrine/index.aspx>.

[4] *Peace Operations*, Royal Netherlands Army Doctrine Publication III, p. 122

[5] P.R. Wilkinson, 'Peace Support under Fire: Lessons from Sierra Leone', ISIS Briefing on Humanitarian Intervention, No. 2, June 2000.

work for an agreed settlement, both suffered from what came to be known as 'mission creep'.

4. Command and control

Command and control is the vital link between the leadership and the troops. It constitutes the analysis, planning, decision making, and communications necessary to direct military operations.[6] The effectiveness of command and control is mainly a function of the quality and teamwork of the headquarters staff – and both of these are far more difficult to achieve when dealing with a collection of multinational forces. A unified effort should be the aim of the command and control arrangements, because without such a unified effort, the military operations are likely to be scattered and indecisive.

Achieving the right relationship between the levels of command is bedevilled by the tendency of superior headquarters to meddle in matters more properly the province of the subordinate headquarters, and by the desire of the political authorities to deal directly with the theatre. As a consequence, of significance are the division of responsibility for various aspects of the operation between national and international authorities, and the introduction into the command-and-control chain of a number of discrete national links with specific national responsibilities. These give governments the power to interfere at the operational and tactical levels and the opportunity to influence the international mission according to their own political agenda.

Where large numbers of countries take part in a multinational force, it is bound to be a fairly complicated undertaking and it would be true to say that a multinational force, particularly a land-based one, is of its nature less efficient than a national defence force. This is due to differences in languages, organisation and logistics.[7] However, in practice, only Headquarters are truly multinational, while the units mostly remain national.

---

[6] T. Durell-Young, 'Command in Coalition Operations', in T.J. Marshall (ed.) *Problems and Solutions in Future Coalition Operations* (U.S. Army College, December 1997) pp. 23-49.

[7] See M. Codner, 'Hanging Together, Military Interoperability in an Era of Technological Innovation', Whitehall Paper 56, The Royal United Services Institute for Defence Studies, 2003.

5. Rules of engagement

Rules of engagement (ROE) are the rules for the application and use of force by military means established for a specific operation.[8] The problems introduced by multinationality stem not only from the extra number of national authorities which must signify agreement to the proposed ROE, but also from the fact that each nation has a different ROE philosophy and interprets the relevant terms, such as 'hostile act' or 'hostile intent', in a different way. For some nations ROE are integral to crisis management, the objective being to avoid taking any action that might escalate the situation, and the firing of a weapon, even in self-defence, is very much an action of last resort. For others, conflict is a less complex affair and the threshold for aggressive reaction is much lower. Russian and US troops, on the one hand, and Canadian and Irish troops, on the other, faced with an identical situation and governed by identical ROE, would in all probability react in different ways. This is not a question of being 'trigger happy', or excessively nervous in the face of danger, but is rather the result of training in a different military culture.

6. Intelligence

Military operations are blind without timely and accurate information. Unfortunately, intelligence support has been a major weakness of most multinational military operations. There is an inherent reluctance to share intelligence because it originates from national organisations that go to great lengths to protect their information, their sources, and their methods.[9] Agency infighting and diplomatic niceties are inevitable, and efforts to release information are often frustrated in the interest of preserving the intelligence regime. The supply of intelligence varies enormously in quality and quantity between the national formations in a multinational operation. In some cases, such as the US, intelligence is comprehensive and can be disseminated quickly to the appropriate commanders, while others have no real capability at all.

---

[8] S. Nambiar, *United Nations Peacekeeping Operations: Problems and Prospects* (New Delhi, Embassy of India, 17 March 1999) p. 7.

[9] J.M. Nomikos, 'Intelligence Requirements for Peacekeeping Operations', Research Institute for European and American Studies, February 2006, <www.rieas.gr/Papers.html>.

7. Logistics

One of the most important problems facing a multinational operation is the way in which logistic support for the operation will be provided and maintained. In such operations, although logistics is a national responsibility, it has become a necessity to ensure maximum efficiency in the jointly conducted operations, to make efforts, in return, to take concerted action to ensure savings in the money spent and to share the logistic support.

Conducting operations in far-flung theatres requires deployable logistics. The bulk of Europe's logistic capabilities, however, having been designed to support Europe's defence against a Warsaw Pact invasion, are not able to get to or to operate in distant or austere environments.

8. Coordination with aid agencies

Multinational peace support operations envisage, among other functions, assistance in the provision of humanitarian aid. As aid agencies are concerned, it is essential that their efforts be coordinated, both in terms of aid effort, as well as the assistance desired from the military. However, most non-governmental organisations (NGOs) appear to have an agenda of their own and are reluctant to subordinate themselves to any other organisation, their argument being that they have to show results to those who fund their activities, and whose aims and purposes may not totally coincide with those of the international community.

9. Rapid deployment

One of the fundamental problems for the UN in peace support operations is that a long period of time is often needed to deploy a multinational force. It is often the case that a conflict has already escalated too far by the time the first troops arrive.

The time it takes to deploy forces must be shortened if there is to be maximum success at minimum cost. A fundamental and recurring problem in multilateral operations has been the proclivity of states to delay action. This delay has occurred for many reasons, such as ambivalence about interfereing in the internal matters of a sovereign state, the lack of political will, uncertainty about public opinion, and the questions whether the crisis at hand poses a direct or sufficient threat to national interests.

10. Article 43 of the Charter

Article 43 of the Charter provides that the member states shall conclude agreements with the Security Council in which forces would be made available to the UN on a permanent basis. In fact, these agreements were never concluded as a result of the East-West confrontation. The Military Staff Committee provided for in the UN Charter, which was to prepare and lead actions of the UN forces, was also condemned to become inactive as a result of the Cold War. The end of the East-West confrontation did not change this situation. Over the years, the lack of an independent UN military force led to a series of proposals to resolve this gap (although on a more modest basis). The first UN Secretary-General, Trygve Lie, launched his idea for a police force as long ago as 1948 and suggested the establishment of a so-called UN legion in 1952. His successor, Dag Hammerskjøld, made several different suggestions for a UN military force in emergency situations. Following the establishment of the UN peacekeeping force for the Middle East (UNEF) in 1956, and the intervention in the Belgian Congo, the ideas about a permanent UN military force were rather forgotten. Up to 1989 the most that could be achieved were the operations of blue helmets in which the permanent members of the Security Council did not participate themselves.

In conclusion, the achievement of Article 43 of the UN Charter as envisaged by the founders of the UN did not seem to be very realistic. After all, no country would be prepared to sign a blank cheque in advance, entailing the risk that its troops would risk their lives in a controversial UN operation.

11. UN Brigade

In November 1994, the Dutch Minister for Foreign Affairs, Hans van Mierlo, and his Canadian colleague, André Ouellet, once again emphasized the importance of rapidly deployable forces in the 49th General Assembly of the UN. Van Mierlo presented the idea of a UN brigade which would be available to the Security Council. This would have to be a 'full-time professional, at all times available and rapidly deployable UN Brigade to enable the UN to save lives in situations such as Rwanda'.[10] Soon afterwards the Secretary-General of the UN came up with the idea of a rapidly employable military force in his 'Supplement to an Agenda for Peace' in January 1995.[11] This would have to be composed of units from the member states which would be trained and equipped in accordance with equal standards, amongst other things. On the whole the response of the international community was rather lukewarm. For many people, making a military force subject to permanent international authority was still a bridge too far. The sovereignty of the UN member states and the related lack of willingness to accept the authority of another state above them will continue to be the main obstacles for the time being to the establishment of a UN Stand-by Force.

12. UNSAS

In order to speed up the deployment of units, another initiative that has been put forward is the UN Stand-by Arrangement System (UNSAS), which was developed in January 1993. The system is based on national promises of units which can be deployed within a short period of time for peacekeeping operations in a UN context. Within a year and a half approximately 50 countries had made promises, so that in principle more than 70,000 troops were available to the UN. However, the system came up against a number of problems, such as the moderate level of preparation for specific military tasks, the lack of interoperability and the fact that the deployment of these units was always subject to national decision making. Thus in May 1994, the Security Council decided to extend the UN Assistance Mission for Rwanda (UNAMIR), but none of the nineteen countries which had appointed UNSAS units at that time were prepared to make a contribution.

13. SHIRBRIG

On a Danish initiative, in 1996, the UN Stand-By Forces High Readiness Brigade (SHIRBRIG) was established. This is a multinational non-standing

[10] See H.P. Langille, 'Renewing Partnerships for the Prevention of Armed Conflict: Options to Enhance Rapid Deployment and Initiate a UN Standing Emergency Capability', A Policy Option Paper Prepared for the Canadian Centre for Foreign Policy Development, Global Human Security Ideas and Initiatives, see <www.worldfederalistscanada.org/langille1.pdf>.

[11] UN Doc. A/50/60/-S/1995/1, 3 January 1995.

brigade with a response time of fifteen to thirty days, whose deployment is limited to *peacekeeping* under chapter VI of the Charter, including humanitarian operations.[12] By putting together units provided for UNSAS by 16 countries, the response time of the UN was increased. Elements of SHIRBRIG were deployed for the first time in the UN Mission in Ethiopia and Eritrea (UNMEE) in 2000. SHIRBRIG forces will deploy for a maximum of six months, following which the deployment is either terminated or they will be replaced by non-SHIRBRIG forces.

As a matter of fact, for the time being, the UN will not be able to lead any peace enforcement operations. Since the mid-1990s it has become established practice that these are contracted out to regional organizations or 'coalitions of the willing' under the leadership of a state, the 'lead nation'.

14. NATO Response Force

In this respect, an important feature in the field of peace enforcement operations is the establishment of the NATO Response Force (NRF).[13] This multinational force is a rapid reaction force intended to be capable of deploying swiftly (in between five and thirty days) in response to any crisis – it is NATO's 'first in, first out' force. The NRF is a standing force made up, in advance, of units which have been made available by member states and which will undergo specialised training to ensure that they are capable of fighting together effectively on short notice. The aim of rapid deployability (a reconnaissance unit within five days, NRF within thirty days) means that decision-making will take place under pressure, but it will be possible to complete the process more quickly because the force has already been constituted in advance. The NRF is to be a 21,000-strong force, with ground, air, and maritime components, to perform high-end missions. It is constituted by countries making units available for a period of six months on a rotational system.

[12] *Peace Operations*, *supra* n. 4, p. 123.

[13] 'The Netherlands and Crisis Management, Three Issues of Current Interests', Advisory Council on International Affairs, No. 34, March 2004, pp. 29-30.

15. EU Battle Groups

A recent development which is most relevant for the UN has been the initiative of the European Union with regard to the establishment of European rapidly deployable military forces (Battle Groups).[14] These will make it possible to fulfil the UN's needs with regard to the rapid deployment of troops more quickly in the future, under Chapter VII of the Charter. A unit comprises about 1,500 military troops with the necessary support, and can be deployed after between five and twenty days for crisis management operations. After a maximum of 120 days they are replaced by a regular peacekeeping force. With the creation of the EU Battle Groups initiative, unit response times can be significantly reduced and the crisis management capacity of the EU and the UN can be significantly increased. Operation Artemis in the Congo in 2003 served as a model for this initiative, in which an EU peacekeeping force served to pave the way for a UN operation. Blue helmets had been stationed in the Democratic Republic of the Congo as part of a UN mission since 1999. Following a serious deterioration in the security and humanitarian situation in the region of Ituri, the Security Council authorized the UN to deploy an interim military force as an emergency measure. This military operation on the African continent made it possible to stabilize the situation in the Bunia region and provided support for a UN observers' mission, the UN Organization Mission, in the Democratic Republic of the Congo (MONUC). The mandate that had been given under SC Resolution 1484 (2003) to an EU response force consisting of 1,500 troops under French command came to an end on 1 September 2003. A strengthened MONUC then took over the peacekeeping operation.

The concept of the EU Battle Groups is reminiscent of the idea of 'peace enforcement units' (PEUs) which Boutros Boutros-Ghali put forward in his 'Agenda for Peace' in 1992.[15] The PEUs would be deployed for restoring and maintaining a ceasefire. Under pressure from the Security Council, which considered that these units went too far, Boutros-Ghali subsequently abandoned this idea.

---

[14] See G. Quille, '"Battle Groups" to Strengthen EU Military Crisis Management?', *European Security Review* (April 2004) pp. 1-2.

[15] UN Doc. A/47/277-S/24111, 17 June 1992.

16. Peacekeepers Inc.

The idea of military provider firms replacing blue helmet troops is one of the most controversial proposals to emerge from the growth of private military firms.[16] Proponents believe that such outscourcing will increase both the effectiveness and efficiency of peace operations.

There are three potential scenarios for the privatization of peacekeeping forces.

The first is privatized protection. The problem of security for relief operations is widespread and pervasive. In fact, this scenario is not all that unlikely, given that several UN agencies already use such firms to provide security for their own offices.

The second possibility is hired units constituted as a 'Rapid Reaction Force' within an overall peacekeeping operation. Wherever recalcitrant local parties break peace agreements or threaten the operation, military firms would be hired to offer the muscle that blue helmets are unable or unwilling to provide. Paid firms might thus provide the short-term coercion necessary at critical junctures in the operation.

The third, and most contentious, scenario is the complete outscourcing of the operation. When a genocide or humanitarian crisis occurs and no state is willing to step forward to send its own troops, the intervention itself might be turned over to regular troops. Upon their hire (by the UN or anyone else willing to pay), the firm would deploy to a new area, defeat any local opposition, set up infrastructures for protecting and supporting refugees, and then, once the situation has stabilized, potentially hand over to regular troops. This idea may sound quite incredible but actually was an option considered by policymakers behind closed doors during the refugee crisis that took place in Eastern Zaire in 1996. Both the UK Department of Peacekeeping Operations and the US National Security Council discussed the idea that, in lieu of UN peacekeepers, a private firm be hired to create a humanitarian corridor. The plan was dismissed when the question of who would actually foot the bill was raised.

---

[16] P.W. Singer, 'Peacekeepers, Inc.', 119 *Policy Review* (June-July 2003), <www.policyreview.org/jun03/>.

17. Common funding

One of the problems within NATO, as well as in the EU, is the funding of the peace support operations.[17] Member states that for obvious reasons cannot make a reasonable military contribution should compensate for this financially as a gesture of solidarity and joint responsibility. Thus, by analogy with the UN system, NATO and the EU should also proceed to draw up a distribution code involving the costs of peace operations to be borne by the member states. Countries actively participating in peace operations would be compensated from this common fund. After all, it is clear that NATO's main task today is no longer the collective defence of the Alliance's territory, but rather to contribute to global collective security. The current 'common funding' system consequently needs to be revised.[18] The fact that NATO and the EU have developed from regional to global players entails consequences for funding military operations. By maintaining the current principle – that is, only participant countries foot the bill – one runs the risks of dealing with gradually diminishing willingness among countries, small countries in particular, to participate in military operations. Past experience teaches us that some countries are more willing to make a military contribution in return for financial compensation.

It is important that NATO and the EU apply a system similar to that commonly used at the UN, where additional costs are paid out of a common fund that is financed by contributions from all the member states, in accordance with their financial strength. This would ensure that there are no 'free riders' in those organisations, sharing the burden of operations equitably between those which contribute forces and those which do not. Such an approach underscores collective solidarity, which is the necessary cement, as it were, for international security organizations to realize their objectives.

18. Cultural interoperability

In any kind of multinational operation, with forces drawn from a variety of societies and thus from a range of different strategic, doctrinal and military

---

[17] M.A. Flournoy and J. Smith, *European Defense Integration, Bridging the Gap Between Strategy and Capabilities* (Washington: Center for Strategic and International Studies, October 2005) p. 51.

cultures, one of the conditions for success will be the meshing of these cultures into a coherent whole.[18] This entails ensuring that any serious problems of 'cultural interoperability' are overcome. They have less to do with weapons systems and platforms and more with the frames of meaning that armed forces bring to bear on the problems they want to resolve, including military doctrine and culture, training and exercises, and the concepts that underpin their intelligence and logistic systems.

In general, commanders and staff officials will therefore come from different countries, which can have repercussions for such aspects as command methods, discipline, etiquette, equipment maintenance, ideas about the deployment of female military personnel and so on.

The maintenance of cohesion in heterogeneous multinational coalitions often requires a considerable degree of tolerance for diversity. This results in lower military efficiency, as well as an understanding of the different cultures, interests and policies, which is sometimes foreign to the traditional military logic and ethics.

The intercultural aspects of international cooperation are most relevant in UN (mandated) operations, as both Western and non-Western nations participate in these operations.[19] In the Gulf War, for example, the most celebrated concern was whether women should be allowed in the theatre of operations, and if so, in what roles. Women have been integrated into most Western forces and are employed in most roles, including combat roles such as air crew. But in Muslim states women are excluded from such activity and there are strict rules governing their mode of living. Such fundamental cultural nervousness can undermine the cohesion of a multinational force, and the need for tolerance and understanding must be emphasized.

Some countries also enter situations with special conditions attached because of domestic considerations. For example, Hindu troops sent in an Indian contingent to Somalia came with the provisio from their government that they might not engage Muslims – for the very understandable reason that such a development might incite difficulties at home.

Another lesson is that the lower the intensity of the operations, the more demanding the maintenance of cohesion.

---

[18] R.H. Palin, 'Multinational Military Forces: Problems and Prospects', ADELPHI Paper 294, The International Institute for Strategic Studies 1995, p. 49.

[19] A. Ryan, *Multinational Forces and United Nations Operations* (Land Warfare Studies Centre, ACT) pp. 5-6.

Media commentators in the field of battle in Iraq noticed differences in behaviour between British and American troops in their contact with Iraqi civilians.[20] British soldiers and marines seemed to be prepared to mingle with the crowd and to talk affably. American troops rarely seemed to behave in this way. They were more likely to remain within the protection armoured vehicles. When they were on foot in the vicinity of civilians, their posture was more confrontational, which was also apparent in multinational operations in the former Yugoslavia, in Bosnia and Kosovo.

19. Language

Linguistic communication within an international force is also a major problem that increases as more nations, particularly those previously under the sway of the former Soviet Union, participate in multinational operations. In multinational force operations a common language is essential in the decision-making chain where tasking is concerned. A further aspect is the vocabulary that needs to be taught and learned. Just as important as the ability to converse colloquially with military partners on a day-to-day basis is the need to be able to speak a military-technical language and to appreciate the military message implicit in an instruction or order. Another difficulty frequently encountered by non-native speakers of English on peace-support operations is that posed by the strong regional accents of many of the native speakers with whom they work.[21] Indeed, many report experiencing greater problems understanding the English of native speakers, complaining that native speakers are never trained to modify their speech when talking with their non-native peers. In other words, native speakers rarely recognise that the common working language in peace-support operatioins is international English, as opposed to their own version of the language.

20. Final thoughts

A number of conclusions can be drawn which are applicable to any multinational force, whether brought together within an alliance or in a coalition.

---

[20] M. Codner, 'An Initial Assessment of the Combat Phase', in J. Eyal, *War in Iraq, Combat and Consequence* (London: The Royal United Services Institute 2003 p. 20.

[21] M. Crossey, 'Improving linguistic interoperability', *NATO Review* (Special Issue, Winter 2005) p. 36.

Predominant is that multinational forces cannot be divorced from either the domestic or the international political incentive. Because each nation works to a different agenda reflecting national military and political cultures, and functions within a dynamic geostrategic environment, the political context in which multinational forces are fashioned or have to operate is unusually complex. The predominance of political factors over the more purely military requirements exacerbates the difficulties of welding disparate national units together. These problems should be recognized at the outset, and special measures adopted, both political and military, to produce a coherent and effective military force.

Whether a multinational military force is established for broad political reasons or for a specific military purpose, the authorities must be prepared to pay the price, both politically and financially.[22]

First, in an alliance context, nations should fulfil their obligations to the multinational formations to which they have committed units. The deeper the levels of multinational integration, the more critical this is. A failure to meet any obligation, be it for constitutional, budgetary or political reasons, undermines the utility of the whole formation.

Second, once nations are committed to a multinational operation they must subordinate themselves to the multinational endeavour and stay the course. Unilateral decision making, and above all unilateral withdrawal, not only reduces the operational capability of the force, but also damages the credibility of the international action.

Third, nations should restrict dealings with their forces in theatre to their direct responsibilities for deployment, discipline, administrative and logistic support, and these should preferably be conducted through an officially accredited national military representative at the operational level headquarters.

Fourth, nations must be prepared to grant the multinational commander more authority in areas of training, exercising and inspection, doctrine and logistics.

Fifth and last, nations should face the inevitable commercial and industrial consequences of adopting a more multinational force structure.

---

[22] Ibid. *supra* n. 15, pp. 76-77.

Chapter 8
UN REFORM AND NATO TRANSFORMATION: THE MISSING LINK

Dick A. Leurdijk*

1. Introduction

From NATO's perspective, Kofi Annan's report *In Larger Freedom: Towards Development, Security and Human Rights for All* at first sight seemed hardly relevant.[1] In dealing with regional organizations, it nowhere explicitly mentioned the North Atlantic Treaty Organization (NATO). This was all the more surprising because Annan thus bypassed NATO's active involvement in the implementation of a number of post-conflict peace-building settlements, based on UN Security Council resolutions, in areas such as Kosovo, Afghanistan and Iraq. In the weeks after the publication of Annan's report, NATO's Secretary-General, Jaap de Hoop Scheffer, on several occasions expressed his support for his UN counterpart's reform package. In a keynote address in Brussels, among others, he argued that 'NATO will increasingly act in concert with other institutions', including the UN, and pointing at NATO's co-operation on the ground in the Balkans and Afghanistan, he added:

> 'However, we need to raise our sights beyond ad hoc cooperation on the ground. We need structured relationships at the institutional level as well – to coordinate

* Senior Research Fellow, lecturer and political commentator at the Netherlands Institute of International Relations 'Clingendael' in The Hague, The Netherlands. His publications include: *The United Nations and NATO in Former Yugoslavia, 1991-1996: Limits to Diplomacy and Force* (The Hague: Netherlands Atlantic Commission/'Clingendael' 1997); (ed.), *A UN Rapid Deployment Brigade: Strengthening the Capacity for Quick Response* (The Hague: 'Clingendael', 1995).

[1] 'In Larger Freedom: Towards Development, Security and Human Rights for All', report of the UN Secretary-General, A/59/2005, 21 March 2005.

O. Ribbelink (ed.), Beyond the UN Charter: Peace, Security and the Role of Justice

strategically, not just cooperate tactically. We need to establish such relationships with the UN.'[2]

In this context, he referred to his address to the Security Council in 2004, the first ever by a NATO Secretary-General, saying 'Kofi Annan's recent proposals for UN reform provide further opportunities for fresh thinking'. However, it is hard, not to say impossible, to find any 'fresh thinking' on the relationship between the UN and NATO in Annan's report. One could even argue that the same holds true for the broader issue of the relationship between the UN and regional organizations. On the one hand, Annan recognized in his report that

> 'a considerable number of regional and sub-regional organizations are now active around the world, making important contributions to the stability and prosperity of their members, as well as of the broader international system'.[3]

NATO had played a key role in this development, given its involvement in the wars in the Balkans in the 1990s. The notion, however, was not further elaborated by Annan. On the other hand, the only recommendation that he made with respect to regional organizations was to create 'strategic reserves' in support of the UN, aimed at improving the UN's deployment options for 'peacekeeping'. Notwithstanding Annan's call for 'a decisive move forward', his recommendation for the establishment of 'an interlocking system of peacekeeping capacities' was but a small step compared to the calls, in recent years, for further clarification and formalization of the relationships between the UN and regional organizations, and has nothing to do with the kind of fresh thinking about which de Hoop Scheffer was talking.

It is against the broader background of evolving relationships between the UN and regional organizations that this paper analyses the relevance for NATO of Kofi Annan's report 'In Larger Freedom', in an extremely dynamic en-

[2] 'Reinventing NATO: Does the Alliance Reflect the Changing Nature of Transatlantic Security?', keynote address by NATO Secretary General Jaap de Hoop Scheffer, 24 May 2005, <www.nato.int/docu/speech/2005/s050524a.htm>. See also 'Liberty as a Security Policy Challenge', speech by NATO Secretary-General Jaap de Hoop Scheffer at the 35th ISC Symposium, 19 May 2005, <www.nato.int/docu/speech/2005/s050519b.htm>.

[3] The publication of Annan's report coincided with a broad international effort to assist the African Union (AU) with its mission in Darfur, involving close cooperation from the UN, the AU, NATO and the European Union.

vironment in which the UN and NATO, since the 1990s, have developed their operational cooperation in the field, in different formats (politically, militarily, legally and conceptually), in areas such as the former Yugoslavia, Kosovo, Afghanistan, Iraq and Darfur.

2. In larger freedom from fear

While emphasizing their complementary roles, in terms of the broader issue of the relationship between the UN and regional organizations, Kofi Annan paid relatively little attention in his report to regional organizations. Their role was discussed in no more than five paragraphs. Furthermore, in supporting a stronger relationship between the UN and regional organizations, it should be emphasized that Annan's recommendations in this respect were strictly limited to 'peacekeeping', as traditionally understood within the UN's conceptual framework. The Secretary-General appealed to member states to 'do more' to ensure that the UN has effective capacities for peacekeeping. In particular, he urged them to improve the UN's 'deployment options' by creating 'strategic reserves' that can be deployed rapidly, arguing that decisions by the European Union to create stand-by battle groups, for instance, and by the African Union (AU) to create African reserve capacities, are 'a very valuable complement to our own efforts'. In suggesting that 'the time is now ripe for a decisive move forward', the UN Secretary-General thus recommended the establishment of '*an interlocking system of peacekeeping capacities* that will enable the United Nations (UN) to work with relevant regional organizations in predictable and reliable partnerships'. In this context, he announced his intention to introduce memoranda of understanding that should govern the sharing of information, expertise and resources, aimed at improving coordination between the UN and individual regional organizations. For regional organizations that have a conflict prevention or peacekeeping capacity, these memoranda of understanding could place those capacities within the framework of the UN Stand-by Arrangement System (UNSAS), Annan wrote, suggesting elsewhere in the report that such regional organizations '*consider the option*' of placing such capacities in the framework of UNSAS.[4]

---

[4] Emphasis added. The system of stand-by arrangements is specifically designed for peacekeeping missions by and under the command of the UN. See D.A. Leurdijk (ed.), *A UN Rapid Deployment Brigade: Strengthening the Capacity for Quick Response* (The Hague: 'Clingendael', 1995).

In presenting this extremely modest recommendation, Kofi Annan followed the reasoning of the High-level Panel. In its report, the Panel paid more attention to the relationship between the UN and regional organizations. It suggested that the UN and any regional organization with which it works do so 'in a more integrated fashion than has up to now occurred'. Among the suggestions that the Panel mentions are formalizing cooperation between the UN and regional organizations in an agreement and, indeed, the placing of peacekeeping capacities from regional organizations in the framework of UNSAS.[5] Furthermore, other than 'In Larger Freedom', the report of the High-level Panel, in discussing regional organizations, contained a separate paragraph on NATO:

> 'In recent years, such alliance organizations as NATO (which have not usually been considered regional organizations within the meaning of Chapter VIII of the Charter but have similar characteristics) have undertaken peacekeeping operations beyond their mandated areas. We welcome this so long as these operations are authorized by and accountable to the Security Council. In the case of NATO, there may also be a constructive role for it to play in assisting in the training and equipping of less-well-resourced regional organizations and States.'

Annan has chosen not to copy this paragraph in his own report, probably deliberately avoiding any discussion beyond the concept of 'peacekeeping'. The paragraph indeed raises a number of questions: in the first place, it identifies NATO (rightly) as a regional organization outside the meaning of Chapter VIII; secondly, it contributes to the all too familiar conceptual confusion regarding the notion of 'peacekeeping' – the reference to NATO's out-of-area 'peacekeeping operations' concerns the deployment of NATO troops in areas such as Kosovo and Afghanistan as part of military missions with a 'peace-enforcement' mandate under Chapter VII of the UN Charter; thirdly, in referring to the issue of authorization for the use of force by regional organizations, the Panel, of course, had in mind NATO's deliberate decision to bypass the Security Council during its actions in Kosovo in 1999; and, fourthly, the reference to NATO's potential contribution to the training and equipping of other 'less-well-resourced regional organizations and States' was probably inspired by the ongoing debate within NATO about the setting

[5] For a comparison of the recommendations of the Panel and of Kofi Annan, see the 'Draft Outcome document of the High-level Plenary Meeting of the General Assembly of September 2005', Annex 1, A/59/L.70, 16 September 2005.

up of Provincial Reconstruction Teams (PRTs)[6] in Afghanistan, in support of both the Afghan government and the UN mission in the country, the establishment of a training mission in Iraq, and a possible supporting role for NATO, in close cooperation with the UN and the European Union, in providing logistics, including airlift, for an AU mission in Darfur, Sudan.

Against this background, there was every reason to believe that Annan would have incorporated a much broader discussion on the relationship between the UN and regional organizations in his report, and more in particular on relations between the UN and NATO, given their agendas in terms of reform and transition, respectively.

3. NATO TRANSFORMATION: THE AFTERMATH OF 9/11

Following the terrorist attacks of 11 September 2001 on the US, NATO's main concern in terms of the 'new threats of the twenty-first century' became international terrorism, linked with the proliferation of weapons of mass destruction. This perception was translated in the formulation of a transformation agenda that was adopted at the Alliance summit in Prague in November 2002. Since then, NATO has been actively engaged in the implementation of this roadmap, aimed at repositioning NATO as a full-fledged instrument in the 'war', the 'fight', or the 'campaign' against international terrorism.

The common element in the responses worldwide to the terror attacks was a reinvigoration of the concept of the right to self-defence, individually and collectively. While the US used the argument as the main justification for the start of Operation 'Enduring Freedom', the UN Security Council, by referring to Article 51 of the UN Charter, at best gave a tacit agreement to the operation in Afghanistan and not an explicit authorization for the use of force, as some have suggested. For NATO, the most immediate consequence of 9/11 was its historic decision on 3 October 2001 to invoke formally, for the first time, Article 5 of the North Atlantic Treaty.[7] With the implementation of this decision, NATO initiated a transformation process that would have profound consequences for its role as a collective defence organization.

---

[6] See *infra*, note 15.

[7] Art. 5 of the North Atlantic Treaty (Washington, DC, 1949) states that 'The Parties agree that an armed attack against one or more of the Allies in Europe or North America shall be considered an attack against them all…'. See <www.nato.int/docu/basictxt/treaty.htm>.

Notwithstanding its invocation of Article 5, the Atlantic Alliance was bypassed by the US when it started its 'war on terrorism' with Operation 'Enduring Freedom' in early October 2001. NATO's contribution, for the time being, was limited to operations in the air and at sea. It sent Airborne Warning and Control Station (AWACS) radar airplanes to the US for 'backfilling' purposes. NATO's maritime contribution – Operation 'Active Endeavour' – was initially aimed at enhancing the security of the sea-lanes in the eastern Mediterranean.[8] Since then, the North Atlantic Council has decided, in two stages, to expand its naval operations, firstly to the Straits of Gibraltar (in February 2003), and finally (in March 2004) to the Mediterranean Sea as a whole.

The North Atlantic Council's position in the immediate aftermath of 9/11 raised a number of fundamental legal questions, such as the identification of the terror attacks as falling under the terms of Article 5. The Council, however, justified its concerns about the attacks in terms of a legitimate interest for the Alliance, by referring to NATO's 1991 and 1999 Strategic Concepts, which already included references to international terrorism as part of its commitment to collective self-defence. The December 2001 semi-annual ministerial meeting thus became the beginning of a new transitional phase, based on a transformation agenda, which aimed at formulating, in the words of (then) US Deputy Secretary of Defense Paul Wolfowitz, a new 'job description' for NATO, saying: 'Fighting terrorism, which has been so clearly linked to weapons of mass destruction, is part of NATO's basic job description: collective defence', adding, 'Article 5 threats can come from anywhere, in many forms'. This meant an effort at repositioning the Alliance as a collective defence organization in a completely new security environment, compared to the time of NATO's establishment, implying profound conceptual, operational and political adaptations with respect to the concept of self-defence, including its traditional 'out-of-area' notion and the notion of 'preemptive attacks'.

As a collective defence organization, NATO's main concern was initially to safeguard the territory of its member states from an armed attack. Its willingness in the early 1990s to support the UN in its peacekeeping efforts in the Balkans was no less than a revolutionary break with its past policies,

[8] Under this operation, NATO air and naval forces have been carrying out patrolling and surveillance activities in the operational area east of Sicily, aimed at safeguarding the ships of NATO nations against the threat of terrorism.

provoking extensive legal discussions on the issue of NATO's legitimacy in acting 'out-of-area' along its periphery. Similar discussions were held during the Kosovo crisis a couple of years later, this time, furthermore, in combination with the question of whether the Alliance was entitled to use force without having explicit authorization from the UN Security Council. The question of NATO's response to 9/11 would lead to a third round of out-of-area discussions, much to the dismay of NATO's (then) Secretary-General Lord Robertson. Where his predecessor, Solana, had suggested in the autumn of 1998 that 'We must not enter into a legalistic debate' on Kosovo, on what he saw as an essentially 'political matter', Lord Robertson explicitly indicated in several interviews in March 2002 that NATO's adaptation to the new security threats would also include a capability to operate far beyond its own borders, presenting this as a kind of logical extension of NATO's performance in south-eastern Europe, its own backyard, in the preceding decade.

NATO's transformation from a regional actor into a global player was formally confirmed by the foreign ministers at their meeting in Reykjavik in May 2002, declaring that the Alliance would confront threats to members' security, no matter what their origin. One year later, Lord Robertson emphasized that the May 2002 decision required that 'NATO should step above its traditional theological squabbles', basically declaring the 'out-of-area' debate as 'dead'. In August 2003 NATO would take over command of the International Security Assistance Force (ISAF) in Afghanistan, the first NATO-led peace-support operation far away from its own territory, and well outside the 'Euro-Atlantic area'.

Another conceptual adaptation, furthermore, was related to the inclusion of 'pre-emptive action' as part of NATO's interpretation of 'self-defence'. Here, again, Lord Robertson quite convincingly supported the position of the Bush administration, disregarding the international legal questions that were being raised by such a broad conceptualization of the concept of self-defence. He explicitly included pre-emption as part of NATO's response to the threats of terrorist attacks, by saying that NATO forces should also be better able 'to deter, pre-empt and defeat' attacks, adding in October 2003 that NATO had already acted pre-emptively in Kosovo in 1999, and concluding that there was nothing new about pre-emption: it had always been a part of NATO's deterrence package, he said.

4. The UN-NATO relationship: Cases of cooperation

4.1 Afghanistan

With the start of Operation 'Enduring Freedom' on 7 October 2001, the United States initiated the first phase in what it called the 'war on terrorism'. The deliberate decision on the part of the Bush administration not to involve NATO was the result of a combination of considerations, such as the US's preference to keep tight control of the military campaign, both because its own national security interests were at stake but also as a consequence of the key lesson of Operation 'Allied Force' as a model of 'warfare by coalition'. At the time, this raised serious questions about NATO's marginalization or irrelevance.

After the fall of the Taliban regime in Kabul, the results of the Bonn Conference, which was held in December 2001, provided for agreement on a phased political transition process for Afghanistan and the deployment of a multinational force –ISAF – initially under the command of the United Kingdom as the 'lead nation', and authorized by the UN Security Council, acting under Chapter VII of the UN Charter.[9]

After some early indications in that direction, in April 2002 NATO offered to carry out the planning for ISAF in an effort to encourage Turkey to take over command of the multinational force from the British in June 2002.[10] The decision was presented as part of a broader effort by NATO 'to make itself more relevant in the campaign against terrorism', as stressed by Lord Robertson,[11] and would lead to growing involvement by the Alliance after

---

[9] S/RES/1378, 14 November 2001; and S/RES/1386, 20 December 2001.

[10] The offer involved identifying the precise forces that are needed from an array of countries and determining when and where they should be deployed. The task is a relatively routine one, in terms of force generation and force planning, for SHAPE, NATO's European military headquarters at Mons in Belgium.

[11] In disclosing the decision, the NATO chief said that the Alliance had been making a direct contribution to fighting terrorism by breaking up al-Qaeda cells in the Balkans and by sending its AWACS planes to patrol American skies, and indirectly by defusing the crisis in Macedonia, thus averting a broader conflict in the Balkans that might have distracted Washington while it was executing Operation 'Enduring Freedom' in Afghanistan. He also asserted that NATO made it easier for European countries and the US to work together in Afghanistan,

more NATO member states took over the command (Italy, and Germany/the Netherlands) and asked for similar support. This development finally led to a decision in spring 2003 that NATO as such would take over full command of ISAF. (Then) US Secretary of State Colin Powell welcomed the announcement in mid-April 2003, saying:

> 'This will be NATO's first significant military operation outside of Europe in its history, and is a sign of the Alliance's new direction and emphasis on confronting the threat of terrorism and weapons of mass destruction from wherever they come … I am pleased that there continues to be broad support for the efforts to stabilize Afghanistan as part of the Global War against Terrorism.'[12]

In early May 2003 on a visit to Washington, Lord Robertson said that the decision was 'undoubtedly another watershed moment, as important as the first NATO involvement in the Balkans', adding that it was now 'quite natural' for NATO to look beyond Afghanistan, to 'consider a possible role for the Alliance in post-conflict Iraq' at a later time. When NATO assumed the leadership of ISAF on 11 August 2003, a NATO press release read:

> 'ISAF's name and mission will not change. NATO will work within the same United Nations mandate as ISAF III and will operate according to current and future UN resolutions. NATO's commitment to the ISAF mission is a reflection of our transformation agenda and the Alliance's resolve to address the new security challenges of the twenty-first century.'[13]

On the same occasion, the US Department of State issued a statement declaring that '[t]his new mission for NATO represents NATO's further transformation as an Alliance that will meet the new security challenges of this century', adding further that 'NATO will run its operations in Afghanistan much as it has managed other successful peacekeeping operations in Bosnia, Kosovo and Macedonia', explaining:

---

underlining the need to close the gap between US and European military capabilities. A Western diplomat was quoted as saying of the plan to offer help to the Turks: 'It shows imagination on the part of the Allies. NATO doesn't have to choose between running the mission itself or doing nothing. There are other things it can do', *International Herald Tribune*, 12 April 2002.

[12] (Then) US Secretary of State Colin L. Powell, *NATO's Takeover of the International Security Assistance Force in Afghanistan* (Washington DC: US Department of State, 18 April 2003).

[13] 3501 *Atlantic News* (21 August 2003).

> 'The Allies will exercise political control in the North Atlantic Council, while NATO's military headquarters will provide military expertise for planning and operations. NATO's new role in Afghanistan demonstrates that the revitalization of the Alliance is becoming a reality, and that NATO will go outside its traditional area of operations to meet threats wherever they may arise.'[14]

NATO's first mission in Asia thus fitted perfectly within the parameters of the sub-contracting model, in this case at the invitation of the provisional Afghan government and formally authorized by the UN Security Council. This was made perfectly clear when NATO, in October 2003, started to mull the possibility of expanding its operations beyond Kabul, and Lord Robertson said that it would first need specific authorization from the Security Council before it could start deploying PRTs.[15] In letters from the Secretary-General of NATO to the President of the Security Council, the Alliance outlined its 'longer-term strategy' in Afghanistan:

> 'The North Atlantic Treaty Organization (NATO) is in Afghanistan in its International Security Assistance Force (ISAF) role in order to support the international community's efforts towards implementation of the Bonn Agreement, as man-

---

[14] Press Statement, P.T. Reeker, Deputy Spokesman, US Department of State, Washington, DC, 11 August 2003.

[15] Initially, PRTs operated in Afghanistan within the framework of the US-led Operation 'Enduring Freedom'. After the fall of the Taliban regime, President Bush promised to reconstruct Afghanistan. As part of a 'hearts and minds' operation, PRTs can be seen as an 'alternative reconstruction model', aimed at providing both security and reconstruction and humanitarian assistance for the local population by combining military and civilian personnel in small, joint missions. According to a NATO Backgrounder, PRTs have successfully introduced a measure of stability to their localities through patrolling, monitoring, influence and mediation, thereby facilitating the reconstruction efforts of other international organizations and allowing the central government in Kabul to extend control to the provinces of Afghanistan. The composition of each team will vary slightly depending on location and will number forty to sixty persons. Composed of civil affairs soldiers who are trained in medicine, psychology, engineering and law, as well as Special Forces and regular army units, the teams will always maintain a 'robust' capacity to defend themselves, as they are being purposely deployed in hostile territory. For more background, see 'ISAF Provincial Reconstruction Teams (PRTs)', 21 *NATO Backgrounder* (21 January 2005) <www.afnorth.nato.int/ISAF/Backgrounder/BackPRT.htm>; 'NATO in Afghanistan', NATO Factsheet, 21 February 2005, <http://nato.int/issues/afghanistan/040628-factsheet.htm>; 'NATO in Afghanistan: How Did This Operation Evolve?', NATO Topics, 15 February 2005, <www.nato.int/issues/afghanistan/evolution.htm>; and 'Reconstruction: The Provincial Reconstruction Team (PRT) in Afghanistan and its Role in Reconstruction', <www.afgha.com/?af=article&sid+33553>.

dated by the United Nations Security Council resolution 1386 (2001). The aim is to assist in the emergence of a united and sovereign Afghanistan, with, *inter alia*, a broad-based, multi-ethnic representative government, integrated into the international community and cooperating with its neighbours.'[16]

The document added that NATO's long-term strategy in this context includes the formulation of an 'Alliance political objective', of a 'desired ISAF end-state' and of 'benchmarks for an Alliance hand-over strategy'. NATO's political objective was formulated as follows:

'Support for implementation of the Bonn process, as mandated by Security Council Resolution 1386 (2001), in cooperation and coordination with key international organizations, in particular the United Nations and the European Union, by assisting the Afghan Transitional Authority (ATA) to meet its responsibility to provide security and order. Additional factors to consider in developing further the Alliance's over-arching political objective include:

1. An expanded ISAF mandate will require a specific United Nations Security Council resolution;
2. The need for enhanced coordination and cooperation between ISAF, the United Nations Assistance Mission in Afghanistan (UNAMA), Afghan authorities, Operation Enduring Freedom (OEF) and non-governmental organizations (NGOs).'[17]

Key components of NATO's 'desired ISAF end-state' included, *inter alia*, completion of the disarmament, demobilization and reintegration (DDR) programme; build-up of the Afghan National Army (ANA); the establishment of a functioning Afghan national police force and judiciary; implementation of effective counter-narcotics activities; the implementation of the constitutional *Loya Jirga* (grand council) and approval of a new constitution; election of a representative government to succeed the Afghan Transitional Authority (ATA) through free and fair elections; removal or modification of the behaviour of the warlords, bringing them into central government institutions; and the resolution of the terrorist threat from the Taliban, al-Qaeda and other extremist groups.[18]

And, indeed, in adopting Resolution 1510 (2003) on 13 October 2003, the Security Council, acting under Chapter VII of the UN Charter, thus autho-

[16] S/2003/970, 8 October 2003.
[17] Idem.
[18] Idem.

rized the expansion of ISAF's mandate 'to allow it, as resources permit, to support the Afghan Transitional Authority and its successors in the maintenance of security in areas of Afghanistan outside of Kabul and its environs'. Following the UN decision in mid-October 2003, NATO initialled the expansion of its assistance from December 2003 onwards, in stages, through the deployment of an increasing number of PRTs, gradually covering the northern and western provinces of Afghanistan respectively. In 2006, NATO planned to finalize stage three, and to be present in the whole of the country, including the relatively dangerous south and south-eastern parts of the territory.

By adopting Resolution 1510 (2003), the UN Security Council also called upon ISAF 'to continue to work in close consultation' with, *inter alia*, 'the Operation Enduring Freedom Coalition in the implementation of the force mandate'. In practical terms, this meant for NATO both the establishment of new PRTs, but also the incorporation of already existing PRTs that were operating under the command of the US-led Operation 'Enduring Freedom'. The transfer of PRTs from 'Enduring Freedom' to ISAF basically lessened the burden on the US military in their hunt for Osama Bin Laden, and established an indirect link between the two missions. Against this background, it was no surprise that in December 2003 both US Secretary of Defense Rumsfeld and (then) US Secretary of State Powell suggested merging the two operations. In early 2004, NATO's new Secretary-General, however, said that he preferred 'synergy', for instance by the appointment of one central commander, rather than a 'real merging' of the missions. The two suggestions raise questions about the relationships between the two missions as initially two different 'tracks', including their mandates, with Operation 'Enduring Freedom' fighting against international terrorism, and ISAF contributing to 'nation building' in a post-conflict peace-building environment. In late February 2004, a NATO official reminded journalists that Article 5 of the Washington Treaty was still in force, and was being used as political cover for many coalition activities in Afghanistan, such as the hunt for al-Qaeda and the Taliban – suggesting implicitly that NATO's role in commanding ISAF could be given an additional dimension by linking it, as Powell had already indicated, to efforts 'to stabilize Afghanistan as part of the Global War against Terrorism'. The discussion on merging the two missions again led to disagreement among NATO's member states, with the US government, supported by Supreme Allied Commander Europe (SACEUR), arguing that there is no point in keeping both structures since the two operations are essentially conducted by NATO member countries, and France and Germany arguing that the two missions' mandates are incompatible, given their respective peace-building and counter-terrorism tasks.[19] In late September 2005, there was no longer talk of merger between the missions but rather how to organize closer cooperation in terms of 'synergy'.[20] In December 2005, NATO reached an agreement on a formula, based on a revision of ISAF's chain of command, establishing a link with Enduring Freedom. At the occasion of their half-yearly meetings, the ministers of defence also reached agreement on a revised operational plan (OPLAN) for ISAF III, the third phase of the deployment of ISAF troops in the southern provinces of Afghanistan. Thus, the ministers recognized the greater security risks, compared to the ISAF I and II deployments, that the ISAF forces would run given the presence of remnants of Al Qai'da and Taliban in the area. This realization provided the basis for an authorization of more robust rules of engagement and the provision of additional security precautions. In their statement, at the end of the meeting, the ministers said:

> 'We are committed to the continuing success of the UN-mandated, NATO-led International Security Assistance Force (ISAF) in all its aspects and have today agreed to move NATO's support for peace and security in Afghanistan to a new level. We have endorsed the operational plan that allows for the continued expansion of ISAF. Provincial Reconstruction Teams are at the leading edge of NATO's effort, supported by military forces capable of addressing security threats where ISAF operates and reinforced by flexible, robust reserve forces, whenever the situation on the ground so requires.'

With the inauguration of Afghan's new parliament, early December 2005, the so-called Bonn-process, which provided for a transition process in the aftermath of the fall of the Taliban-regime, came to an end. Afghanistan entered a new stage in its post-conflict peace-building efforts – in close cooperation both with the UN and NATO.

4.2 Iraq

NATO as such was not involved in Operation 'Iraqi Freedom' in 2003. That was not to say, however, that 'Iraq' was not relevant for the Atlantic Alliance.

[19] 3602 *Atlantic News* (August 2004) and 3616 *Atlantic News* (14 October 2004).
[20] 3706 *Atlantic News* (13 September 2005).

On the contrary, the issue led to sharp differences of opinion among its members as a direct consequence of the debates within the UN Security Council on the conditions for use of force under the UN Charter. In their Prague Summit Statement on Iraq on 21 November 2002, NATO's heads of state and government committed themselves 'to take effective action to assist and support the efforts of the UN to ensure full and immediate compliance by Iraq, without conditions or restrictions, with UNSCR 1441' – implying that NATO, if necessary, would be prepared to enforce by military means Iraqi compliance to UN Security Council demands. Since then, US policy-makers, both in the administration and in Congress, discussed the possibilities for a NATO role in Iraq, during Operation 'Iraqi Freedom', during the occupation, and after the formal transfer of sovereignty at the end of June 2004. In mid-January 2003, the US administration, formally requesting NATO support in case of an attack on Baghdad, presented several 'options' for assistance.[21] In February 2003, against the background of increasing build-up of troops in the area and growing disagreements among the Allies, Turkey invoked Article 4 of the NATO Treaty.[22] After much controversy, the Allies decided to assist it by providing air surveillance (AWACS), deploying theatre anti-missile defences (Patriots) and NBC assets against the possible use of weapons of mass destruction. In May 2003, shortly after the fall of Saddam Hussein and the deployment of the Stabilization Force (SFIR), the North Atlantic Council decided to accept Poland's request for support in commanding one of the multinational divisions of SFIR, more or less along the lines of the 'technical assistance', including force generation and logistics, that NATO was giving to ISAF in Afghanistan. With the security situation in Iraq deteriorating, there was no consensus among NATO's members about more support to the coalition forces, which were operating under an occupation regime,[23] notwithstanding calls for such support in the US Congress in mid-2003. In December 2003, (then) US Secretary of State Colin Powell said that it was time to 'begin examining what we might be able to do in Iraq beyond support of the Polish Division'. One of the options, he said, might include

[21] The options for protecting Turkey against Iraqi counter-attacks, ranging from the use of AWACS aircraft, use of command facilities, and base and over-flight rights from NATO Allies, were formally presented to the NAC.

[22] Art. 4 states that the allies will consult 'whenever, in the opinion of any of them, the territorial integrity, political independence or security of any NATO country is threatened'.

[23] S/RES/1483 (2003), 22 May 2003; and S/RES/1511 (2003), 16 October 2003.

having NATO assume full command of the Polish-led sector in Iraq, coinciding with Spain's expected replacement as lead nation in August 2004.[24] In March 2004, Jaap de Hoop Scheffer also pointed out that 'momentum is growing' for the Alliance to do more, especially in the perspective of the end of the formal occupation period:

> 'Should we do more? My answer to this question is clear: If a sovereign Iraqi government, with the support of the United Nations, were to request NATO to play a greater role, then we should do more. For I do not see how we could abdicate our responsibilities if such a request were made.'[25]

In the following months, however, NATO shifted its focus towards a possible contribution to the reconstruction of Iraq by setting up a training mission for rebuilding Iraqi security forces after the formal transfer of authority to the new Iraqi government in June 2004. NATO's first concern at this stage of the decision-making process was to ensure that the political and international legal conditions for possible deployment would be fulfilled. In adopting Resolution 1546 on 8 June 2004, the Security Council, 'welcoming the beginning of a new phase in Iraq's transition to a democratically elected government, and looking forward to the end of the occupation and the assumption of full responsibility and authority by a fully sovereign and independent Interim Government of Iraq by 30 June 2004', recognized that the multinational force, whose presence 'is at the request of the incoming Interim Government of Iraq', would also assist 'in building the capability of the Iraqi security forces and institutions, through a programme of recruitment, training, equipping, mentoring, and monitoring'. In this context, the Security Council requested member states and regional organizations to assist both the multinational force and the government of Iraq in building the necessary capabilities.[26] Indeed, under these circumstances there was broad consensus among NATO member states that the Alliance should play a role

[24] It is worthwhile to note that NATO's SACEUR, General Ralston, already in August 2003 in an interview with Reuters, suggested that NATO would assume command of the Polish-led force of 9,000 troops operating in south-central Iraq; 3502 *Atlantic News* (28 August 2003).

[25] 'NATO's Transforming Agenda', by NATO Secretary-General Jaap de Hoop Scheffer, at the Diplomatic Academy, Warsaw, 4 March 2004. See <www.nato.int/docu/speech/2004/s040304a.htm>.

[26] S/RES/1546 (2004), 8 June 2004.

in Iraq after the transfer of sovereignty from the occupying authorities (the Coalition Provisional Authority) to the Iraqis at the end of June 2004, taking into account the parameters of the sub-contracting model, including a formal invitation by the new Iraqi government and authorization by the UN Security Council.[27] At its summit in Istanbul in June 2004, NATO decided 'to offer assistance to the government of Iraq with the training of its security forces', without, however, clarifying for the time being the details of the mission. In a separate statement that the heads of state and government issued on Iraq, they fully supported the independence, sovereignty, unity and territorial integrity of the Republic of Iraq, adding that NATO 'supports unreservedly' Resolution 1546 (2004) of the UN Security Council and 'offers its entire cooperation to the new sovereign interim government in its efforts to strengthen internal security and prepare for holding national elections in 2005.'[28]

Given the political sensitivities of a possible NATO presence on the ground among the member states (related to security concerns, political will and availability of instructors), the mission's modalities were extensively discussed within NATO in the months to come, following intense diplomatic wrangling. While the activation order for the mission was given on 15 December 2004 by SACEUR, it would take until mid-February 2005 before NATO was officially able to announce that all 26 member states would in some way participate in the programme, either by dispatching instructors to Iraq or by training outside Iraq, or by the provision of equipment or financial contributions. The agreement also had a strong symbolic significance, reflecting the decision by NATO members, in President Bush's words, 'to put the past behind them', thereby pointing at the sharp differences of opinion among the Allies during the war against Iraq. NATO's small training mission (with no more than 150 personnel), which is specifically intended for the training of senior officers, would complement the much larger training mission set up by the US-led multinational force to train units of Iraqi soldiers and police officers.[29] Both missions aim at building up effective Iraqi secu-

---

[27] Strictly speaking, from an international legal point of view such a formal authorization would not be necessary, once an official request has been made by the government of the host state.

[28] 3588 *Atlantic News* (29 June 2004).

[29] NATO decided to establish a provisional training centre in Baghdad's Green Zone instead of on the outskirts of the city. It therefore needed less staff than the 300-person mission originally foreseen. The interim staff college should begin to 'train the trainers' in April 2005

rity and police forces, thereby ultimately creating conditions for the withdrawal of foreign forces from Iraq's territory as soon as circumstances would permit.[30] In a statement read to the press by the Council's President at the end of May 2005, Denmark's ambassador to the UN said that the Security Council members had discussed the mandate of the Multinational Force in Iraq, authorizing an extension of its mandate 'until the completion of the political process', welcoming 'the progress made in recruiting, training and equipping Iraqi security forces', while looking forward 'to those forces progressively playing a greater role and ultimately assuming responsibility for Iraq's national security', thus, again, explicitly endorsing NATO's training mission.[31] In 2005, the mission trained 1,000 mid- and senior-level officers in the country, and close to 500 in NATO facilities in Europe. The aim was to train another 1,500 Iraqi officers in 2006.[32]

4.3 Darfur

Since initial contact was made by phone at the end of August 2004 between the Secretary-Generals of the UN and NATO, the UN Under-Secretary-General for Peacekeeping Operations called NATO in September 2004 to 'ask what NATO can do', according to a NATO official.[33] NATO's Secretary-General reacted favourably, committing himself to finding out what options NATO held. The 'open request', implying that each form of assistance would be welcome, paved the way for close contacts in the months to come among the UN, NATO and the European Union, and the AU as the lead organization, and establishment of a military mission, authorized by the Security Council and set up to monitor the implementation of a cease-fire as agreed

and it was foreseen that by September 2005 the Iraqi trainers would begin to give their first courses to Iraqi officers; 3654 *Atlantic News* (23 February 2005).

[30] In April 2005, President Bush said that US forces would pull out of Iraq once the representative government is in place. 150,000 members of the Iraqi security forces have been trained and equipped, President Bush was quoted as saying by AFP, adding that at the moment the Iraqi army, police and security forces exceed the US armed forces in number, which is the beginning of a 'new phase' in US operations in Iraq, according to Bush; 3668 *Atlantic News* (14 April 2005).

[31] Press Release SC/8403, IK/495, 31 May 2005. The announcement was quite exceptional, in the sense that, usually, the Security Council lays down its formal decisions in the form of resolutions!

[32] 3743 *Atlantic News* (24 January 2006) and 3745 *Atlantic News* (31 January 2006).

[33] 3607 *Atlantic News* (16 September 2004).

by the conflicting parties in Darfur.[34] It would take until April 2005 before the AU formally requested NATO's support. In the meantime, in January 2005 at a security conference in Munich (Germany), UN Secretary-General Kofi Annan repeated his call to assist the AU in its mission in Darfur, without, however, making a formal request. He stressed that the AU's ability to meet security needs was negligible compared to the size of the challenge, saying: 'People are dying every single day, while we fail to protect them', while adding, 'Those organizations with real capacity – and NATO as well as the EU are well represented in this room – must give serious consideration' to what they can do, he said.[35] In March 2005, US Secretary of State Condoleezza Rice argued that if the AU was to request NATO support, she hoped that NATO would provide it. Others, such as French Minister of Foreign Affairs Michel Barnier, responded, however, by saying that he would prefer a role for the EU, highlighting the experience gained by the EU in the Balkans and the Democratic Republic of Congo (DRC). NATO Secretary-General Jaap de Hoop Scheffer underlined that he was waiting for an initiative from the African Union. At the end of the month, the African Union formally asked NATO for 'logistic support' for its mission in Darfur. The request was made by the President of the African Union in a letter addressed to the NATO Secretary-General.[36] NATO ambassadors agreed to look at the possibility of providing support through the start of 'exploratory discussions' with the AU, realizing that if such support was to happen, it would be the first time that NATO would be involved in a mission on the African continent – alongside other international organizations, including the UN and the EU.

The President of the AU announced his presence in Brussels on 17 May 2005, both at NATO headquarters and to visit the EU for further discussions. After the visit, NATO undertook to give an answer 'as quickly as possible' to the AU's request for logistical support. 'The principle is, should be and will be that the AU is leading the mission', Jaap de Hoop Scheffer said. The President of the AU Commission, Oumar Konare, acknowledged that 'we are fully aware that we need support when it comes to capabilities and logistics'. More specifically, the AU called for aid in order to strengthen logistics in terms of transport, housing, training and communications, given the inten-

34 S/RES/1556, 30 July 2004.

35 3651 *Atlantic News* (15 February 2005).

36 3674 *Atlantic News* (28 April 2005).

tions to expand its mission from 2,000 to more than 7,700 troops in the course of the year.

At a special meeting in Addis Ababa to discuss the further deployment of the mission, NATO's Secretary-General stressed both the AU's leadership regarding Darfur and the need for close liaison with the AU and other donors, in part with the EU, to ensure maximum complementarity and effectiveness. After exploratory contacts with the AU, NATO's military authorities had identified three areas in which the Alliance could do its part for the international assistance effort:

> '– first, we could help to deploy the AU forces, in particular in the field of strategic airlift. NATO members indeed possess considerable airlift capabilities and could set up an appropriate centre for such an operation;
> – second, we could help to train the AMIS headquarters' staff in important areas such as command and control or operational planning;
> – and finally, if the AU so wishes, we could assist in the field of intelligence with training, for instance.'[37]

That same day, the North Atlantic Council agreed on these initial military options for support to the African Union.[38] The details still had to be worked out after additional clarification of the AU's needs. The decision opened the way for NATO's first mission to Africa, despite initial resistance from some members, such as France and Belgium (both former colonial powers), which argued that support for the AU should come from the EU and not from NATO.[39] NATO spokesman James Appathurai, emphasizing that the AU

---

[37] 'Speech by the Secretary-General at the Pledging Conference for the AU Mission in the Sudan', Addis Ababa, Ethiopia, 26 May 2005, NATO Speeches.

[38] 3681 *Atlantic News* (26 May 2005). On the eve of a new meeting in the series of talks between the AU, NATO, EU and UN in Addis Ababa, a number of former foreign ministers, including Madeleine Albright, strongly urged NATO to make an even greater commitment to the African mission, one that would include putting NATO troops on the ground under UN authorization. In addition, they suggested, NATO should seek authority from the Security Council for a new Chapter VII resolution establishing a no-flight zone over Darfur, which NATO aircraft would enforce; *International Herald Tribune*, 26 May 2005.

[39] Jaap de Hoop Scheffer was quoted as saying: 'NATO and the EU are entering into a very good example of what I would say is practical and pragmatic cooperation. Let's not have theology. Let's do it. The AU came to NATO and the AU came to the EU. There is no room for competition. There is plenty of work to be done ... The decision could ... also be an important test case for much closer cooperation between NATO and the EU'; *International Herald Tribune*, 9 June 2005.

had always been adamant about the presence of only African soldiers on the ground, said that NATO (like the EU) would not send troops, adding that both organizations would keep a low profile since neither Sudan nor the Arab League wanted Western troops in Darfur.[40] By providing strategic airlift, NATO thus started mid 2005 to contribute to the deployment of AU forces on the ground in Darfur. However, at the end of the year, there were increasing doubts about the effectiveness of the mission, given its inability to end the atrocities in the area. These criticisms opened the floor for a discussion on a possible transfer of the mission from the AU to the UN. In January 2006, UN Secretary-General Kofi Annan urged for a larger, more robust and more mobile force than the AU, while president Bush supported the idea of increasing the level of forces, 'probably under the auspices of the UN and with NATO involvement'. While the US Secretary of State Condoleezza Rice, at the time, restated that 'Our position is that a genocide has been committed and that it is continuing in practice', the US Senate adopted, on 2 March 2006, a resolution, urging NATO to send troops to Darfur, asking the President to see to it that NATO would ensure respect of a no-fly zone over Darfur. However, NATO's Secretary-General Jaap de Hoop Scheffer ruled out sending NATO troops, saying that he could only see a role for NATO in the field of logistics.

5. Conclusion

Since the end of the Second World War in 1945, the international political system has seen two major turning-points: the end of the Cold War; and the terror attack of 9/11. Both events have had a profound impact on the position and performance of NATO, including the formulation and implementation of 'transformation agendas' in completely different security environments. The end of the Cold War has contributed to defining the contours of NATO's institutional and operational relations with the UN, highlighting its inherently ambivalent character as a collective defence organization, which is also willing and capable of performing as an instrument of the collective security system, as embodied in the UN Charter. The contours were shaped as a result

[40] Although the AU had always been adamant about the presence of only African soldiers on the ground, NATO support could possibly require the presence of a few soldiers, NATO sources stated; 3681 *Atlantic News* (26 May 2005).

of NATO's performance in Bosnia, both before and after the signing of the Dayton Peace Agreement, Operation 'Allied Force' and the deployment of Kosovo Force (KFOR) in Kosovo, and its presence in Macedonia in supporting the implementation of the Ohrid Agreement. This series of consecutive missions can be construed in two 'models': the so-called sub-contracting model and the autonomy model. Under the sub-contracting model, the Atlantic Alliance is prepared, responding to a request of the UN, to assist in the implementation of Security Council resolutions, while recognizing the Council's primacy in maintaining international peace and security under the UN Charter. NATO's decision, however, in 1999 to execute Operation 'Allied Force' in Kosovo, according to its own rules under the autonomy model, made clear that the Alliance basically reserves its right as a collective defence organization to use force without the explicit authorization of the Security Council – a decision that was formalized in NATO's 1999 New Strategic Concept. The message was clear: while NATO is prepared to act within the parameters of the sub-contracting model, the bottom line is that it is not willing to subordinate itself to the UN under all conditions. The Kosovo debate, heated as it was, to a large extent was reminiscent of the discussions in 1949 among NATO's founding fathers about the wording of the preamble to NATO's treaty in the run-up to the establishment of the Alliance.

The two models, as developed in the 1990s, have thus laid down the framework for the relationships between NATO and the UN in the aftermath of 9/11. NATO's current transformation agenda is determined by international terrorism as the main security threat of the twenty-first century. This might very well lead to a shift from the sub-contracting model of the 1990s to a renewed focus on the autonomy model, with more emphasis on NATO's character as a collective defence organization and its right to self-defence under Article 5 of the Washington Treaty. Responding to the terrorist attacks of 9/11, NATO's decision to invoke this article for the first time in its history is still operational, as illustrated by the recent decision to expand Operation 'Active Endeavour' to cover the whole of the Mediterranean Sea.[41] NATO's position as an autonomous instrument in the fight against international terrorism was also underlined by its wish (as expressed in Reykjavik in May 2002) to become a 'global player', capable of acting wherever forces are

[41] NATO's AWACS support to the US ended in April 2002; *Atlantic News*, No. 3379.

needed,[42] leaving behind its 'out-of-area' syndrome, and the acceptance of the concept of pre-emptive attacks, which is in line with the US national security strategy. At the same time, NATO's involvement in ISAF fits perfectly in the so-called sub-contracting model, just like the (initial) idea to task NATO with the command of a multinational force in Iraq after the end of the occupation regime. Although the latter task did not materialize, NATO's training mission in Iraq is similarly being embedded within the same framework, including an explicit request from the acting government of the host-nation and formal authorization by the UN Security Council. What is striking is that all of these developments reflect a certain eagerness on the part of NATO, or so it seems to me, to take on new responsibilities in the aftermath of 9/11 as part of its transformation agenda. In the case of Afghanistan, NATO offered support to Turkey, even before Turkey itself had taken a decision about accepting a 'lead nation' role, followed by similar offers to other member states, and its willingness to take over full command of ISAF. In the case of Iraq, NATO committed itself to enforcing Security Council demands in the case of non-compliance by Saddam Hussein, assisted Poland in its role in SFIR, operating under an occupation regime, has been considering taking over the command of a multinational force as soon as the occupation regime comes to an end, and is currently involved in a training mission in parallel with the US-led Stabilization Force in Iraq (SFIR). It is surprising to note how these far-reaching decisions have been, and are being, taken and implemented without a serious public debate on NATO's transformation agenda.

In March 2004, UN Secretary-General Kofi Annan quite unexpectedly called upon NATO to support the UN in Africa, saying that if the UN undertakes new peacekeeping operations in Africa, support from NATO would be 'tremendously helpful'. Annan welcomed the willingness of the Alliance to 'go global', citing its recent work in Afghanistan as an example. Anticipating 'a surge' of new peacekeeping operations across Africa in the year ahead, he added:

---

[42] N. Burns in the *International Herald Tribune* wrote that in 2003 NATO added vital new military capabilities that 'will revolutionize our strategic reach', thus underlining two accomplishments: on 1 December 2003 NATO inaugurated the new Czech-led CBRN battalion, which is designed to safeguard 'our' civilian populations from a WMD attack; and on 1 October 2003 the Alliance launched the new NATO Reaction Force, which will for the first time in its history give NATO a quick-reaction force for hostage rescue, peace interventions and combat operations far from Europe.

> 'NATO might be employed in a "peace enforcement" role, much as the European Union deployed 'Operation Artemis' in the Democratic Republic of the Congo (DRC) as a bridging force before the deployment of a UN operation.'[43]

At the time, Annan also praised NATO's preparedness to send troops to Iraq if requested. While thus welcoming the role of NATO as a 'global player', he added that the UN and NATO would continue to discuss the world's collective security system as well as peace-support operations. One year later, in January 2005, Kofi Annan again urged NATO to consider seriously becoming active in Africa, this time, however, by assisting the African Union in its mission in Darfur. Annan's calls for greater NATO involvement in Africa were made against the background of increasing cooperation between the UN and regional organizations that were focused on either seeking direct support to the UN by deploying before, alongside, or after a UN operation, or the long-term enhancement of regional and sub-regional organizations' capacity for peacekeeping, particularly in Africa (giving as examples Ivory Coast and Liberia – Economic Community of West African States (ECOWAS) – and the DRC – the European Union). In this context, Annan spoke of the need to reinforce 'strategic partnerships' with regional organizations.[44] Two months later, Jean-Marie Guehenno, UN Under-Secretary-General for Peacekeeping, presented a plan to strengthen UN peacekeeping through the rise of what he termed 'partnership peacekeeping' – the UN working alongside regional organizations like NATO, the EU and ECOWAS.[45] Without giving further details, in 'In Larger Freedom' Kofi Annan called for the establishment of an 'interlocking system of peacekeeping capacities' as part of the UN System of Standby Arrangements (UNSAS), through 'partnerships' with regional organizations. Taking into account the conceptual and operational limits of UNSAS, the High-level Panel's report, which argued in favour of a stricter formalization of the UN's relations with its regional partners, was more ambitious than Annan in his report. And even Jaap de Hoop Scheffer was much more outspoken when, responding to Annan's recommendations, he underlined the need to develop 'structured relationships at the institutional level' between NATO and the UN, in order to 'coordinate strategically, [and] not just cooperate tactically'.

---

[43] 'Annan Invites NATO Support for Anticipated African Peacekeeping Missions', UN News Centre, 9 March 2004.

[44] UN News Centre, 27 February 2004.

[45] *International Herald Tribune*, 20 April 2004.

In terms of the actual cooperation between the two organizations, in its deployments in Bosnia, Kosovo, Afghanistan and Iraq, NATO already went far beyond the scope of the so-called 'interlocking system of peacekeeping capacities'. Other than by calling for 'a decisive step forward', with his recommendation on the establishment of 'an interlocking system of peacekeeping capacities', Annan basically set the clock some ten years back. In the early 1990s, after an extensive discussion on the idea of the establishment of a UN rapid reaction force in the aftermath of the genocide in Rwanda, the Security Council made it clear that 'the first priority in improving the capacity for rapid deployment should be the further enhancement of the existing stand-by arrangements', thereby declining any initiative beyond the UN Standby Arrangement System for peacekeeping operations.[46]

Where Annan is extremely reluctant in recommending further formalization of the relations between the UN and regional organizations beyond 'peacekeeping', there is an additional reason for him when it comes to the relationship between the UN and NATO. This has to do with NATO's 'status apart' among the so-called 'regional organizations' – outside the purview of Chapter VIII of the UN Charter. While NATO in the last decade has presented itself as a powerful military instrument of the UN's collective security system, it has simultaneously made it abundantly clear that, given its character as a collective defence organization, it retains the right under all circumstances to use force without UN Security Council authorization, thereby neglecting the Council's primacy in maintaining international peace and security. Both organizations could continue with 'business as usual' on the ground, without any further formalization of their mutual relationships. Looking at NATO's future, however, one can assume that the Alliance will increase its out-of-area missions. Anticipating more calls for assistance in the years ahead, US Ambassador Nicolas Burns, in early 2005, thought it highly likely that 'in one or two years from now, most NATO troops will be outside Europe'.[47]

This raises the question of whether there is greater need than ever before to formalize relationships between the two organizations as the missing link between UN reform and the transformation of NATO.[48] Nevertheless, as far

---

[46] D.A. Leurdijk (ed.), *A UN Rapid Deployment Brigade: Strengthening the Capacity for Quick Response, supra*, note 4, p. 11.

[47] 3641 *Atlantic News* (13 January 2005).

[48] The *Draft Outcome Document, supra*, note 5, used as a basis for the deliberations in the General Assembly on the recommendations of Kofi Annan, supports a 'stronger relationship' between the UN and (sub-)regional organizations 'pursuant to Chapter VIII of the Charter',

as the UN-NATO relationship is concerned, the 2005 World Summit Outcome document seems to suggest that there is no need to go beyond ad hoc cooperation on the ground – no need for fresh thinking whatsoever, in other words. At the same time, one should not dramatize the outcome: it will not prevent the UN and NATO from future forms of cooperation along the (*ad hoc*) lines of the past, reflecting both organizations' interests.

---

suggesting to 'Expand consultation and cooperation between the UN and regional and sub-regional organizations through formalized agreements between respective secretariats, regularized involvement of regional organizations in the work of the Security Council, and participation of relevant regional organizations in the Peace-building Commission'. For a comparison of the paragraphs on regional organizations in the three reports of the High-level Panel, Kofi Annan and the 'Draft Outcome Document', see Annex 1 with the Draft Outcome document.

Chapter 9
LEGITIMATION OF MILITARY OPERATIONS

Leon Wecke*

1. Definition

The legitimation of military operations is more important than is often realized. The hypothesis seems plausible that one of the main factors in the national decision-making process on participation in military operations is the problem of the legitimacy of these operations. Especially in Western democracies, the legitimacy of governmental decisions on military operations is turning into an increasingly crucial condition. Of course, in general, the necessity of the precondition of legitimacy differs according to time and place. Dictators and absolute monarchs, governing by the grace of God, may have less need for the legitimacy of their behaviour, although even for them legitimacy is a positive circumstance – even Saddam Hussein would have been pleased by it. Also in the case of parliamentary democracy, one can pose the question whether legitimacy is a necessary condition. One can follow the reasoning that the public expressed its will by means of elections after which the chosen representatives and the democratically formed government act in the name of the people and do not need any further legitimation.

Of course, it all depends on the definition of legitimacy. How can one define it?

There are many definitions and opinions. Sociological definitions, which characterize legitimacy as an attribution of a social institution to realize majority support; policy-oriented definitions, underlining that means are legitimate if they lead to the intended results; and also traditional legitimacy, based

* Centre for International Conflict Analysis and Management (CICAM), Radboud University Nijmegen.

O. Ribbelink (ed.), Beyond the UN Charter: Peace, Security and the Role of Justice

only on the very existence of definite practices and behaviour. A possible subdivision into two categories is the following: on the one hand, the objectivist visions of a mainly philosophical heritage: they give objective, substantial criteria in answering the question whether something is legitimate; on the other hand, a behavioural category, in which case the subject itself determines what is right or wrong.

The category of classical and more recent politico-philosophical views (e.g., Plato, Aristotle, Thomas of Aquino, Bodin, Hobbes, Locke and Hannah Arendt) is characterized by considering the criteria for evaluating the political system irrespective of the subject, the population or the citizen; whereas the behavioural category speaks of legitimacy whenever the citizen considers the political system to be right. In the former case the observer concludes whether a system is right or wrong, measured according to definite universally acknowledged values and norms. In the latter case the opinion of the citizen is decisive.[1] Values, norms, interests and expectations are the criteria of the individual citizen.

The latter view implies that a political system, but also a governmental policy, a decision, a minister and, for instance, a military operation are legitimate if they are perceived as right by the majority of citizens.

Legitimacy may concern a total political system as well as a part or a specific aspect of its structure, proceedings, decisions and implementations. Measured by universal values and norms, a definite policy may be inhuman and wrong. But legitimate authority, in our view, need not be identical with a right authority, measured according to universal, objective criteria.

Following Friedrich, we will speak of legitimacy as such: 'when a given rulership is believed to be based on a good title by most men subject to it'.[2]

Not only a given rulership, but all aspects of its behaviour may be the object of public evaluation and may be found legitimate or illegitimate. Legitimacy concerns a congruency of the citizen's values, norms, expectations and interests and the object to be judged. It ought to involve a majority of the

[1] L. Wecke, 'Legitimacy as Limiting Factor in Governmental Decision Making: The Case of the Cruise Missiles', in I.Th. Snellen (ed.), *Limits of Government* (Amsterdam, 1985) pp. 99-133 and 'Legitimiteit van de Nederlandse krijgsmacht', in B. Bomert and H. de Lange (eds.), *Jaarboek Vrede en Veiligheid 1998* (Nijmegen) pp. 253-267.

[2] C.J. Friedrich, *Man and His Government: An Empirical Theory of Politics* (New York 1963) p. 234.

people. If there is a parliamentary majority you may label it as political legitimacy. Legitimacy is reserved for the majority support in public opinion. But: what about a passionate minority? They can ruin the policy of the government and in the case of a civil war the whole political system. Nevertheless, we will stick to our definition: a majority is required.

Our preference for a 'subjectivist' definition is based on our view that public opinion is important for and often crucial to the possibility of military operations: the decision to deploy and the continuation of the action. Sometimes a decision to intervene by military means cannot be taken or must be postponed, or will depend on certain conditions, because of its illegitimacy. Apart from this, it is of the utmost importance, although this is often neglected, to be aware of the legitimacy or illegitimacy of a military intervention in the host country and also in other countries, whether or not they may be allies.

2. Measuring legitimacy

How do we know whether a planned operation is legitimate or not? Legitimacy can be measured by means of public opinion polls. When the questions are not suggestive and reliable and valid and more polls produce more or less the same results, one may assume that they are accurate. Indications of legitimacy or illegitimacy may be inferred from the behaviour of the government. For example, when it hesitates in taking a decision, this may be an indication of the government's feeling that its behaviour lacks public support. The behaviour of citizens may be indicative too, among other things when a planned or taken governmental decision leads to large demonstrations or even unrest in society. For example, in the early 1980s the Dutch Government postponed for many years the decision to deploy 48 cruise missiles, because of the evident illegitimacy of this legally valid decision. More recently, because of the supposed political and public illegitimacy of the decision to send troops to the province of Uruzgan in Afghanistan, the government tried to shift the decision-making process to Parliament.

3. Justifying images

The arguments either in favour of or opposed to military operations – and all other matters – consist of images in the minds of people, images which have definite characteristics.[3] One main characteristic in the case of justifying images is their importance. What is their relevance for behaviour? What is the intensity of the (il)legitimacy in specific cases? On the one hand, it is important to know the percentage of citizens who perceive a military action as right or wrong. On the other hand, it is important to know the intensity of their feelings and how much they are involved in their judgment. Are public actions to be expected in case the government takes or implements its decision? What is the emotional and what is the rational component of the arguments in favour or against a planned operation? What dimension do the arguments have? Are political, economic, moral and, for instance, religious dimensions to be discerned? Do the arguments have an idiosyncratic character, in other words: are they isolated from or connected with other beliefs and attitudes? And how accurate are they for the holders concerned? Are they clear indications for them? These and more characteristics are important to know for those who want to foster illegitimacy as well as for those who want to underline the legitimacy of a governmental policy.

Other important aspects are the elements which, in the eyes of citizens, are inherent in the object 'military operation'. People can agree or disagree with the procedure which led to the definite decision, the decision itself or, for instance, its implementation. People can agree with the action and its goal but not with the armament of the military units concerned. In that case one speaks of partial legitimation.

The legitimacy of military operations can be determined more completely if at least five questions are answered:

1. What are the legitimizing values, norms, interests and expectations of the people?
2. In which elements is the military operation subdivided by the people?
3. Which criteria are applied in assessing the operation?
4. How large is the share of the population which approves or disapproves of the military operation?
5. How involved are the citizens sharing this opinion?

[3] L. Wecke, 'Enemy Images in Public Opinion', in H-J. Rebel and L. Wecke, *Friends, Foes, Values and Fears* (Nijmegen/Amsterdam, 1987) pp. 143-186, 150-151.

4. Legitimation

Legitimation is the process which makes legitimacy. This process may consist of information, propaganda, but also of lies to justify military operations; it may consist of all kinds of manipulative communication contents, limiting and misleading the press, false interpretations and/or distributing one-sided and incomplete pictures of political and military reality. The last-mentioned may be in good or bad faith. Actors in the legitimizing process are not only governments. Especially the media may function as simple distributors of arguments, but also – consciously or unconsciously – as co-propagandists and co-misleaders. Patriotism and all other understandable barriers to the ideal of an objective press make the media receptive as instruments for the legitimation of governmental decisions such as on military operations. All kinds of institutions varying from political parties, trade unions, churches, interest groups and individual experts and persons with social prestige may be elements in the process of legitimation.

Furthermore, not only subjective factors, but also particular events may be a factor in the legitimation process. Sometimes specific events, such as the shelling of a marketplace in Sarajevo, the murder of a well-known and beloved statesman, images of a supposed genocide, or supposed preparations for nuclear armament can facilitate the justification to take or implement decisions to send troops abroad.

Up to the present the most important instrument of legitimation of military operations is still an enemy or at least a serious threat. Unfortunately, after the fall of the Berlin Wall, a real enemy in the sense of a military threat no longer exists for nearly all countries. The Soviet Union no longer exists, and by way of a joke, I may add that the Germans had their turn and a second opportunity for the Vikings is not probable! A well-known Dutch columnist in the *NRC Handelsblad*, Jerome Heldring, wrote in 1986:

> 'but when everything runs according to the intentions of Michail Gorbachov – or let me say, according to what they seem to be – then it is clear from the dogma of a common enemy that NATO will not survive. The reason for its existence will have disappeared.'

He was right. After the collapse of the Soviet Union, NATO became a solution searching for a problem. Of course by means of the new Strategic Concept of NATO and in view of its actions in Kosovo and presently in

Afghanistan one may say that NATO found some justification for its continuation, although not convincing to everyone.

In the same year, 1986, in an interview in the same newspaper – *NRC Handelsblad* – our then Chief of Staff, General Huijser, stated:

> 'Given the economic interests and considering the specific political agreements, we buy military material in proportion to the funds available. Subsequently, we adapt our force structure and finally we consider which threat fits in'.

Legitimizing threats does not necessarily have to be true. Crucial is the fact whether people believe it to be true or not. The illegal, but in the beginning for the American people legitimate, attack on Iraq was justified by non-existent weapons of mass destruction. An argument that was enforced by making people believe in a non-existent relationship between Saddam Hussein and Osama bin Laden.

The so-called 'Thomas Theorem' cannot be underlined enough; it runs: 'If men define situations as real, they are real in their consequences'.[4]

Permit me to illustrate this *theorem* with a common event in which I participated myself. Some time ago I went by train from The Hague to Nijmegen. I did so in the company of a colleague in communication science. In our compartment a German man, a woman and three children were also present. They asked us: does this train go to Oberhausen?' We, who had to go to Nijmegen, answered; 'No, this train goes to Nijmegen'. In Arnhem, the last stop before Nijmegen, the German, his wife and three children hurried to leave the train. It took much more time for us to realize, and subsequently too late, that our train had already crossed the border in the direction of Oberhausen. In legitimizing military operations people are often put on the wrong train.

Terrorism is a common threat for all peoples and states, but in relation to the amount of victims of other threats for mankind, it is peanuts. Look at the many millions of victims each year as a consequence of hunger, illness, poverty and pollution of the environment. The chance of becoming a victim in The Hague traffic is a million times more probable than becoming a victim of a terrorist attack in the Netherlands. But this is statistical reasoning. And Churchill once observed: 'I believe only those statistics which I have forged myself'.

---

[4] W.I. Thomas, 'Social Behavior and Personality', in E.H. Volkart (ed.), *Theory and Social Research* (New York: Social Science Research Council 1951).

Of course, depending on the character of the military operation, the justifying goals and values will differ.

5. Goals and legitimations

A distinction which is as clear as possible must be made between short and longer-term goals of military operations and legitimations, which sometimes have little or nothing to do with these goals. Another category of relevant data is the ideological and personal drives behind the goals, as well as, of course, a potential situation which may be a decisive factor for implementing long-cherished plans.

Frequently, it is difficult to make a distinction between the goals of an operation and its legitimation which is often not related to these goals. Maybe a further specification in primary and secondary goals is required. But in the case of the recent war in Iraq it seems less difficult to distinguish goals and false legitimations.

When the hypothesis is valid that this war is meant to be waged in accordance with the content of the 'National Security Strategy of the United States' and this content is mainly a reflection of the neo-conservative agenda,[5] the goals of the recent Gulf War are evident. It implies: 'fostering and/or strengthening of the hegemony of the United States in the world and especially in the Middle East'. Regime change is mentioned, and also 'the task of the military to ensure and expand the "zones of democratic peace", to deter the rise of a new great power competitor, defend key regions of Europe, East Asia and the Middle East, and to preserve American pre-eminence through the coming transformation of war, made possible by new technologies'.[6]

Content analyses of the State of the Union, inaugural and other speeches by President Bush before the attack on Iraq and thereafter, teach us that although freedom, democracy and free enterprise are the verbal goals of American foreign policy, in the case of Iraq the weapons of mass destruction were the main argument.[7] Only after the exposure of the weapons of mass de-

---

[5] National Security Council, 'The National Security Stategy of the United States of America', The White House, September 17, 2002.

[6] 'The Project of the New American Century, Rebuilding America's Defenses, Strategy, Forces and Resources for a New Century', Washington, DC, September 2000.

[7] See my article: 'Democratie als voorgewende legitimatie van de Derde Golfoorlog', 1 *Civis Mundi* (2006) pp. 37-42.

struction (WMD) justification did democracy and the liberation of the Iraqi people take their predominant places.

Military operations are legitimized preferably by impressive threats or high values: to relieve humanitarian needs, freedom, democracy, security, God, international order and human rights are all well-known elements in the justification of military operations. Of course, people ought to believe in them and if they do not, the process of legitimacy is aimed at fostering that belief.

During the Nuremberg Trial, Hermann Goering, stated:

> 'Of course the people don't want war. But after all, it's the leaders of the country who determine the policy, and it's always a simple matter to drag the people along, whether it is democracy or a fascist dictatorship. Voice or no voice, the people can always be brought to the bidding of the leaders. That is easy. All you have to do is tell them they are being attacked, and denounce the pacifists for lack of patriotism, and exposing the country to greater danger.'

'Who is not with us, is with the terrorists', is a more recent slogan.

6. Operations and soldiers

In speaking about the legitimacy of military operations we must distinguish between the legitimacy of the operation itself, the military concerned and, of course, the procedure of decision-making and the implementation of that decision.

For instance: the Dutch army has a high degree of legitimacy. According to ten years of research by the Society and Armed Forces Institute ('Stichting Maatschappij en Krijgsmacht') we may state that three quarters of the Dutch population accept the Dutch army as necessary or a necessary evil.[8] The quality of the assessment of the latter category is of course less high. Nonetheless, concerning the operations of Dutch forces, the legitimacy differs considerably. Answering in September 2005 the question whether during the Second World War the deployment of Dutch troops was right or not, 95.7 per cent agreed.[9] This percentage for deployment in Indonesia (1945-1950) was

[8] Stichting Maatschappij en Krijgsmacht, *Trends publieke opinie*, <http://www.smk.nl/mkop.html>, zie ook: *Veteranenmonitor* 2005 t.b.v. SVI, Blauw Research, September 2005.

[9] *Veteranenmonitor* 2005, 'Terechtheid inzet militairen', p. 8.

47.4 per cent, for New Guinea (1950-1962) 44.4 per cent, for Lebanon (1979-1985) 52 per cent, for Srebrenica (1994-1995) 58.2 per cent, for Afghanistan (2001-present) 51.5 per cent and for Iraq (2003-2005) 42 per cent.

The legitimacy of the action as such is one thing, but the legitimacy of the military is something else. The question of what about the appreciation of the military involved was asked. It turned out that even if the action as such is illegitimate, the military are not valued in the same way. Much, or very much, appreciation (66.4 per cent) was given to the military involved in the operations in Iraq, and 66.8 appreciated those who participated in the operation in Srebrenica.[10] It might be worth mentioning that a poll, organized by our institute six weeks after the fall of Srebrenica, showed that 68 per cent of the Dutch were in favour of the continuation of UN operations and 62 per cent were in favour of the continuation of operations in Yugoslavia; this in spite of the press and politicians who would have liked to make people believe that the disaster of Srebrenica had created a Srebrenica trauma.[11]

High percentages in favour of Dutch military operations belong to the past. Speaking about Iraq, public opinion researcher Jan Schoeman stated: 'This is no longer an accident; the Netherlands does not want that war'.[12] A recent mission by Dutch marines and commandos to Afghanistan received the approval of 45 per cent, against were 49 per cent.[13] Furthermore, scores of those approving will undoubtedly be lower when serious losses and/or losses which catch the imagination of the public are to be regretted. The Mueller or casualties hypothesis is still valid.[14] Mueller found on the basis of analyses of public opinion during the Vietnam and Korea Wars that support for war decreases as a logarithmic function of casualties. During the 1990s we tested his hypothesis by means of public opinion polls in the Netherlands.

---

[10] *Veteranenmonitor* 2005, 'Mate van waardering voor ingezette militairen', p. 10.

[11] B. Schennink and L. Wecke, 'De Nederlandse publieke opinie over VN-vredesoperaties', in M.F.A. Cras and L. Wecke (eds.), *Vijftig jaar VN-vredesoperaties, tussen nationaal belang en internationale rechtsorde* (Nijmegen 1996).

[12] J. Schoeman, 6 *Carré* (2005) p. 25.

[13] Opinieonderzoek Maurice de Hond, *de Volkskrant*, 19 March 2005.

[14] J. Mueller, *War, Presidents and Public Opinion* (New York: Wiley 1973); J. Mueller, 'Trends in Popular Support for the Wars in Korea and Vietnam', 65 *American Polical Science Review* (1971) pp. 358-375.

7. The Mueller hypothesis

In November 1993 we asked the Dutch public its opinion about the acceptability of actions by Dutch forces in favour of three goals, namely: the defence of our territory, the defence of international order, and actions to protect Dutch interests.[15] The first question was on the acceptability of deterrence by means of the armed forces for the three goals mentioned. It turned out that 69 per cent answered 'yes' to the acceptability of deterring by means of the armed forces in order to defend the territory and the international order. A much lower percentage were in favour of deterring with the armed forces to protect national interests. The next question for those who had answered 'yes' to the first question had to do with the acceptability of the actual use of the armed forces for the same goals. About 60 per cent were in favour of using the forces to defend its own territory and the international order; 38 per cent were for the defence of national interests. The third question for the respondents in favour of using the armed forces was what their opinion would be in the case of heavy losses on the side of the other party or parties. In case of substantial losses the original majority changed into a minority: 41 per cent were for international order and 38 per cent were for defending the territory. Twenty per cent remained in favour of using the armed forces to defend national interests. The next question for those who still belonged to the 'yes' category was: 'What is your answer in the case of substantial losses on our own side?' The percentage shrunk to 33 per cent for international order, 31 per cent for the defence of our own territory and 19 per cent for national interests. The next question: 'what is your opinion in case your family and acquaintances belong to the victims?' Of course this led to even less enthusiasm. The percentages for own territory and international order shrank to below the 30 per cent mark and national interests only received 15 per cent. The last question was of course: 'what is your answer in case you are a victim of the operation?' In that case the enthusiasm was the lowest.

When the first battalion of the Dutch Air Mobile Brigade departed for former Yugoslavia, we reformulated our questions and asked about numbers instead of percentages of casualties. The information given to the respondents was a battle situation for the battalion in case a possible peace agree-

[15] L. Wecke, 'Legitimiteit en vredesoperaties', in H.J. van der Graaf, D.K. Schut and H.W. Bomert (eds.), *Het vredesproces in beweging, nieuwe uitdagingen voor VN-vredesmachten* (Nijmegen 1994) pp. 169-196.

ment had to be enforced. The question was: 'How many casualties out of the total of about 1,000 men are acceptable: one, ten, twenty, more?' Of the respondents 42 per cent answered no casualties are acceptable, 21 per cent one to ten – the usual number of road traffic victims in such a big operation; and only two lunatics answered: 'in our opinion the whole battalion is allowed to die'.

In 1995 the question about the acceptability of casualties was posed again. This poll was held about six weeks after Srebrenica. But this time a distinction was made between military and civilian casualties. Furthermore, we did not speak about serious losses, but only losses. As was expected, military victims were more acceptable than civilian casualties. Of the respondents 52 per cent, a slight majority, answered 'yes' to the acceptability of military losses and 46 per cent to civilian casualties.

We repeated the Mueller question in 1999 with more or less the same results.

In our opinion there are enough indications for the plausibility of the Muller hypothesis that Dutch public opinion will not accept heavy losses in military operations, assuming that some of the Mueller hypothesis undermining factors are absent. Nonetheless, if they are present the acceptance degree will be higher. These undermining factors are:

- A successful operation through which quick results are achieved.
- An operation of short duration; people know the end is nearby.
- An enemy which is seen as very dangerous and threatening.
- Political unanimity: government and opposition are strongly united in the decisions taken.
- A one-sided press in favour of the military operation
- Successful neglect of casualties, no governmental attention to them.
- Transformation of serious losses into patriotic manifestations.
- A culture and history with less value attached to individual human lives.

From many studies it is evident that even serious losses do not or do not immediately influence public support for military operations.[16]

[16] The casualties hypothesis is commented upon in various chapters of P. Everts and P. Iserna (eds.), *Public Opinion and the International Use of Force* (London/New York 2001). See also: PH.P. Everts, 'Het maatschappelijk draagvlak voor militaire vredesoperaties. De

Explanations for the unwillingness to accept casualties are:

1. A real threat to one's own existence is no longer perceived;
2. A real positive effect of risky operations has not yet been registered by the public;
3. In an individualistic society human rights are valued highly;
4. Death and suffering of war victims have, through television images, led to an awakening of consciousness, more so than to indifference;
5. De-Christianization means that our earthly life is seen as more valuable, at least as more valuable than our heavenly life;
6. Organizations like Amnesty International have contributed to the notion of the value of individual lives;
7. In Western countries families are becoming smaller. After the killing of a son, parents have lost, in most cases, 50 per cent of their children.
8. The goal of the operation is not sufficiently explained or is not to be explained to the people.
9. The military operation is publicly judged to be of marginal importance.

Looking back at the loss of nearly 6,000 lives in the military operation in Indonesia, we may conclude that the acceptance of such losses is unthinkable in our time. Compare this with the more recent the disasters in Somalia, where 18 American soldiers were killed and two bodies were dragged through the streets of Mogadishu, and the blast at the Marines Headquarters in Beirut, Lebanon, killing 214 marines at once. Both events resulted in the ending, or ending earlier than foreseen, of the military operations concerned.

The fact that only recently the Iraq war lost it legitimacy in the United States has its explanation in experiencing a very dangerous enemy. But nowadays as the fear for Iraq turned out to be misplaced and losses are increasing, the illegitimacy of that operation is a fact.

---

slachtoffer hypothese nader bekeken', 25/1 *Transaktie* (1996) pp. 44-70 and Ph.P. Everts, 'The "Bodybag Hypothesis" as an Alibi. Public Support for UN Military Operations in the Netherlands: The Case of Bosnia-Hercegowina', 6/1 *Politics, Groups and the Individual* (1996) pp. 57-84. See also J. van der Meulen and M. de Konink, 'Nooit meer sneuvelen. Precisering van de slachtofferhypothese', 27/2 *Transaktie* (1998) pp. 191-209.

8. Neglecting illegitimacy, the case of Uruzgan

Of course, governments may and often must neglect the majority opinion of their people. Public emotions are often understandable, but in many cases the government would be well advised to retain its own line. Nonetheless, if not because of democratic principles, in certain cases the government will do the right thing by following the opinion of the majority. This is especially the case when there is a large and highly involved majority on a basic issue. Such a majority can be reflected in immediate or near future political illegitimacy and may bring the policy concerned, if not the government itself, to an end. An interesting theory about governmental behaviour in case of high costs of military operations is formulated by Donna J. Nincic and Miroslav Nincic.[17] They state that governments act as investors and the public as consumers in relation to the course of a military operation. In the face of mounting casualties, the initial reaction of governments, dealing with a long-term perspective, will be escalation. Public opinion, however, acting from a short-term perspective, wants to terminate the intervention.

After long hesitation and confused discussion in Parliament, the Dutch Government decided to send forces to the dangerous province of Uruzgan in Afghanistan. First, there was a clear majority which disapproved of that decision. Later on, when the parties in Government and a part of the opposition underlined the legal character – a UN mandate and a NATO obligation – and legal procedures in case of prisoners of war and military assistance in case of emergency were assured, public opinion in favour of the operation increased. Basic values in the public mind, as well as international order and human rights, undoubtedly also played a role in convincing people to favour a positive decision. Nevertheless, more people disapproved than approved.

Although in its briefing to Parliament the Government mentioned the very dangerous situation, it concluded that this situation in Uruzgan is nevertheless acceptable.[18] The many points of attention on the governmental and parliamentary checklist for deployment outside NATO territory, and about the military and political feasibility, did not lead to the rejection of the planned operation. The Government concluded with an intention to go, and also at-

[17] D.J. Nincic and M. Nincic, 'Commitment to Military Intervention: The Democratic Government as Economic Investor', 32/4 *Journal of Peace Research* (1995) pp. 413-427.

[18] 'Artikel 100-brief inzake Nederlandse bijdrage aan ISAF in Zuid-Afghanistan', DVB/CV-388/05, 22 December 2005.

tempted to place the decision-making process in the hands of Parliament, instead of first taking a decision, which is then subsequently discussed in Parliament.

Political legitimation was achieved, in spite of, or rather thanks to hearings in which mainly supporters of the operation participated and in spite of the cancellation of parliamentary visits to South Afghanistan because of the insecure situation. Another forgotten aspect is the legitimacy, or illegitimacy, of the planned operation in the eyes of the Afghan people. This is regrettable, because the opinion of the people of the country of deployment should be an important factor in decision making and the implementation of military operations.

The Dutch participation in the International Security Assistance Force (ISAF) is part of the further expansion of ISAF, after ISAF already expanded beyond Kabul. The Afghan public opinion about this planned operation should have been subject to Dutch parliamentary discussion, instead of the opinion of more or less selected persons. Nonetheless, the data were apparently not present. A public opinion poll in Afghanistan in November/December 2005 measured the degree of legitimacy of the new ISAF mission. The question to be answered was: 'As you may know the NATO peacekeeping forces known as ISAF have recently expanded their presence beyond Kabul to several areas. Do you approve or disapprove of this expansion?'[19] Of the respondents 60 per cent approved, 18 per cent disapproved, and 16 per cent refused to answer.

Eighteen per cent of 16 million Afghanis is not a slight number. Moreover, it must be taken into account that 30 out of the 34 provinces were represented in the sample. In Uruzgan, however, nobody was asked about his or her opinion.

The answers to a sequel question were even more interesting. Respondents who had approved of the first expansion of ISAF were asked: 'Would you favour or oppose expanding the ISAF presence to more areas?' In favour of expanding the ISAF presence to more areas were 59 per cent, opposed to expanding ISAF presence to more areas were 5 per cent, and 2 per cent refused to answer or did not know.

---

[19] World Public Opinion, *Poll of Afghanistan*, November-December 2005.

Therefore, the percentage of the Afghan population in favour of further ISAF expansion is 59 per cent of 66 per cent, which is 38.4 per cent. This is a clear minority even without an 'Uruzgan correction'. In any case Dutch troops will participate in a military operation which is illegitimate in the eyes of the Afghan people. Nevertheless, the public opinion of the Afghan people did not play any role in the parliamentary discussion in the Netherlands.

A decisive role in the discussion was reserved for the opposition Labour party; a party whose voters were in the majority against the planned operation. In spite of this fact, in the end the Labour party agreed to the Government's decision.

It was clear that more factors played a role than only the points on the governmental checklist and the themes discussed publicly in Parliament.

9. Intervening variables

Matters of political opportunity may be decisive for political legitimation. Although this will not be admitted by politicians, political interests and conditions for possible future coalitions do play a role even in the decision-making about military operations. The perspective of a possible future coalition between Labour and Christian Democrats must be one of the explanations for the Labour vote in favour of the operation, but of course it is not the only one.

Governments risk being punished for neglecting a highly involved public opinion, but, as the Blair case teaches us, when there is no alternative and there is success in other fields, such as the economy, public punishment may not occur. In the Dutch situation both the Government and the political parties could risk neglecting the majority.

Nonetheless, this can change following unexpected serious losses. The undermining conditions of the Mueller hypothesis are absent. Moreover, the basic attitude of the Dutch people is that they accept military operations, but especially peace-keeping and not peace enforcement. The Dutch Minister of Defence, Henk Kamp, is of the opinion that 'in the future the Netherlands will participate in actions during the early phases of conflict, also at a high level in the spectrum of violence'. A question in a public opinion poll concerning this point read as follows: 'Do you agree with the proposal to have Dutch troops participating in frontline battles in the early stages of a conflict'.[20] Of the respondents 24 per cent agreed and 69 per cent disapproved, while 7 per cent did not know. Another question concerned the tasks of the army: 'Do you think that the Dutch army has to limit itself to humanitarian tasks and should not be engaged in missions aimed at enforcing peace by means of violence?' Of the respondents 58 per cent answered in the affirmative, 37 per cent in the negative and 5 per cent did not have an opinion. It is one of the many indications that losses, and certainly heavy losses, will foster the already present illegitimacy of our Uruzgan mission.

A problem for legitimizing military operations is the public opinion concerning the allies. Does the public opinion trust its own allies and does it agree with their policies? Even if the people approve of a military action, the answers to these questions may undermine the quality of any possible legitimacy.

The Netherlands will always be one of the participating allies in military operations. Our great ally is undoubtedly the United States. When a distinction is made between the United States, the Americans, and the President of the United States and his current foreign policy, it is clear that the latter two attract more disapproval than approval, not only in the Netherlands but in the whole world. The recent Iraq policy of the United States does not have legitimacy, not in the world and not at home in the United States. Already in his first term three quarters of the Dutch people did not trust the American President. In a TNS-NIPO poll in May 2005, the following statements were put to the respondents:

1. 'President Bush is a danger to world peace'.
   - Answer: agree 56 per cent, disagree 42 per cent.
2. 'The attitude of the United States concerning other countries frightens me more than ever'.
   - Answer: agree 64 per cent, disagree 35 per cent.
3. 'The European Union, the Netherlands included, must compensate the United States'.
   - Answer: agree 71 per cent, disagree 27 per cent.

---

[20] Enquete, De Ochtenden, Radio 1, January 10, 2004. ≤http://sea2fd.sea2.hotmail.msn.com/cgi-bin/getmsg?curmbox=f000000001a=9ffab564>.

4. 'The Bush government exerts too much pressure on other states to become or remain an ally of the United States'.
    - Answer: agree 71 per cent, disagree 17 per cent.

And, finally,

5. 'The Dutch government behaves as the lap-dog of the United States'.
    - Answer: agree 68 per cent, disagree 31 per cent.

One of the results of a poll by the PEW, Global Attitudes Project, in June 2005, reads:

> 'There is a big gap between Americans and other civilians over whether the United States should remain the sole global military superpower, or if it would be better if a country or group of countries emerges as a rival of the United States.'

Majorities and often big majorities in all 16 countries surveyed, besides the United States, favour another country challenging America's global military supremacy.[21]

It might be clear that in some way the image of the current administration of the United States has its influence on the process of legitimizing military operations together with the United States. Participation of the Dutch Government in discussions on the future American military strategy, also implying definite agreements on mutual assistance, will not favour a future legitimacy of possible military operations.[22] It neglects the United Nations, while international order is a key value of Dutch public opinion. It will not help relations with European allies, which are not invited, to say nothing of the relations with the Muslim and Arabic world. It goes without saying that the present opinion about the United States is not a contribution to the legitimation of Dutch participation in American-led military operations.

10. A FINAL REMARK

The public willingness to accept casualties is not identical to the readiness of soldiers to be killed, although sometimes both are confused. The former concerns the acceptance of the public and the politicians to have their soldiers

[21] PEW, 'Global Attitudes Project', June 2005.

[22] 'Militaire alliantie VS "hachelijk"', *de Volkskrant*, 22 March 2005.

killed. The latter implies the personal readiness of the professional soldier to fall in battle. The public willingness to accept losses depends on the degree that public opinion is convinced of the legitimacy of the action. Professional soldiers know that they have to obey their government, even in risky situations, and in operations which, because of different reasons, they may not favour at all. The illegitimacy of an operation will decline if there is a public willingness to accept casualties. In addition, the illegitimacy will have an influence on the morale of the soldiers in action. In the case of an endless operation and high losses the military themselves will become demotivated. This will be even worse when there is a strong sense of illegitimacy in the minds of citizens in the country of deployment. When the military are not seen as peacekeepers or liberators, but as occupiers and oppressors, there will be a serious problem, if not a barrier to achieving the goals of the operation.

Legitimacy and illegitimacy are intervening variables in the decision-making process, as well as the course of military operations. They are not static but developing processes. A military operation may have full public support at the beginning, but may have to be terminated because of an emotional majority against its continuation.

11. Post Scriptum

It is often, and rightly, stated that the Dutch do not have a heroic military tradition. Moreover, referring to the Srebrenica disaster, some people totally and unjustifiably labelled the Dutch Blue Helmets as terrified and cowardly. Years ago, we asked a representative sample of Dutch professional soldiers whether they would be prepared to die for their country. About 50 per cent answered that they would be prepared to make the highest sacrifice. The most enthusiastic category proved to be the very high-ranking military with many years of service. This is the group which will be the last to do so. However, those of low rank and with limited years of service have the same opinion: this is the group which still has to learn about the real risks of military life, and, of course, about the relationship between military operations and legitimacy.[23]

[23] Answers to the KMA questionnaire in B. Bomert and L. Wecke, *Van Vijandbeeld naar Vriendbeeld! Van diensplicht naar beroepsleger?* (Nijmegen/Amsterdam 1991) p. 125.

Part III
A Case Study on Rwanda: How to Re-Establish Peace and Security after Genocide

Chapter 10
LA RÉPRESSION DU GÉNOCIDE DES RWANDAIS TUTSI : D'ARUSHA VERS LES COLLINES RWANDAISES

Fançois-Xavier Nsanzuwera*

Ce génocide et ces massacres sont une honte pour l'humanité entière, non seulement en raison de leur nature, mais aussi parce qu'ils se sont déroulés en présence des Casques bleus des Nations Unies.

François-Xavier Nsanzuwera in Jean-François Dupaquier (Réd.), *La justice internationale face au drame rwandais* (Paris, Karthala 1996)

1. Introduction

Dans sa Résolution 1503(2003), le Conseil de sécurité des Nations Unies a demandé au Tribunal pénal international pour le Rwanda de terminer ses jugements en première instance en 2008 et en 2010 ses jugements en appel :

> « [...] Demande au Tribunal pénal international pour l'ex-Yougoslavie et au Tribunal pénal international pour le Rwanda de prendre toutes mesures en leur pouvoir pour mener à bien les enquêtes d'ici à la fin de 2004, achever tous les procès de première instance d'ici à la fin de 2008 et terminer leurs travaux en 2010 (Stratégies d'achèvement des travaux). »[1]

Douze ans après sa création et quatre ans avant sa fermeture, cette juridiction pénale internationale ad hoc était-elle justifiée ? Aura-t-elle en 2010 répondu

* Ancien Procureur de la République à Kigali, ancien Secrétaire général de la Fédération Internationale des Ligues des Droits de l'Homme (FIDH), Conseiller juridique, Section d'appel, Bureau du Procureur, TPIR. Les idées exprimées dans cette communication n'engagent que l'auteur.

[1] S/Res/1503 (2003), 28 août 2003.

O. Ribbelink (ed.), Beyond the UN Charter: Peace, Security and the Role of Justice

aux attentes de la Communauté internationale qui l'a soutenue et particulièrement aux espoirs des rescapés du génocide et à leur soif de justice ?

Aura-t-elle contribué à la réconciliation du peuple rwandais avec lui-même ?

2. La mission confiée à la communauté internationale ou le mandat du TPIR

2.1 Un tribunal international chargé de juger en priorité les responsables du génocide

La mission de juger les responsables, en particulier, les planificateurs du génocide des Rwandais tutsi et les crimes contre l'humanité commis envers les Rwandais hutu opposés à l'exécution du génocide revenait et revient toujours au tribunal pénal international pour le Rwanda.

Pour mémoire, le Tribunal pénal international pour le Rwanda a été créé, en vertu du chapitre VII de la Charte des Nations Unies, par le Conseil de sécurité des Nations Unies. Le Conseil de sécurité :

> « Décide par la présente résolution, comme suite à la demande qu'il a reçue du Gouvernement rwandais (S/1994/1115), de créer un tribunal international chargé uniquement de juger les personnes présumées responsables d'actes de génocide ou d'autres violations graves du droit international humanitaire commis sur le territoire du Rwanda et les citoyens rwandais présumés responsables de tels actes ou violations commis sur le territoire d'Etats voisins, entre le 1er janvier et le 31 décembre 1994, et d'adopter à cette fin le Statut du Tribunal criminel international pour le Rwanda annexé à la présente résolution. »[2]

Le génocide des Rwandais tutsi s'est déroulé en la présence des casques bleus des Nations Unies. La communauté internationale, incapable d'arrêter ce génocide, ne devait pas laisser impunis ses auteurs dont les cerveaux s'étaient réfugiés dès la fin des massacres et de la guerre à l'étranger, loin de la compétence juridictionnelle du nouveau pouvoir rwandais.[3]

---

[2] S/RES/ 955 (1994), 8 novembre 1994.

[3] Les autorités judiciaires rwandaises ont demandé l'extradition de plusieurs présumés génocidaires sans résultat, notamment en raison du fait que la peine de mort figure dans

Contrairement à la thèse des génocidaires et de certains de leurs défenseurs, la tragédie qui a ensanglanté le Rwanda d'avril à juillet 1994 n'était pas un événement spontané suite à l'attentat du 6 avril 1994 contre l'avion du Président Juvénal Habyarimana mais belle et bien un génocide pensé, préparé et organisé systématiquement par un groupe politico-militaire qui voulait garder à tout prix les rênes du pouvoir et ses privilèges, quitte à exterminer une partie de la population rwandaise. Le génocide des Rwandais tutsi et les massacres des Rwandais hutu qui s'y opposaient a été exécuté du sommet de l'Etat jusqu'aux échelons inférieurs. Face à l'ampleur du génocide, confronté au nombre impressionnant de victimes et de bourreaux, l'appareil judiciaire rwandais, décimé pendant le génocide,[4] n'était pas capable de répondre à un tel besoin de justice.

En effet, à la fin du génocide et de la guerre en juillet 1994, le Rwanda était un pays dévasté : infrastructures détruites, un appareil judiciaire presque totalement anéanti.

Seule une juridiction internationale pouvait poursuivre et juger les bourreaux du peuple rwandais. Les cerveaux du génocide des Rwandais Tutsi, vaincus, s'étaient réfugiés à l'étranger surtout au Congo où ils rêvaient de revanche.[5] Seul un tribunal international établi par la Communauté internationale était en mesure d'arrêter et de juger les cerveaux du génocide rwandais.

---

l'arsenal juridique rwandais. Seule l'Ethiopie a livré au Rwanda Karamira Froduald, ancien vice-président du parti Mouvement Démocratique Républicain (MDR), auteur du slogan « Hutu power » qui fut chanté par des miliciens pendant le génocide. Karamira fut condamné à la peine capitale et exécuté au stade de Nyamirambo.

[4] Le premier magistrat du Rwanda, M. Joseph Kavaruganda, président de la Cour de cassation et président de la Cour constitutionnelle du Rwanda fut assassiné le 7 avril 1994 par la Garde présidentielle. D'autres magistrats furent tués, d'autres parvinrent à s'enfuir. Selon la loi fondamentale de la République rwandaise (article 3 alinéa 3 de l'Accord de Paix du 4 août 1993), il revenait de droit à la Cour constitutionnelle de constater la vacance du pouvoir à la demande du Gouvernement de transition suite à l'attentat contre l'avion du Président Habyarimana (attentat qui lui a coûté la vie). Les auteurs du coup d'État du 7 avril 1994, en assassinant le président de la Cour constitutionnelle et le premier ministre Agathe Uwiringiyimana créaient ainsi un vide constitutionnel pour enfin mettre sur pied un gouvernement qui exécutera le génocide. Pour plus de détails, consulter, entre autres, le livre du Général Roméo Dallaire, *J'ai serré la main du diable. La faillite de l'humanité au Rwanda* (Canada : Libre Expression 2003).

[5] En 1996, les restes de l'Armée génocidaire (ex-FAR) et les miliciens interahamwe commencèrent des attaques contre le Rwanda à partir du Congo. Ces attaques visèrent principalement les préfectures du nord mais également le centre du Rwanda. Ces attaques cesseront avec le démantèlement des camps de réfugies par l'Armée patriotique rwandaise dans des conditions controversées.

Il fallait aussi à ces personnes accusées de porter les plus hautes responsabilités dans le génocide un tribunal capable de garantir des procès équitables, un tribunal qui respecte l'égalité entre les parties. Il fallait éviter des procès sommaires. Il fallait montrer aux auteurs présumés du génocide que même les auteurs des crimes les plus abominables avaient droit à des procès équitables. Le juriste et philosophe Antoine Garapon écrit avec raison que :

> « Les bourreaux ne doivent être ni diabolisés ni rejetés hors de l'humanité, mais jugés. Le jugement est une manière de ré instituer un rapport politique : le procès est une instance de reconnaissance, non seulement pour la victime à laquelle il donne acte de sa souffrance, mais aussi pour l'accusé, auquel il reconnaît une faculté d'agir et d'user de sa liberté. »[6]

Et contrairement au Tribunal militaire de Nuremberg, le Tribunal pénal international pour le Rwanda n'est pas un tribunal des vainqueurs. Aucun juge rwandais ne siège à Arusha. Les pays dont sont originaires les juges n'ont pas pris part au conflit rwandais, lequel d'ailleurs est qualifié de conflit armé non international. Même si le Tribunal n'a pas encore jugé les auteurs présumés de violations graves de droit international humanitaire dans le camp du vainqueur, le Tribunal a mandat pour juger les auteurs présumés de ces crimes graves commis par l'une ou l'autre partie belligérante. Les combattants du Front Patriotique Rwandais passibles de poursuites sont concernés par l'article 4 du Statut du Tribunal :

> « Le Tribunal international pour le Rwanda est habilite a poursuivre les personnes qui commettent ou donnent l'ordre de commettre des violations graves de l'article 3 commun aux conventions de Genève du 12 août 1949 pour la protection des victimes en temps de guerre, et du Protocole additionnel II aux dites Conventions du 8 juin 1977. »

Plusieurs critiques négatives ont été formulées à l'égard du Tribunal, principalement, la lenteur et la lourdeur des procédures et le harcèlement des témoins de l'accusation par les avocats de la défense. S'il est vrai que les débuts ont été difficiles, aujourd'hui, tous les observateurs reconnaissent l'importance du travail accompli par le Tribunal. Mais il y a un apport qui passe largement inaperçu alors qu'il devrait figurer parmi les principaux acquis de ce tribunal. C'est l'action humanisante de cette juridiction internationale :

---

[6] A. Garapon, *Des crimes qu'on ne peut ni punir ni pardonner. Pour une justice internationale* (Paris : Editions Odile Jacob 2002) p. 184.

> « L'action de la justice se veut [..] doublement humanisante : non seulement pour la victime, dont elle reconnaît la souffrance mais aussi pour l'accusé, à qui est offerte l'opportunité d'entrer à nouveau dans la communauté des humains, c'est-à-dire de personnes qui répondent de leurs actes. »[7]

Ce face à face entre les victimes et les accusés, malgré les mauvais souvenirs ravivés devant la Cour, participe au processus de réconciliation à travers l'établissement des faits et la recherche de la vérité

2.2 Un tribunal pour favoriser la réconciliation nationale au Rwanda

Dans la Résolution 955(1994) créant le Tribunal pénal international pour le Rwanda, le Conseil de sécurité des Nations Unies a insisté sur la nécessité de la réconciliation nationale, le rétablissement et le maintien de la paix :

> « Convaincu que, dans les circonstances particulières qui règnent au Rwanda, des poursuites contre les personnes présumées responsables d'actes de génocide ou d'autres violations graves du droit international humanitaire [...] contribueraient au processus de réconciliation nationale ainsi qu'au rétablissement et au maintien de la paix. »

Dans la détermination de la peine, les juges rappellent cette mission du Tribunal et en tiennent compte. Les exemples sont multiples :

Dans le jugement « Le Procureur contre Juvénal Kajelijeli », la Chambre de première instance II du Tribunal déclare qu'elle a gardé à l'esprit la Résolution 955 du Conseil de sécurité, particulièrement en ce qui concerne les impératifs de dissuasion, de justice, de réconciliation et de rétablissement et maintien de la paix.[8] Les juges continuent en déclarant :

> « En décidant de la peine à infliger à Kajelijeli, la Chambre a attentivement examiné tous les facteurs susceptibles de contribuer à la réalisation des objectifs précités. Compte tenu de la gravité des crimes commis au Rwanda en 1994, il importe au plus haut point que la communauté internationale les condamne d'une manière permettant d'en éviter la répétition ou que ce soit, au Rwanda ou ailleurs. La réconciliation entre Rwandais, à laquelle les activités du Tribunal devraient contribuer, doit aussi être dûment prise en considération par la Chambre au moment de prononcer la sentence. »[9]

---

[7] A. Garapon, op. cit., p. 184.

[8] *Affaire le Procureur* c. *Juvénal Kajelijeli*, Chambre de 1re instance, par. 944.

[9] *Affaire le Procureur* c. *Juvénal Kajelijeli*, Chambre de 1re instance, par. 945.

Dans le jugement « *Le Procureur* c. *Sylvestre Gacumbitsi* », la Chambre de première instance III du Tribunal a considéré, lors de la sentence, les impératifs de dissuasion, de justice, de réconciliation et de rétablissement et maintien de la paix.[10] La réconciliation entre Rwandais, à laquelle le mandat du Tribunal doit contribuer selon les termes de la Résolution 955 sera prise en considération, précise la Chambre dans l'affaire Gacumbitsi.[11]

Soucieux de cet impératif que constitue la réconciliation[12] entre Rwandais, le Tribunal a, également, jugé important d'établir une hiérarchie des peines. Cette constatation est confirmée par les différentes peines prononcées par le Tribunal dans les différentes affaires. Par exemple : le Tribunal a condamné l'ancien premier ministre du Gouvernement intérimaire, Jean Kambanda, à une peine d'emprisonnement a vie alors que l'ancien conseiller de secteur Vincent Rutaganira a été condamné à six ans d'emprisonnement. En 2010, le Tribunal, sur décision du Conseil de sécurité terminera son mandat. Malgré un bilan largement positif,[13] un nombre important d'auteurs présumés du génocide de la catégorie des planificateurs seront toujours en liberté. A qui le Tribunal Pénal International pour le Rwanda (TPIR) passera-t-il le flambeau ?

2.3 La passation du flambeau : d'Arusha vers les juridictions nationales

L'article 11 bis du Règlement de procédure et de preuve prévoit que le Tribunal international pour le Rwanda peut renvoyer des affaires devant d'autres juridictions :

---

[10] *Affaire le Procureur* c. *Sylvestre Gacumbitsi*, Chambre de 1re instance, par. 335

[11] *Affaire le Procureur* c. *Sylvestre Gacumbitsi*, par. 336.

[12] La Résolution du Conseil de sécurité utilise le terme « réconciliation ». Nous aurions préféré l'expression « cohabitation » car elle répond à la réalité de la vie. Les blessures laissées par le génocide ne seront jamais cicatrisées et il sera impossible pour les rescapés de tourner cette page qui a bouleversé toute leur vie mais une nation doit penser bien sûr à une politique qui libère son peuple d'un passé si lourd.

[13] Concernant particulièrement l'apport du TPIR dans la Réconciliation nationale au Rwanda, voir notre article 'The ICTR Contribution to National Reconciliation', 3 *Journal of International Criminal Justice* (2005) pp. 944-949. L'un des legs important du Tribunal est la reconnaissance judiciaire du génocide des Rwandais tutsi et la neutralisation des politiques négationnistes et révisionnistes. Le Tribunal va laisser au Rwanda et à la Communauté internationale une documentation sans pareille pour la constitution d'une histoire objective du génocide, une histoire qui fera obstacle aux versions négationnistes.

> « Apres la confirmation d'un acte d'accusation, que l'accuse soit place ou non sous la garde du Tribunal, le Président peut designer une Chambre de première instance qui détermine s'il y a lieu de renvoyer l'affaire aux autorités de l'Etat :
> i. sur le territoire duquel le crime a été commis ;
> ii. dans lequel l'accuse a été arrête, ou
> iii. ayant compétence et étant dispose et tout a fait prêt a accepter une telle affaire, afin qu'elles saisissent sans délai la juridiction appropriée pour en juger. [..] »

Dans le passé, plusieurs pays, ont déjà jugé des personnes accusées de génocide rwandais. Il s'agit de la Belgique[14] et de la Suisse. Le Canada emboîtera le pas à ces pays. Malheureusement aucun pays africain n'a jamais eu jusqu'à présent le courage ou la capacité de juger des présumés génocidaires se trouvant sur le continent africain. Plusieurs raisons sont avancées comme l'absence de moyens humains et financiers mais les obstacles politiques restent les plus sérieux. Mais quelle que soit la bonne volonté des pays à juger les auteurs présumés du génocide réfugiés en dehors du Rwanda, il revient principalement au Rwanda de prendre la relève.

2.4 D'Arusha vers les Collines Rwandaises : les juridictions Gacaca

Quand le Rwanda se dota d'une loi organique pour la répression du crime de génocide en 1996, les prisons rwandaises comptaient plus ou moins 150.000 personnes attendant d'être jugés. Si depuis les prisons rwandaises ont été désengorgées avec les libérations de dizaines de milliers de prisonniers, aujourd'hui, les autorités rwandaises estiment à des centaines de milliers le nombre de personnes suspectées de participation au génocide.[15] Aucun pays au monde, surtout un pays qui sort d'un génocide ne peut juger un nombre si impressionnant de présumes avec les moyens et les méthodes de la justice

[14] Pour en savoir plus sur les deux procès qui ont eu lieu en Belgique, il faut lire en autres le livre de L, de Vulpian, *Rwanda, un génocide oublié ? Un procès pour mémoire* (Bruxelles : Editions Complexe 2004).

[15] En réalité personne ne sait le nombre exact de personnes impliquées dans le génocide. Il nous semble qu'il reviendra aux Juridictions *Gacaca* de déterminer ce nombre à travers des jugements. Il ne faudrait pas que les Juridictions *Gacaca* en arrivent à demander à chaque Rwandais de répondre de ses éventuelles omissions ou compromissions. Si, un jour nous avons écrit que chaque Rwandais porte une responsabilité dans la tragédie rwandaise, il faudra éviter d'en arriver en la changer en responsabilité pénale.

classique. Et pourtant la demande de justice était une des premières revendications des rescapés du génocide si ce n'est la seule.

Deux ans après le génocide, nous écrivions ces mots qui, aujourd'hui, gardent leur sens et leur urgence :

> « Faut-il toujours répéter qu'un des seuls moyens de permettre aux Rwandais de retrouver une paix stable, d'oeuvrer à la réconciliation nationale et de construire la démocratie, c'est de rétablir la confiance en mettant sur pied un véritable appareil judiciaire indépendant et en engageant toutes les procédures légales visant à la sanction de tous les coupables, à l'élargissement des innocents et enfin à l'indemnisation des victimes. »[16]

Face au refus de l'impunité et face au besoin de justice des rescapés du génocide, le Rwanda fut obligé de penser un nouveau système pour faire face au lourd contentieux du génocide. Il s'agit des juridictions *Gacaca* un mélange de justice traditionnelle rwandaise et de justice classique.

Les Juridictions *Gacaca* furent créées par la loi organique no 40/2000 du 26 janvier 2001 portant création des « Juridictions *Gacaca* » et organisation des poursuites des infractions constitutives du crime de génocide ou de crimes contre l'humanité, commises entre le 1er octobre 1990 et le 31 décembre 1994. Cette loi organique fut modifiée par la loi organique no 16/2004 du 19 juin 2004 portant organisation, compétence et fonctionnement[17] des Juridictions *Gacaca*. Nous n'entrerons pas dans les détails du fonctionnement de ces juridictions à moitié traditionnelle et à moitié modernes. Nous soulignerons leurs aspects spécifiques qui les distinguent des juridictions

[16] J-F. Dupaquier (Réd.), op. cit., p. 228.

[17] Les théoriciens du droit affirment avec raison que les lois ont leur sens si elles sont adaptées aux situations qu'elles régissent. Les résultats escomptés avec les Juridictions *Gacaca* dépendront toujours de l'application effective de la loi organique régissant ces juridictions. Le système *Gacaca* est loin de faire l'unanimité surtout au sein de la diaspora rwandaise mais tous les observateurs estiment que ces juridictions constituent aujourd'hui la seule alternative. Ceux qui critiquent le système n'avancent malheureusement aucune alternative à la place. L'un des reproches réguliers est l'absence de conseils de la défense. Ce rôle est joué par l'Assemblée générale de la juridiction *Gacaca*, c'est-à-dire l'ensemble de la population. Et s'il est vrai que le choix des Juridictions *Gacaca* relève d'un choix politique, il n'empêche que le processus est judiciaire. La population rwandaise, l'Etat rwandais, les pays donateurs et les organisations de défense des droits de l'homme qui aident à la bonne marche du processus doivent être vigilants pour éviter certains dérapages comme n'importe quel système judiciaire peut en connaître.

classiques.[18] Les juridictions *Gacaca* se distinguent des juridictions classiques rwandaises par la composition de leurs juges, le rôle de la population dans le processus judiciaire, la catégorisation des auteurs présumes du génocide, la nature des peines et la place des victimes.

2.4.1 *Des intègres ou citoyens modèles*

Contrairement aux juridictions classiques, les juridictions *Gacaca* sont composées de juges non professionnels. Il s'agit de citoyens ordinaires considérés comme intègres et élus par leurs concitoyens. D'après la loi organique sur les juridictions *Gacaca*, est intègre, tout Rwandais remplissant les conditions suivantes :

- n'avoir pas participé au génocide ;
- être exempt d'esprit de divisionnisme ;
- n'avoir pas été condamné par un jugement coulé en force de chose jugée à une peine d'emprisonnement de six (6) mois au moins ;
- être de bonne conduite, vie et mœurs ;
- dire toujours la vérité ;
- être honnête ;
- être caractérisé par l'esprit de partage de la parole (article 14 de la loi organique).

Les gens ne participent pas seulement à l'élection des juges mais participent également aux procès en témoignant sur ce qu'ils ont vu ou vécu pendant le génocide.

2.4.2 *Le devoir de témoigner*

Les témoins aiment rappeler que le génocide s'est passé en pleine journée au vu et au su de tous. Les victimes étaient pourchassées et tuées sauvagement en public. Ceux qui n'étaient pas visés par les massacres et qui n'ont pas

---

[18] Malgré la modification de la loi organique portant création des juridictions *Gacaca*, les aspects développés dans notre article « Les juridictions *Gacaca*, une réponse au génocide rwandais ou le difficile équilibre entre châtiment et pardon », restent actuels. Cet article a été publié dans *La répression du génocide rwandais,* sous la direction de L. Burgorgue-Larsen (Bruxelles : Editions Bruylant 2003) pp. 109-119.

participé ont quand même vu ce qui se passait. La loi organique régissant les juridictions *Gacaca* demande à toute la population de participer à cette œuvre de justice. L'article 29 de cette loi stipule que :

> « Participer aux activités des Juridictions Gacaca est une obligation pour tout Rwandais.
> Toute personne qui omet ou refuse de témoigner sur ce qu'elle a vu ou sur ce dont elle a connaissance, de même que celle qui fait une dénonciation mensongère, est poursuivie par la Juridiction Gacaca qui en fait le constat. Elle encourt une peine d'emprisonnement allant de trois (3) à six (6) mois…. [..]. »

2.4.3 *La catégorisation des auteurs*

Le génocide des Rwandais tutsi et les autres crimes contre l'humanité sont l'œuvre d'un régime politique, qui a mis son appareil étatique au service du crime. Des ministres, des préfets, des bourgmestres, des officiers supérieurs de l'armée, de la gendarmerie, des religieux participèrent au génocide. Mais également la population participa aux massacres. Si le point commun aux différents auteurs est la monstruosité du crime, la responsabilité individuelle devrait différer selon la catégorie sociale a laquelle appartenait l'auteur. La loi organique sur les Juridictions *Gacaca* classe les auteurs présumés en catégories. La loi organique de 2001 créait quatre catégories qui ont été ramenées à trois catégories par la loi de 2004. Nous n'allons pas entrer dans les détails que le lecteur trouvera dans la loi. En résumé, la première catégorie comprend les planificateurs, les organisateurs, les incitateurs, les superviseurs et les encadreurs des crimes tandis que la troisième catégorie qui est la dernière comprend les personnes ayant commis des infractions contre les biens.

Cette catégorisation répond au souci du législateur d'édicter des peines « permettant aux condamnés de s'amender et de favoriser leur insertion dans la société rwandaise sans entrave à la vie normale de la population » (Préambule de la loi organique).

2.4.4 *La resocialisation des auteurs*

L'opinion s'étonne souvent du nombre important d'auteurs présumés du génocide. En effet, presque chaque colline a été touchée par les massacres. Il sera impossible de juger tous les génocidaires. Nous pensons également qu'il faut donner une chance à des milliers d'exécutants entraînés par les responsables politico-administratifs. La loi sur les Juridictions *Gacaca*, dans son préambule, met en avant la nécessité d'assurer les poursuites et le jugement rapide des auteurs et de leurs complices mais également la nécessité de réhabiliter la société rwandaise.

Dans ce souci de resocialisation des auteurs, la loi prévoit le plaidoyer de culpabilité, de repentir et d'excuses qui assure a l'accusé une réduction sensible de la peine. L'échelle des peines va de 30 ans à une année d'emprisonnement. Seuls les auteurs de la première catégorie n'ayant pas recouru au plaidoyer de culpabilité encourent la peine de mort ou la perpétuité. Les prévenus accusés d'avoir commis des infractions contre les biens sont condamnés a la réparation des dommages causés aux biens d'autrui. Mais une des particularités la plus importante de la loi *Gacaca* est la place réservée aux victimes du génocide.

2.4.5 *La reconnaissance des victimes*

A Nuremberg, les victimes avaient le rôle de témoins. A Arusha, presque un demi-siècle après, les victimes continuent d'éclairer les juges sur les faits. Devant les juridictions *Gacaca*, la victime est un acteur important du processus judiciaire. Bien plus, les juridictions *Gacaca* participent à la mémoire des personnes tuées durant le génocide.

Parmi les attributions de l'Assemblée générale de la Juridiction *Gacaca* de la Cellule figure la confection des listes de personnes, qui ont été, dans la Cellule, victimes du génocide, des personnes qui résidaient dans la cellule mais qui ont été tuées à d'autres endroits. La loi exige de tous les habitants de la Cellule de relater les faits qui se sont produits notamment là ou ils habitaient et de fournir des preuves en dénoncent les auteurs et en identifiant les victimes (article 33).

Grâce aux témoignages des gens et principalement grâce aux aveux des auteurs, des familles ont pu trouver des corps des leurs dans des fosses communes et ont pu les enterrer dans la dignité. Ces aveux des bourreaux permettent aux victimes d'adoucir leur deuil.

3. Conclusion

Le 7 avril 2006, douze ans après, les Rwandais et toute la Communauté internationale se souviendront pour la douzième fois des centaines de milliers de victimes du génocide. Pour la douzième fois, nous constaterons que le « Plus jamais ça » prononcé à Nuremberg reste un vœu mais un vœu qui nous aide à espérer dans un monde moins désespérant. Mais ce triste anniversaire confirmera la Communauté internationale dans sa volonté et dans sa détermination de ne pas laisser impunis les auteurs de génocide et de crimes contre l'humanité.

Cette douzième commémoration se déroulera à un moment où l'on parle de la stratégie d'achèvement du Tribunal pénal international pour le Rwanda. Cette commémoration doit rappeler au Conseil de sécurité en particulier et à la Communauté internationale dans son ensemble que les juridictions nationales doivent continuer à traquer et à juger les auteurs présumés du génocide des Rwandais tutsi. La fermeture programmé du Tribunal devra être à ce prix : que les États membres des Nations Unies prennent leur responsabilité afin de continuer l'œuvre de justice enclenchée par le TPIR.

Les victimes ne devraient pas être aigries du fait que ce Tribunal ferme. Il aura laissé derrière lui un patrimoine judiciaire et jurisprudentielle considérable. Cette communauté de juristes de différents pays avec différentes cultures juridiques aura posé un socle pour les générations futures. Puisse cet héritage guider les juridictions nationales et particulièrement les juridictions rwandaises dans la continuité de cette œuvre de justice pour toutes les victimes du génocide.

> « Cette justice est une garantie de la cohabitation harmonieuse des Rwandais en permettant de départager coupables et innocents. Elle constituera un rempart contre la globalisation dans la désignation des auteurs présumés du génocide. Cette justice devra respecter les droits de la défense, la présomption d'innocence. »[19]

Ces mots, que nous écrivions il y a dix ans, continuent d'avoir leur sens.

---

[19] J-F. Dupaquier (Réd.), op. cit., p. 234.

Chapter 11
LA CONTRIBUTION DES FEMMES RWANDAISES À LA CRÉATION D'UNE NOUVELLE SITUATION DE PAIX

Jacqueline Rusilibya*

L'organisation que je représente est un Collectif dénommé *Pro-Femmes/Twese Hamwe* regroupant 43 associations rwandaises œuvrant pour la promotion intégrale de la femme, de la paix et du développement. Les associations membres comptent actuellement plus de 50.000 membres effectifs et le nombre de bénéficiaires s'élève à plus de 250.000 sans compter celui de bénéficiaires indirects qui sont en fait toute la population en général et les femmes en particulier. Le Collectif *Pro-Femmes/Twese Hamwe* est né en 1992 dans un contexte politique de conflit armé causé par une politique basée sur la discrimination ethnique et régionale, qui a abouti au génocide de 1994.

Ce génocide a laissé un pays complètement ruiné, un peuple traumatisé par la mort violente de plus d'un million de Rwandais, des milliers de veuves, orphelins et handicapés. Dans une situation pareille, ce sont les femmes et les enfants qui en payent le lourd tribut.

Le contexte tel que décrit ci-dessus ne pouvait pas laisser indifférentes les femmes rwandaises qui venaient de prendre conscience que leur rôle dans la gestion des conséquences du génocide et le rétablissement d'une paix durable était primordial.

Comme dit un proverbe français « l'union fait la force », le Collectif *Pro-Femmes/Twese Hamwe* qui regroupait 13 associations jusqu'en 1994, a ouvert ses portes aux autres associations qui voulaient s'associer à cette noble lutte, notamment celles qui avaient été créées dans les pays d'exil (Congo, Burundi,

* Présidente du Collectif *Pro-Femmes/Twese Hamwe*, Collectif des Organisations Rwandaises de Promotion de la Femme, de la Paix et du Développement.

O. Ribbelink (ed.), Beyond the UN Charter: Peace, Security and the Role of Justice

Uganda, Kenya, Tanzanie) ainsi que d'autres qui venaient d'être créées par les rescapés du génocide. Toutes ces associations n'avaient pas eu le même passé historique ni les mêmes préoccupations, plusieurs événements pouvaient les séparer.

Mais les femmes rwandaises ont décidé de surmonter les barrières et de tenir compte de leurs points communs : être femme, avoir un même pays, la même culture. Face aux conflits armés, la femme est toujours la cible privilégiée des auteurs d'une guerre qu'elle n'a pas déclenchée.

Cette volonté de reconnaître les valeurs d'autrui et de dépasser les barrières historiques a prévalu aux femmes du Rwanda qui étaient représentées par *Pro-Femmes* le « Prix UNESCO Mandajeet Singh pour la Tolérance et la Non Violence » en Novembre 1996.

En 2003, nous avons également reçu un autre prix octroyé par la Fondation Peter Gruber, des Etats-Unis, pour avoir eu le courage de militer pour les droits de la femme dans un pays endeuillé par le génocide. Ce prix, nous l'avons partagé avec Madame Navi Pillay, de la Cour Pénale Internationale, ici présente. Je renouvelle mes félicitations à Madame Navi Pillay pour sa lutte pour les droits de la femme dans son pays et en particulier au TPIR ; le prix qu'elle a reçu est le symbole de cette noble mission. En effet, le 16 Novembre de chaque année, le Collectif *Pro-Femmes/Twese Hamwe* célèbre la Journée Internationale de la Tolérance et mène une réflexion sur les différentes activités pour voir s'il mérite encore ces prix. Pour nous, la tolérance est le premier signe de la résolution d'un conflit.

Nous avons instauré la « Remise du flambeau de la paix » Le Collectif *Pro-Femmes/Twese Hamwe* remet ce flambeau à un groupe qui s'est distingué par de bons actes de culture de la paix ou à des groupes qui ont été accusés de violences mais qui ont pu se ressaisir et s'orienter vers un changement positif.

Dans un pays, aussi meurtri que le nôtre, il faut un travail continu de sensibilisation, de recherche et de formation. C'est ainsi que le Collectif *Pro-Femmes/Twese Hamwe* a commencé par sensibiliser la femme sur son rôle dans l'édification de la paix dans le Rwanda nouveau à travers un Programme « Campagne Action pour la Paix » qui vise à construire une Société égalitaire où règne une paix durable. Grâce à ce programme, les femmes rwandaises ont pris en charge les groupes vulnérables sans distinction d'ethnie ou de religion dont les orphelins, les veuves, les femmes en prison, les femmes victimes de violences, les rapatriés, les sans abris, les femmes dont les maris sont en prison, les enfants en circonstances difficiles.

Les femmes ont également osé faire des travaux qui autrefois étaient effectués par les hommes, notamment la construction des villages. Nous pouvons donner l'exemple de l'association *Duhozanye* dont les membres ont commencé à construire seules leurs propres maisons et qui par ailleurs a reçu le prix pour un meilleur habitat. La particularité de cette association, dont le nom signifie « Consolons-nous mutuellement », est composée d'une part des veuves tutsi dont les maris et enfants ont été massacrés pendant le génocide et d'autres part les femmes hutu mariées aux tutsi tués également avec leurs enfants par leurs beaux parents ou leurs beaux frères. Ces femmes ont eu le courage d'accuser ces bourreaux en justice même si cela risque de les mettre en conflit avec leur propre famille.

Permettez- moi de présenter toute ma gratitude à la Coopération Néerlandaise et à NOVIB qui, à travers la SNV, nous a prêté main forte dès la première heure juste après le génocide. Son appui moral, technique, matériel et financier nous a permis de reconstruire le Collectif *Pro-Femmes/Twese Hamwe*, de l'agrandir et de le décentraliser jusqu'à la base car le génocide de 1994 avait emporté certains de ses membres, d'autres avaient connu l'exil et les biens des associations pillés. Ce soutien nous a permis spécialement d'initier le Programme Campagne Action Pour la Paix qui, jusqu'à ce jour, fait parler de lui dans notre pays et dans la Région des Grands Lacs.

Vous comprenez bien combien je suis heureuse d'être parmi vous dans ce pays afin d'être la porte-parole de toutes les femmes qui se sont mobilisées pour léguer à leurs enfants un Rwanda indemne de discrimination, caractérisé par l'égalité et l'équité entre l'homme et la femme dans le processus de développement dans un contexte d'une société stable et paisible. En effet, la plupart des pays africains connaissent actuellement des guerres et conflits divers à travers lesquels un fait commun demeure : les femmes et les enfants sont les plus affectés et les plus meurtris. C'est pourquoi nous, les femmes, sommes interpellées afin de bâtir des sociétés africaines paisibles, démocratiques et prospères.

Des efforts de résolution de ces conflits se remarquent ici et là en Afrique. Le combat des femmes africaines pour la paix s'inscrit surtout dans la dynamique de la société civile, dont les ONGs et les associations féminines constituent la majorité. De nos jours et même traditionnellement, le rôle des femmes en tant que artisanes de la paix est reconnu comme essentiel dans la prévention des conflits, la lutte contre la violence spécialement dans la reconstruction des sociétés après les conflits. En effet, selon la tradition africaine, la femme constitue le cœur et le trait d'union entre les familles. Elle est mère, épouse et éducatrice. Elle donne la vie, donc elle a le devoir de la protéger.

La culture de paix constitue une attitude, un comportement, une façon de penser et d'agir dans un monde où cohabitent de multiples cultures dans un climat de compréhension, de tolérance et de solidarité. La culture de la paix implique le partage et l'utilisation des méthodes non violentes pour gérer les conflits, grâce au dialogue et à la recherche d'une solution pacifique ainsi que la concertation.

Un ancien du village de Mozambique à un représentant de l'UNESCO disait ceci : « Vous pouvez nous livrer la culture guerrière par avion, l'aide humanitaire par camion mais vous ne pouvez pas nous apporter la culture de la paix parce que c'est un arbre profondément enraciné dans notre terre ». Nous pouvons dire la même chose pour le Rwanda qui, dans sa tradition, compte parmi les héros des femmes qui se sont distinguées pour résoudre les conflits entre pays voisins pour ramener la paix. Nous commémorons également les femmes reconnues comme Héroïnes pour avoir marqué un visage de paix et de courage dans les moments les plus durs de l'environnement politique Rwandaise, comme Madame Niyitegeka Félicité, qui a accepté de perdre sa vie alors que son frère qui avait le grade de colonel voulait la sauver. Elle a préféré mourir avec ses frères Tutsi en disant à son frère « si tu ne peux pas sauver tout le monde je préfère mourir avec eux, je vous remercie pour cette gentillesse, on se rencontrera au ciel».

Madame Uwiringiyimana Agathe, ancien Premier Ministre, farouchement assassinée dans son domicile n'a pas mâché ses mots en interpellant le gouvernement de l'époque à signer les accords de paix d'Arusha pour cesser la guerre, elle a toujours lutté contre la discrimination ethnique et régionale.

Toutefois, malgré ces efforts fournis pour recoudre le tissu social, le bout du tunnel est encore loin. Le poids des conséquences du génocide étant encore lourd, nous continuons à promouvoir encore la culture d'une paix durable, de tolérance et de justice sociale à travers la promotion d'une bonne gouvernance et de renforcement du rôle de la femme dans les mécanismes de prévention et gestion des conflits. Les clubs de dialogue pour une culture de la paix ont été initiés dans les établissements scolaires dans le but d'éduquer la jeunesse en particulier les filles porteuses des valeurs de la non discrimination et la tolérance que lui attribue la société rwandaise « *Nyampinga* ».

Nous souhaitons que la génération future puisse vivre dans un pays de paix où chaque citoyen jouit de ses droits fondamentaux. La paix étant un préalable pour tout développement, nous privilégions la négociation, la médiation et la gestion pacifique des conflits. Notre perspective, peut-être encore difficile à atteindre, est de construire un monde sans guerre, sans violence où règne le respect de la diversité et la tolérance.

Le Collectif *Pro-Femmes/Twese Hamwe*, a effectué des recherches qui lui servent d'outils de plaidoyer auprès des décideurs. A titre d'exemple:

- Recherche sur les « racines et la genèse du confit rwandais » qui a permis de comprendre l'histoire du Rwanda et surtout d'échanger sur certains sujets tels que la discrimination, les ethnies, le régionalisme, lors des clubs de dialogues pour la paix qui ont été mis en place, à cet effet, dans toutes les provinces en 1998 et 1999.
- Recherche sur « le rôle de la femme dans les mécanismes traditionnels de résolution des conflits. »
- La recherche faite sur «l'implication de la femme dans les instances de prise de décision». Actuellement le Rwanda est le premier pays au monde à avoir un grand nombre des femmes au Parlement (48%).
- La recherche menée sur les violences faites aux femmes et d'autres....

Toutes ces recherches ont permis aux femmes rwandaises de comprendre leur histoire afin de mieux gérer les conséquences du génocide car elles sont décidées de prendre part à la vie politique du pays, à jouer un rôle actif dans les instances de prise de décision afin d'éviter d'être des éternelles spectatrices. Aujourd'hui, la femme Rwandaise continue à jouer un rôle actif dans la résolution des conflits, notamment dans les Juridictions *Gacaca*.

Le génocide Rwandais de 1994 a emporté un nombre impressionnant de victimes. Aussi, un nombre assez important de Rwandais a participé de près ou de loin au génocide ; plus de 100.000 personnes présumées coupables sont en prison. Tout le monde réclame que « justice soit faite ». Le souci majeur actuel est de recoller le tissu d'une société complètement décomposée pour arriver à la cohésion sociale et au développement du pays.

La justice s'avère un passage obligé vers cette société où règne l'harmonie sociale. Cela nécessite l'appréhension, la poursuite et le jugement de tous les auteurs du drame, l'objectif étant de punir les vrais coupables, rétablir les victimes dans leurs droits, de mettre fin aux suspicions pour enfin reconstruire la société sur des bases solides. La justice classique conçue pour répondre aux situations normales ne permettant pas seule d'atteindre cet objectif (il faudrait au moins 350 ans), il fallait recourir à une justice unique en son genre « *Gacaca* » inspiré du système traditionnel rwandais de règlement des différends qui recherchait non seulement la punition du coupable mais aussi et surtout l'entente, l'harmonie et la cohésion sociale. Ce système est une justice et une réconciliation pour la population et par la population.

La société rwandaise a adopté *Gacaca* comme mécanisme de prévention et gestion des conflits. Le *Gacaca* constituait le premier échelon dans les instances judiciaires et était composé des juges choisis parmi les plus intègres. Pour appuyer ce mécanisme, si important pour notre pays, le Collectif *Pro-Femmes/Twese Hamwe* a élaboré et exécuté un projet de « Renforcement du rôle des femmes dans les Juridictions *Gacaca* » qui mobilise la communauté rwandaise en général et les femmes en particulier à participer massivement et activement aux Juridictions *Gacaca*. Ce projet a été exécuté en collaboration avec International Alert avec le financement de l'Union Européenne pendant 3 ans. Il a pu installer dans les districts 318 leaders communautaires à raison de 3 par district. Ces femmes formées en prévention et transformations des conflits et en technique d'animation ont pu toucher dans trois ans presque un million de population (1.000.000).

L'impact est très grand sans parler du nombre important de femmes ayant participé dans les juridictions et mêmes des femmes juges. Nous connaissons des associations qui se sont formées grâce à la sensibilisation des leaders communautaires. Ces associations regroupent les rescapées du génocide et les ex-prisonniers auteurs du génocide libérés qui avouent et demandent pardon et se réconcilient avec l'autre partie.

En plus de ces activités de sensibilisation, le Collectif *Pro-Femmes/Twese Hamwe* a initié, en collaboration avec les autres acteurs de la Société Civile, un projet de monitoring des Juridictions *Gacaca*. Dans le contexte actuel, le génocide de 1994 a occasionné une déchirure du tissu social faisant plus d'un million de morts, plusieurs milliers d'orphelins et de veufs d'un côté, et une population carcérale considérable de l'autre côté ; tout ce monde attend que justice soit faite. Les rwandais ont opté pour les juridictions *Gacaca* comme seul outil pouvant permettre de lever ces défis avec une valeur ajoutée, la participation de la femme comme citoyen, témoin et même victime.

Nous osons dire que les juridictions *Gacaca* ont parfois permis de connaître la vérité et de réconcilier les groupes des rescapés du génocide avec ceux ayant participé au génocide. Suite aux juridictions *Gacaca*, certains rescapés ont pu enterrer dignement leurs morts, et peuvent ainsi aller de temps en temps se recueillir sur les tombes des membres de leurs familles car pour les Rwandais vivre son deuil, c'est quelque chose de très important.

Ces deux dernières années, les membres de *Pro-Femmes/Twese Hamwe* ont eu l'occasion de s'entretenir avec environ 36.198 ex-prisonniers libérés dont environ 800 femmes dans le but de les préparer à vivre pacifiquement avec les autres membres de la population. Les femmes victimes de violences ont été aussi sensibilisées pour qu'elles puissent témoigner dans les juridictions *Gacaca* et au TPIR; malheureusement parfois elles sont maltraitées et subissent des humiliations.

Dans le but de réduire l'impunité, le gouvernement du Rwanda a initié les travaux d'Intérêt Général (T.I.G.) en faveur des prisonniers ayant fait l'aveu et demandé pardon pour avoir participé au génocide. Ces prisonniers qui n'ont pas tué ou violé les femmes peuvent bénéficier d'une libération provisoire mais acceptent de faire les travaux d'intérêt général, 3 fois par semaines pendant une durée équivalente à la moitié de leur peine (Construction des routes, écoles dispensaires...). Ces travaux d'intérêt général permettent aux prisonniers libérés de s'intégrer progressivement dans la vie et de se réconcilier avec les rescapés du génocide tout en contribuant au développement du pays. Le Collectif *Pro-Femmes* organise les journées d'échange et de dialogue avec les groupes concernés sur les valeurs de la culture de la paix, la tolérance, la non violence et la cohabitation pacifique et l'implication de la femme dans la réconciliation.

Nous pouvons nous réjouir d'avoir une constitution qui tient compte de la dimension gender, ceci est le fruit du travail des femmes Rwandaises qui ont participé à tout le processus depuis son élaboration jusqu'à son référendum. Actuellement, il est appliqué surtout à son article qui stipule qu'au moins 30% de places doivent être réservées aux femmes. Bien que la loi électorale tienne compte de, au moins, 30%, notre rôle est de sensibiliser les femmes pour leur droits en tant que électrices et candidates et leur doter des capacités afin de bien mener leurs campagnes électorales. C'est comme ça que nous avons 48% des femmes au Parlement et 42% dans les organes de décision à la base.

Pour nous, la paix n'est pas seulement l'absence de la guerre, elle est également le résultat de tout un bien être moral. C'est pourquoi le Collectif *Pro-Femmes/Twese Hamwe* s'investit dans la lutte contre les fléaux qui menacent notre société.

Malgré les efforts faits par les femmes, le gouvernement et les différents partenaires, nous avons encore le fléau du VIH/SIDA qui tue un grand nombre de population active spécialement les femmes à cause de la culture qui fait que les femmes ne prennent pas encore de décisions en matière de santé reproductive, du manque d'informations et des problèmes de pauvreté. Il est également prouvé que le paludisme et la tuberculose tuent un grand nombre de femmes et d'enfants ; c'est pour cela que les associations membres du Collectif *Pro-Femmes/Twese Hamwe* sont très impliquées dans la campagne de lutte contre le paludisme, la tuberculose et le VIH/SIDA. Tous ces programmes contribuent à la paix.

Le Rwanda est un pays enclavé qui vit essentiellement des aides extérieures. En plus, le niveau d'éducation et de savoir- faire généralisé au sein de la population en général et chez les femmes en particulier, font que plus de 80% de la population s'attelle à l'agriculture de subsistance comme seul atout de survie. Le Collectif *Pro-Femmes/Twese Hamwe* a participé à la conception de la Stratégie Nationale de réduction de la pauvreté. C'est à ce titre que les associations membres sont impliquées dans l'encadrement des femmes pour les projets générateurs de revenus, les coopératives d'épargne et crédits, nous avons même un comptoir spécial pour les femmes à la banque populaire. Mais malgré tous ces efforts, le problème de pauvreté reste de taille.

Le Collectif *Pro-Femmes/Twese Hamwe*, assure la vice-présidente de la plateforme de la société civile et fait partie du comité de suivi de la Conférence Internationale sur la Paix, la Sécurité et le Développement sur la Région des Grands Lacs (CIRGL). Il a participé avec les autres membres de la société civile à l'élaboration du document national dans lequel ils ont introduit les préoccupations et les attentes de la population rwandaise spécialement des groupes spécifiques tels que les femmes, les jeunes, les handicapés etc.

Afin d'assurer le processus démocratique de notre pays, 8 collectifs de la société civile dont *Pro-Femmes/Twese Hamwe*, ont initié un programme d'observatoire des élections au Rwanda (POER). Celui-ci est chargé de faire le suivi de tout le processus électoral et de faire le rapport d'observation des élections.

Nous ne pouvons pas prétendre ramener, et maintenir la paix dans notre pays lorsque les conflits armés ont touché plusieurs pays africains spécialement la Région des Grands Lacs, c'est pourquoi nous avons jugé nécessaire de nous associer avec d'autres femmes africaines qui mènent le même combat que nous. Ainsi nous faisons partie d'un réseau dénommé

« Concertation des Collectifs des Associations œuvrant pour la Promotion de la Femme dans la Région des Grands Lacs (COCAFEM/GL) regroupant les collectifs du Burundi, de la RDC et du Rwanda. Cette concertation nous sert de cadre de réflexion sur le rôle de la femme dans le rétablissement, le maintien et la consolidation de la paix dans la Région des Grands Lacs. La Fédération des Réseaux des Femmes Africaines pour la Paix (FERFAP) dont nous sommes membres fondateurs nous permet aussi d'élever notre action de solidarité au niveau africain et de faire une action de plaidoyer pour que la femme africaine soit impliquée dans les négociations de paix et la médiation des pays en conflits.

Depuis l'an 2000 *Pro-Femmes* est impliqué dans tout le processus de la marche mondiale des femmes pour la paix et a participé à toutes les rencontres internationales de suivi de la mise en œuvre des recommandations.

La dernière a eu lieu à Kigali – Rwanda, du 4 au 12 Décembre 2005 où la charte mondiale des femmes a été adoptée incluant 5 valeurs à savoir: la solidarité, la liberté, la justice, la paix et la tolérance.

A Kigali, en mars 1997, nous avons abrité une Conférence Panafricaine sur le thème « Genre, Paix et Développement » qui a eu lieu en mars 1997 à Kigali, où chaque déléguée a recousu son pays déchiré par les conflits armés, aussi avons-nous construit une carte d'Afrique reconstruite par les femmes comme un idéal et une perspective à atteindre dans le but de montrer que la paix en Afrique devrait être le garant de la synergie entre les femmes africaines. Ainsi toutes nos activités visent à atteindre cet idéal, un Rwanda guérit de toutes les blessures et une Afrique en Paix.

Que vive la paix au Rwanda, en Afrique et dans le monde entier.

Chapter 12
HOW THE INTERNATIONAL CRIMINAL TRIBUNAL FOR RWANDA IS A CRUCIAL ELEMENT IN THE RE-ESTABLISHMENT OF A NEW SITUATION OF PEACE AND SECURITY IN RWANDA

Hassan B. Jallow*

1. Introduction

I want to highlight the vital role that the International Criminal Tribunal for Rwanda (ICTR) plays in the search for a new situation of peace and security in Rwanda. I will also discuss the challenges the ICTR faces and perspectives for the accomplishment of its mandate.

In a meeting with Tanzania's Head of State, H.E. President Jakaya Kikwete on 17 March 2006, near the seat of the Tribunal in Arusha Tanzania, senior ICTR officials thanked the host government for the assistance and cooperation so far received, and published the latest statistics of the work accomplished by the ICTR. The Tribunal had completed cases involving 27 accused since the first trials started in January 1997, whereas cases involving 27 accused are on-going. 15 accused are awaiting trial at the detention facility of the Tribunal in Arusha, Tanzania.

In regard to the deadline imposed by the UN Security Council for the completion of the work of the ICTR, the expectation of the ICTR is that by the end of 2008, all trials will be completed and by 2010, all appeals will also have been concluded, and that between 65 and 70 accused will have their cases completed by the end of 2008.

* Prosecutor of the ICTR. Paper presented on behalf of Justice Hassan B. Jallow, by William T. Egbe, Senior Trial Attorney, Office of the Prosecutor of the ICTR.

O. Ribbelink (ed.), Beyond the UN Charter: Peace, Security and the Role of Justice

Security Council Resolution 955 (1994)[1] established the International Criminal Tribunal for Rwanda to prosecute persons responsible for genocide and other serious violations of International Humanitarian Law committed in the territory of Rwanda and Rwandan citizens responsible for genocide and other such violations committed in the territory of neighboring States, between 1 January 1994, and 31 December 1994.

Resolution 1503 (2003)[2] specifically called on States, to cooperate with the ICTR in apprehending all indicted persons who are still at large and to accept the transfer of cases to national jurisdictions for trial in order to achieve the objective of completing investigations by the end of 2004, all trial activities at first instance by the end of 2008 and all cases on appeal by end of 2010.

In both Security Council Resolutions, the objectives remain accountability, deterrence and the promotion of national reconciliation and peace. It is against these objectives that the work of the ICTR will be evaluated today.

2. The key achievements of the ICTR

2.1 The context for evaluating the achievements

The United States Institute of Peace in early 1995 estimated at approximately 100–300, the number of persons who planned and organized the Rwandan genocide.[3] The Security Council in its Resolution 955 made no determination as to the range of culpable individuals, leaving it to its organ of international justice to do the due diligence required. However, the list published by the Rwandan Government in 2001 and revised in 2003 and 2005, containing the names of individuals sought for their involvement in the genocide, mentions approximately 300 individuals who live outside Rwanda.[4] This figure excludes persons already tried or currently appearing before the *Gacaca* courts.

Evidently, in debates on the evaluation of the legacy of the ICTR, the question of numbers comes up frequently, hence the need to advance a thought about this question, at this forum.

---

[1] SC Res. 955 (1994), 8 November 1994.

[2] SC Res. 1503 (1994), 28 August 2003.

[3] United States Institute of Peace, Special Report 13, January 1995.

[4] Official list published in 2001 and 2003, 1re Cat 13(1)03.2001.

History reminds us that in Nuremberg only 22 defendants were indicted with many suspects allowed to walk away avoiding prosecution. Essentially, suspects of non-German nationality avoided accountability for their crimes. Yet the legacy of Nuremberg as the catalyst in the evolving foundation for contemporary international criminal law on war crimes is a reality. The Special Court for Sierra Leone (SCSL) decided to indict only 13 individuals, attracting the criticism that it operated an overly narrow understanding of its own mandate.

Lessons in history teach modesty about what the law can accomplish – the law will never be a panacea for crimes perpetrated by mankind against his kind, just as criminal trials cannot be the only response to the criminality of mass atrocities. The case of Rwanda, where it was a recognized sovereign government that chose to murder its own citizens on a large scale or to acquiesce in their murder, is no exception. Admittedly, the notion of mass atrocities conjures up the idea of mass complicity. Nevertheless, the Rwandan experience informs us of an essential historical truth, which is that establishing an indisputable historical record of the planning and execution of the genocide at the highest level of the Rwandan State, is not predicated on the number of persons tried.[5] As an example, the single event of the confession before the ICTR and subsequent conviction of Prime Minister Jean Kambanda,[6] head of the government that presided over the genocide, had a domino effect that triggered several confessions in prisons inside Rwanda.

As we evaluate the achievements of the Tribunal, we need to focus the discussion on two essential questions, the first being what the Tribunal has contributed to the struggle to establish peace and security in Rwanda and the second, on the socio-politically level, the relevance of the Tribunal to the lives of persons who were affected by the heinous crimes perpetrated in Rwanda in 1994. To both questions, the view expressed in this paper is that the Tribunal is and continues to be an indispensable forum, in addition to the national courts of Rwanda, for the search for peace and justice for the victims of the crimes of 1994.

---

[5] Twenty-seven persons have been tried so far, the cases of 27 accused are ongoing, while 15 accused are in detention awaiting trial. Note the domino effect of Kambanda's confession and how it triggered several confessions in Rwandan prisons.

[6] See *Prosecutor* v. *Jean Kambanda*, Case No. ICTR 97-23-S, Judgment and Sentence, 4 September 1998. Kambanda affirmed that (a) his guilty was voluntary, (b) he clearly understood the charges against him and the consequences of his guilty plea, and (c) his guilty plea was unequivocal, in other words, the said plea could not be refuted by any line of defence.

2.2 The achievements

2.2.1 *Genocide*

The first judgment by an international court for the crime of genocide was delivered on 2 September 1998, by the ICTR in *Prosecutor* v. *Jean-Paul Akayesu*[7] Applying Article 2 of the Statute of the ICTR[8] which provides a definition of genocide similar to that in the Genocide Convention, the Trial Chamber found that the crime of genocide does not require the actual extermination of a group in its entirety. Genocide is committed once any of the prohibited acts mentioned in Article 2 is committed with the intent to destroy the group in whole or in part.[9] The Trial Chamber also found that genocide is unique among crimes because of its special intent or *dolus specialis* component. The special intent lies in the intent to wholly or partially destroy a national, ethnical, racial or religious group, as such.[10]

Since the rendering of the *Akayesu* judgment, the Tribunal has rendered judgments in the cases of twenty six other accused in which the crime of genocide, including its inchoate crimes, has been decided.[11] The precedent of *Akayesu* was followed by the ICTY when it delivered its first conviction for the crime of genocide on 2 August 2001 in the case of Radislav Kirstic. In that case, the Trial Chamber held that 'by deciding to kill all men of fighting age, a decision was taken to make it impossible for the Muslim people of Srebrenica to survive.'[12] Stated otherwise, what was ethnic cleansing became genocide.

---

[7] *Prosecutor* v. *Jean-Paul Akayesu*, ICTR-96-4-T, Judgment by Trial Chamber I, 2 September 1998.

[8] In article 2, the discriminatory intent must be on national, ethnical, racial or religious ground while the prohibited acts included *inter alia*, the killing of members of the group.

[9] *Prosecutor* v. *Jean-Paul Akayesu*, ICTR-96-4-T, Judgment by Trial Chamber I, 2 September 1998, Para. 497.

[10] *Akayesu* judgment, Para. 498.

[11] Art. 2, Para. 3 of the ICTR Statute punishes the following inchoate crimes: conspiracy to commit genocide, direct and public incitement to commit genocide, attempt to commit genocide and complicity in genocide. The ICTR has never indicted any one for attempt, favoring complicity with its component of aiding and abetting to achieve a conviction.

[12] Summary of the judgment of the ICTY in the Krstic case, quoted in M. Simons, 'General Guilty in Srebrenica Genocide', *The New York Times*, 3 August 2001, p. 1.

2.2.2 *Sexual violence and rape*

The *Akayesu* judgment represented the first time an individual was convicted by an International Tribunal for the crime of rape as a specific crime under the definition of crimes against humanity. The Nuremberg Charter did not criminalize rape.[13] The International Military Tribunal for the Far East, on its part, admitted evidence of sexual violence and rape against women of Nanking, the Philippines, etc but dealt with these atrocities as inhumane treatment under crimes against humanity.

The legal definition of rape provided in the *Akayesu* judgment represented a 'first' in International Humanitarian Law. In the judgment, the Trial Chamber stated:

> 'The Chamber defines rape as a physical invasion of a sexual nature, committed on a person under circumstances which are coercive. Sexual violence, which includes rape, is considered to be any act of a sexual nature which is committed on a person under circumstances which are coercive.'[14]

The *Akayesu* definition of rape, which was not disturbed by the Appeals Chamber of the ICTR and ICTY, has been cited by subsequent decisions in both *ad hoc* Tribunals, notably, in the ICTY cases of *Furundzija,*[15] *Celebici*[16] and *Kunarac*[17] even though the ICTY continues to favor the conservative judicial approach that defines rape in terms of body parts.[18]

Finally, the *Akayesu* judgment made judicial history by defining rape as an act of genocide. This ruling derived from the finding that rape was systematically used as a weapon in the campaign to destroy the Tutsi by violating Tutsi women and whether the victims died in course of the rapes or were just simply killed, the clear intent established was to kill or inflict mental or bodily harm as part of the process of destroying an ethnic group in whole or in part.

---

[13] See paper by K. Chiedu Moghalu: 'No peace without justice: The role of the International Criminal/Humanitarian Law in Conflict Settlement and Reconciliation', 2001, p. 17.

[14] Akayesu judgment, paragraphs 596-598.

[15] *Prosecutor* v. *Anto Furundzija*, Case No. IT-95-17/I-T, Judgment, 10 December 1998.

[16] *Prosecutor* v. *Delalic et al,* Case No. IT-96-21-T, Judgement, 16 November 1998.

[17] *Prosecutor* v. *Kunarac et al*, Case No. IT-96-23/2, Judgment, 22 February 2001.

[18] See *Furundzija* judgment, op. cit., where the ICTY's Trial Chamber II reviewed national laws on rape 'to arrive at an accurate definition of rape based on the criminal law principle of specificity' (Para. 177).

Following *Akayesu,* there have been other cases before the International Criminal Tribunal for Rwanda in which charges of rape were proffered against accused persons. The current OTP record on the prosecution of rape and sexual violence related crimes is as follows:

i. 5 of the 27 accused in completed cases;
ii. 19 of the 27 accused currently on trial; and
iii. 8 of the 15 accused awaiting trial.[19]

By equating rape to genocide and meting out appropriate punishment, the Tribunal's jurisprudence has contributed in a significant manner in highlighting the particularly evil nature of the crime and eased the process of closure for the victims.

2.2.3 *No sovereign immunity for genocide – the case of Prime Minister Jean Kambanda*

The international community, through the ICTR, made a strong statement in the *Kambanda* judgment[20] to the effect that 'sovereign impunity' will no longer be explained away under the 'act of state doctrine', otherwise known as sovereign immunity.

Prime Minister Jean Kambanda was head of the Interim Government in place from 8 April 1994 until about 17 July 1994, the period of the genocide. He was arrested and handed over to Tribunal officials in July 1997 and indicted for Genocide, Conspiracy to Commit Genocide, Direct and Public Incitement to Commit Genocide, Complicity in Genocide, and Crimes against Humanity. In the pleadings, the Prosecution also alleged that as Prime Minister he exercised *de jure* and *de facto* authority and control over the members of his government, senior civil servants including *Préfets* (regional governors), and senior officers in the military and that he incited massacres of Tutsi and moderate Hutu at public meetings and through the media.

---

[19] See article by Dr. Alex Obote-Odora, 'Rape and Sexual Violence in International Law: ICTR Contribution', 12/1 *New England Journal of International and Comparative Law* (2005) p. 134.

[20] See *Kambanda* judgment, Case No. ICTR 97-23-S, 4 September 1998. The Appeals Chamber confirmed the judgment and sentence on 19 October 2000, thus sending a strong message against sovereign impunity.

On 1 May 1998, at his initial appearance before the ICTR, Kambanda pleaded guilty to the six counts on which he was indicted. Based on his guilty plea, he was convicted and sentenced to life imprisonment on 4 September 1998, which sentence was confirmed by the Appeals Chamber on 19 October 2000.

The *Kambanda* case was thus the first confession by an individual for the crime of genocide, fifty years after the Genocide Convention. It confirmed that the criminal enterprise that was Rwanda's genocide was a State-sponsored plan aimed at wiping out the country's ethnic minority.[21] *Kambanda's* confession destroyed the credibility, such as existed, of a small number of revisionist historians and lawyers in certain quarters who claimed that there was no genocide in Rwanda. As stated earlier, the confession and judgment had an impact on the more than 100,000 genocide suspects imprisoned in Rwanda's jails by triggering a significant number of confessions from some of these suspects in the immediate aftermath of the judgment.

On the international scene, the *Kambanda* judgment was cited by human rights groups in the case against General Augusto Pinochet, former Head of State of Chile, when in 1998, the House of Lords in the United Kingdom ruled that the General was not immune from prosecution for international crimes such as crimes against humanity, torture and hostage-taking, overruling a lower court.[22] The *Kambanda* judgment also served as a precedent for the 1999 indictment by the Hague Tribunal, of Slobodan Milosevic, former President of the Federal Republic of Yugoslavia.

3. THE CHALLENGES

3.1 Determining whom to indict

In the discharge of the Prosecutor's functions under the ICTR Statute,[23] determining whom to indict is a significant challenge which calls for the exer-

[21] See K. Chiedu Moghalu, 'Rwanda Panel's Legacy: They Can Run But Not Hide', *International Herald Tribune*, 31 October-1 November 1998, p. 6.

[22] *Regina* v. *Bartle and the Commissioner of Police and Others* (Appellants) *Ex Parte* Pinochet (Respondent); Evans and Another and the Commissioner of Police and Others (Appellants) *Ex Parte* Pinochet (Respondent), Decision of the House of Lords on appeal from a Divisional Court of the Queen's Bench Division, 25 November 1998.

[23] Arts. 15(2), 17(4) and 18(1) of the ICTR Statute.

cise of prosecutorial discretion. The said Statute provides the juridical bases for the exercise of this power, yet the power is not absolute.[24]

At the pretrial stage, the Prosecutor must submit his indictment to a Confirming Judge for review and if the evidence therein establishes a *prima facie* case, the indictment will be confirmed. Where the threshold in not met, the Prosecutor may have to, *inter alia*, resubmit the indictment with additional information to the Confirming Judge.

At the trial stage, in the case of amendment of an indictment with the inclusion of additional charges,[25] the Prosecutor must also seek the approval of the Trial Chamber.

Additionally, since the coming into force of Resolution 1503 in August 2003, the need to review and arrive at a realistic workload that can be achieved within the deadlines imposed has meant that the boundaries for the exercise of the Prosecutor's discretionary powers have become arguably narrower. In the selection of targets, for instance, the Prosecutor must undertake a higher standard of review for quality and strength of evidence, and make a judgment on the chances of securing a conviction before retaining the case for trial.[26] This implies that only the most serious cases are being retained for trial at the Tribunal.

So far, a former prime minister, several cabinet ministers, senior military officers, MRND leaders and civil administrators have been indicted and have either been tried, are on trial, or are awaiting trial in Arusha. In the list of indictees at large, the same category of individuals appears. The Prosecutor's selection of cases for trial continues to take into account the fact that almost every administrative unit of the country was affected, hence the need for geographical spread with regard to the targets and the crime scenes. Obvi-

---

[24] See H.B. Jallow, 'Prosecutorial Discretion and International Criminal Justice', 3 *Journal of International Criminal Justice* (2005) pp. 145-161.

[25] In *Akayesu,* the Prosecutor's original indictment confirmed on 16 February 1997, did not contain a rape charge. The testimonies of two women during the trial, showed graphic references of sexual violence against Tutsi women during the genocide, and in the case of Akayesu, some of the incidents occurred in the Bureau Communal. As a result of these testimonies the Prosecutor conducted further investigations and amended the indictment during the trial on 17 June 1997, specifically charging Akayesu, *inter alia*, with rape as a Crime against Humanity in Count 13 of the indictment and rape as a Violation of Art. 3 common to the Geneva Conventions in Count 15. The Trial Chamber accepted the amendment.

[26] See Art. 18 of the Statute.

ously, in the exercise of his functions, the Prosecutor has a duty to be fair and to some critics, the fact that only Hutus have so far been prosecuted calls into question the impartiality of the Prosecutor.

In the *Ntakirutimana* case,[27] in response to the claim that the Prosecutor was engaged in selective prosecution, it was held that the Defence had failed to establish by evidence that the Prosecutor had a discriminatory or otherwise unlawful or improper motive in indicting the accused. Judge Shahabuddeen in his separate opinion in *Barayagwiza (2nd Appeal),* reiterated that the Prosecutor is a party to a case although he is not partisan. The Judge went on to state that by requiring the Prosecutor to disclose all exculpatory information, for instance, the Rules ensure that Prosecutors bear themselves 'in the character of ministers of justice' assisting in the administration of justice.[28]

3.2 The trial process

Another area of significant challenge is the trial process. The Prosecutor wins his case when justice is done, whether the verdict is 'guilty' or 'not guilty' and in this regard, it must be said that the highest priority is that the truth be told. The need to respect due process and the right of the accused to a fair trial, has resulted in trials often being lengthy and slow. Yet a slow trial that guarantees respect for the rule of law, and in the case of Rwanda, that leads to accountability, is preferred to the rule of force.

The *Kambanda* trial represented accountability for political leadership at the national level. At the Provincial level Prefect Kayishema was held accountable. Akayezu at the community level took responsibility for his crimes at the level of the *Commune*. Thus, even though the ICTR is criticized for being slow, its contribution to a new situation of peace in Rwanda is evident in the healing process that its trials bring.

Unlike at the International Criminal Court (ICC),[29] the victims of Rwanda, given the horrors they survived and the pain they continue to suffer, are not

[27] Decision on the Prosecutor's Motion to Join the Indictments, *Ntakirutimana* (ICTR-96-10-I and ICTR-96-17-T), Trial Chamber, 22 February 2001, Paras. 870-887.

[28] Separate opinion of judge Shahabuddeen, Decision, Barayagwiza (ICTR-97-19-AR72), Appeal Chamber, 31 March 2000, Para. 68.

[29] Art. 68 (3), Rome Statute. This provision was meant to be an improvement on the failure of the ICTR Statute to bring victims into the trial process.

part of the trial process. Such lack of participation by the persons most affected by the greatest crimes of the 20th Century, evidently posed major challenges to the legacy of the ICTR. One key way the Tribunal has sought to address the discussion in this area is through the outreach program which was put in place in 1999 by the Tribunal. The outreach program has improved dissemination of vital information about the trial process to the people of Rwanda, in the expectation of advancing the healing process and today, that program is also involved in capacity building for the Rwandan judiciary.

4. Towards completing the mandate

4.1 Cooperation with States

For the Prosecutor to adequately discharge his mandate under the relevant UN Security Council Resolutions,[30] it is essential that Member States of the UN cooperate with the Tribunal in two key areas. First, in the area of arresting and transferring indicted fugitives and secondly, in accepting cases for transfer to national jurisdictions for trial.

With no police force and prisons of its own, the ICTR concept was founded on cooperation with member states. Article 28(2) of the Statute deals with cooperation and judicial assistance and makes it mandatory for States to comply without undue delay with any request for assistance in the identification and location of persons, the taking of testimony and production of evidence, the service of documents, arrest or detention of persons and the surrender or the transfer of the accused to the International Criminal Tribunal for Rwanda.

Security Council Resolution 1503 urged all States, within the imperatives of the completion strategy, to cooperate with the ICTR in apprehending all indicted persons who are still at large. With currently 18 indicted fugitives at large, among them political, military and administrative leaders and planners of the genocide, it is important that States cooperate in arresting and delivering them for trial. One notes the political and military support received by the ICTY in the search for Karadic and Mladic and would only have hoped for similar support for the ICTR notably in the arrest of the likes of Felicien Kabuga, a leading mastermind of the Rwanda genocide, as alleged in his indictment.

---

[30] Art. 2, Security Council Resolution 955 November 1994 and 1503 August 2003.

In relation to transfer of cases for trial by national courts, cooperation from States is vital. Rule 11 *bis* of the ICTR Rules provides for referral of the indictment to a national court. It provides that if an indictment has been confirmed, whether or not the accused is in the custody of the Tribunal, the President may designate a Trial Chamber which shall determine whether the case should be referred to the authorities of a State. The States concerned will be those in whose territory the crime was committed, those in which the accused was arrested or those having jurisdiction and being willing and adequately prepared to accept such a case.

It is noted here that several states in Africa, Europe and North America have extended cooperation to the ICTR as envisaged by the Statute of the ICTR. Individuals sought by the Tribunal have been arrested and transferred from Belgium, Benin, Burkina Faso, Cameroon, Cote d'Ivoire, Denmark, France, Kenya, Mali, Namibia, the Netherlands, South Africa, Switzerland, Tanzania, Togo, the United Kingdom, the United States and Zambia. In view of the imperatives of the completion strategy imposed by Resolution 1503, for the Prosecutor to complete his mandate States need to accept to take on some of the cases of the 15 persons currently awaiting trial and the cases of the 18 fugitives who have been indicted.

On 15 February 2006, the Prosecutor filed his first motion under Rule 11 *bis,* requesting the Trial Chamber to transfer the case of Michel Bagaragaza to the Kingdom of Norway for trial. The indictment against Bagaragaza was confirmed on 28 July 2005, and he surrendered to the Tribunal on 16 August 2005 and pleaded not guilty to charges of genocide, conspiracy to commit genocide and complicity in genocide, whereupon he was transferred the detention unit of the ICTY in the Hague. As the Prosecutor recalled in his motion for transfer, the UN Security Council mandated both *ad hoc* Tribunals in Arusha and The Hague on 28 August 2003, to conclude all trials at first instance by 2008. Resolution 1503 specifically requests that the transfer of cases to national courts be an element of the completion strategy.

Whereas the ICTY has gone ahead with plans to transfer 14 or more defendants to Bosnia and 2 to Croatia under conditions stipulated in the Rule 11 *bis of* the ICTR Statute, the ICTR has not yet found many willing States. Rwanda has, however, offered to try some of the cases, but it is yet to provide the required guarantees, such as the guarantee that the death penalty will not be applied and that the trials conducted inside the country will be free and fair.

The Prosecutor continues to make the argument that transfers to national jurisdictions other than Rwanda provide for a wider understanding of how the genocide occurred and will improve the process of development of ideas on prevention, deterrence and effective intervention. These transfers and prosecutions in national courts also effectively counter the voices that deny that there was genocide in Rwanda in 1994, or dismiss it as a spontaneous eruption of inter-ethnic violence.

4.2 **Guilty pleas**

Confessions or guilty pleas will significantly advance the work of the Tribunal in the context of the completion strategy. So far, the Tribunal has rendered judgment on guilty pleas in four cases,[31] and is yet to deliver sentence in regard to two other cases that are pending.[32] Critics have charged that guilty pleas deprive the public of an accurate portrayal of the criminal behavior that is being punished. Others emphasize the powerful incentives plea bargaining provides to Prosecutors, Defense Attorneys, and Judges to sacrifice the interests they are charged to protect in favor of expediency. Still others charge that plea bargaining can result in excessive leniency for dangerous defendants and excessive punishment for defendants who exercise their right to trial.[33]

Yet the advantages are obvious. Quite apart from the administrative and cost reducing component of guilty pleas, truth-telling is a valuable means of promoting healing and reconciliation. The Trial Chambers have considered a guilty plea as evidence of honesty[34] and of an 'acknowledgement of [the defendant's] mistakes and crimes,' which 'is a healthy application of reason and sentiment'.[35] In other words, guilty pleas that are motivated by sincere remorse and a genuine acknowledgement of wrong-doing are much more likely to encourage dialogue and forgiveness.

Kambanda himself provides a perfect example. Before being sentenced, Kambanda

---

[31] *Kambanda* in 1998, *Serushago* in 1999, *Ruggiu* in 2000 and *Rutaganira* in 2005.

[32] Sentencing in the cases of *Bisengimana* and *Serugendo* is pending.

[33] Alschuler, *Implementing the Criminal Defendant's Right to Trial,* at pp. 726-728.

[34] *Prosecutor* v. *Erdemović*, ICTY Case No. IT-96-22-T, Sentencing Judgment, March 5, 1998, Para. 16(ii); *Ruggiu* Sentencing Judgement, at Para. 55.

[35] *Ruggiu* Sentencing Judgement, at Para. 55.

> 'declare[d] that his prime motivation for pleading guilty [was his] profound desire to tell the truth ... [and] his desire to contribute to the process of national reconciliation.'[36]

Building on this theme at the pre-sentencing hearing, Kambanda's lawyer read a letter from a woman whose husband and three children were killed in the genocide. After recounting her loss, she stated:

> '[N]aturally, I would always have reasons to hate you until the end of my days. I have every reason to become an extremist. However, your [guilty plea] rekindles hope in me particularly because the perpetrators of the genocide if they recognize their guilt, reconciliation among Rwandans would become inevitable.' [sic][37]

5. Conclusion

Of course, no criminal justice system lacks difficulties or critics. Yet thanks to the ICTR and as the Rwandan tragedy once more demonstrates, the enterprise of justice is a collaborative effort between the victim society and the wider international community. By virtue of the instruments of international cooperation among States, persons otherwise out of the reach of Rwandan justice have been brought to court and have accounted for their crimes. These achievements have been possible through ICTR jurisprudence that has contributed to peace and reconciliation through individualization of guilt as opposed to collective criminalization, a process that blocks avenues for reconciling and bringing peace to fractured societies.

> 'If there is no establishment of who is guilty, that means there is no establishment of who is innocent' Des Forges said. 'That leads to a globalization of guilt-that all Hutus are guilty-and the consequence of that for any kind of future reconciliation is of course, very, very serious.'[38]

---

[36] *Kambanda* Plea Agreement, at Paras. 4-5.

[37] *Kambanda* Transcript, at 28.

[38] 'Rwanda, Ten Years Later: Justice Is Elusive Despite Peace', by Stefan Lovgren, for *National Geographic News*, April 6, 2004.

Chapter 13
THE IMPORTANCE OF TRUTH AND RECONCILIATION COMMISSIONS TO THE PROCESS OF RE-ESTABLISHING A NEW SITUATION OF PEACE AND SECURITY IN RWANDA

Howard Varney*

1. Introduction

Countries emerging from periods of armed conflict or authoritarian rule have typically suffered significant violations of human rights and humanitarian norms. Sometimes the scale of violations has been massive such as in Rwanda.

'Transitional justice' is the field that has developed as a response to the dilemma of what to do about the past. The aim of transitional justice is to confront legacies of abuse in a broad and holistic manner that encompasses criminal and restorative justice. It recognizes that a responsible justice policy must include measures that seek to achieve both accountability for past crimes and the prevention of new crimes. It is also recognizes that the demand for criminal justice is not an absolute, but must instead be balanced with the need for peace, democracy, development and the rule of law.

The reality is that countries recovering from periods of mass abuse face the almost certain prospect of 'flawed justice.' In a number of cases, transitional governments are effectively forced to choose between justice and the continuation of peace. Even where such threats are less prominent, the massive scale of past abuse, the weakness of the local justice system, the adop-

* Advocate, South Africa. Former Chief Investigator, Sierra Leone Truth & Reconciliation Commission. Consultant, Truth & Reconciliation Commission, South Africa.

O. Ribbelink (ed.), Beyond the UN Charter: Peace, Security and the Role of Justice

tion of amnesty laws, and severe limitations in human and financial resources often make ordinary justice impossible. For the fact is that justice systems are designed for crime as an exception, not a rule. If crime becomes the rule, no system is robust enough to cope. Consequently, in most if not all transitional justice contexts, other tools of accountability will be required, going well beyond the courts.

In theory and in practice, transitional justice focuses on four main mechanisms: trials (whether civil or criminal, national or international), fact-finding bodies (such as truth commissions), reparations (whether symbolic or restitutionary) and justice reforms (including reforms of laws, institutions and vetting of personnel). Transitional justice also encompasses other topics such as amnesty, disarmament, the combating of corruption and achieving national reconciliation.

The path of each transition, whether it was brought about by foreign intervention, negotiation between the parties, or armed resistance, determines to some extent the prospect of consolidating democracy or peace and, in turn, the prospect of advancing reconciliation.[1]

2. Key lessons

A key lesson learned from past experiences is that the pursuit of transitional justice is in most cases highly beneficial. The most 'successful' democratic and post-conflict transitions have been those in which successor governments have, at some risk and against the odds, made a bona fide attempt to confront the abuses of the past.

Successor governments should generally endeavour to make the most of transitional 'moments', when significant international resources and attention are focused on the country and when political and social backing for transitional justice measures is often at its peak.

Successor governments should not put expediency ahead of principle in dealing with past crimes. If there is to be a true break with the past, then justice, whether retributive or restorative must be meted out fairly.

Successor governments should endeavour to keep public expectations in check. Much can go wrong – important trials can be lost, truth commission

[1] This section has been adapted from a policy briefing paper prepared by Mark Freeman, 'Reconciliation in Times of Transition: The Role of Parliaments and Inter-Parliamentary Bodies', March 2004.

recommendations are often ignored, victim compensation can be unaffordable and reconciliation can be slow or superficial.

Successor governments should not lose sight of the complex relationships among transitional justice mechanisms. For example, it may or may not be desirable: to allow sharing of information between courts and truth commissions; or to commence with commissions or trials before a process of disarmament, demobilization and reintegration has concluded; or to empower a truth commission to grant amnesty or provide compensation. These and other issues deserve careful consideration from the outset to ensure complimentary rather than conflicting relationships between mechanisms, and to guard against public confusion over their purpose and operation.[2]

3. Truth commissions

The mechanism most closely associated with transitional justice is the truth commission. Truth commissions are temporary non-judicial fact-finding bodies, usually in operation for one to two years. Typically they are established and empowered by the state, usually at moments of democratic or post-conflict transition. Truth commissions focus on the investigation of patterns as well as specific instances of past human rights abuse committed during a defined period. They operate in a victim-centered fashion, and usually conclude their work with the delivery of a final report containing findings and recommendations.

While truth commissions may not be appropriate in every context, they have the potential to assist societies in transition. Under optimal conditions they may help establish the truth about the nature and scale of past human rights violations, and serve as a guard against nationalist or revisionist accounts of the past. They may foster the accountability of perpetrators by collecting and preserving evidence and publicly identifying those responsible. They may recommend detailed victim reparations programs and necessary legal and institutional reforms. Truth commissions can also provide a public platform for victims to directly address the nation with their personal stories. They can inform and catalyze public debate about how to deal with the past and how to ensure a better future. And they can cultivate reconciliation and tolerance at the individual and national level.[3]

---

[2] Ibid.
[3] Ibid.

4. ARE TRUTH COMMISSIONS A SUBSTITUTE FOR JUSTICE?

There is no clear answer to this question. It is certainly true that some truth commissions were created in contexts where it was not possible to seek justice or even unwise to do so. In this sense there are cases of truth commissions acting as substitutes for justice. This has sometimes been the experience in Africa. In Latin America while truth commissions and investigations into disappearances may have been viewed initially as a substitute for justice, many of those commissions in fact recommended the vigorous prosecutions of offenders. Human rights activists in countries such as Argentina, Chile and Peru have been fighting long battles to achieve the delivery of justice, with a measure of success. We have experienced situations where truth commissions (or similar bodies) have operated without criminal justice follow up; where criminal justice initiatives have taken place without a wider a truth initiative; where attempts have been made to carry out both truth and justice initiatives simultaneously; and where it was decided to do neither.

4.1 **Hard choices**

Commissions are set up at times because of the inability to deliver criminal justice due to lack of resources and skills *or* because the justice process is curtailed to keep the peace *or* it is excluded to end war. In most post conflict countries there is little or no prospect of taking most cases to court. In some countries, such as South Africa, the commission process with its truth for amnesty formula was designed because of the need to keep the peace process on track and because of the impracticality of taking all cases to court. In other countries like Sierra Leone – the court process was initially excluded in order to end bloody conflict. That commission was seen as an alternate means of holding role-players accountable.

4.2 **Addressing impunity**

It should be noted that impunity is not only addressed through the courts. A truth commission that engages in thorough research and investigation can play a significant role in tackling impunity. A truth commission can do this by assigning responsibility for abuses and violations through a meticulous process of 'naming names'. When the public and indeed the world are aware of who did what in the conflict it will have a major impact on the standing and reputation of those implicated. Pressure will be placed on senior perpetrators to relinquish or not to assume positions of authority. Their room for maneuver will be substantially limited. While there is no doubt that the most effective means of addressing impunity is through the courts we should recognise the severe limitations under which they operate. Justice is a cumbersome and expensive affair. The donor community has reached something of a funding fatigue after pouring of hundreds of millions of dollars into international criminal tribunals and other international courts.

4.3 Historical fidelity

Even when there is a robust judicial response to crimes of the past it does not necessarily do away with the need for a detailed examination of the wider facts, which truth commissions offer. In courts little judicial notice is taken of context and background unless it can be shown to be directly relevant to the proving or disproving of an element of the crime. Most courts will prefer to paint the context in broad sweeps rather than in detail. Courts generally deal with a very small number of cases and in those cases, a relatively small number of counts. Dealing with a small number of incidents makes it difficult for a Court, constrained to apply a stringent standard of proof, to draw conclusions on patterns of violations. Prosecutions cannot be relied upon to supply the impartial historical record of a conflict. While prosecutions ought to be strategic in that they should illustrate patterns of violations and they ought to expose the chain of command we should look to other mechanisms, not constrained by the legal process, to provide the full context, history and patterns.

4.4 Integrated approach

There is much to be said for an integrated approach involving both truth commissions and courts, so long as they are carefully designed and planned so as not to produce conflicts of objectives and interests. There are different models and formulas that can be explored involving demarcating areas of responsibility along mandated periods of time or categories of crimes Prosecutions and other transitional justice mechanisms can work side by side dealing with all matters over the same time period if their objectives are properly harmonized. For example, a truth and reconciliation process can identify those cases where a prosecution would be inappropriate; it can also produce deserving cases that are ripe for prosecution.

It seems to me, however, that there is room for both responses in virtually all circumstances. We need however to be alive to the limitations of the truth and justice options and to employ them in a way that best meets the needs and demands of the country at hand. To simply drop both into the mix without such preparation is to invite failure.

5. A TRC for Rwanda?

When posing the question of whether a TRC should be set up for Rwanda, many will ask whether a truth process can ever be commensurate with the massive level of criminality that took place in Rwanda?[4] In short, can a truth commission adequately address the gravity of crimes such as genocide? The question is however somewhat academic, as aside from the international justice efforts through the ICTR, Rwanda itself has opted for a domestic justice model through its national tribunals and the *Gacaca* tribunals. The question then is really whether there is a role for a truth commission in Rwanda, over and above the justice measures, or as a complementary body to the institutions of retributive justice.

It is arguable that the Rwandan approach to transitional justice already, and more than adequately, incorporates the objectives of truth seeking and national reconciliation through the *Gacaca* tribunals, the National Unity and Reconciliation Commission and the Rwandan Demobilisation and Reintegration Commission. The Unity and Reconciliation Commission was established to build unity and reconciliation and the *Gacaca* courts were established to facilitate the search for truth and justice.

Rwanda has firmly placed justice as the key pillar upon which reconciliation rests. In justifying this approach, Antoine Rutayisire, the Vice-President, National Unity and Reconciliation Commission has distinguished the circumstances of Rwanda from other conflicts. Rutayisire says that

> '…the South African Truth and Reconciliation Commission was hailed as a great success by the whole world, it became like a trend and many countries now recovering from traumatic experiences like Sierra Leone, Burundi, even Kenya want to embrace it. Many have even been asking why Rwanda is not adopting the same approach as it proved expedient and effective for South Africa.

---

[4] R. Brody, 'Justice: The First Casualty of Truth?', *The Nation*, 30 April, 2001.

One great mistake people make in apprehending the Rwanda problem is to look at it, as just another genocide, and equate its solutions to the solutions that have been used for other mass crimes and genocides. But the Rwandan situation presents some specific particularities that make it unique.

1. One, the genocide was not just a political or military system that was turned against the victims like in the case of the Holocaust in Germany or the Khmer Rouges in Cambodia. The Rwandan genocide was so well organised and turned neighbours against neighbours, husbands against wives and parents against their own children. This complicates the matter of justice and reconciliation
2. The second particularity is that the genocide was stopped not by external forces as in most of the other cases but by part of the Rwandese population. The RPF was primarily made up of a majority of Tutsi and their victory was not hailed and celebrated by the world but was rather criticised....
3. The third great particularity is that the family of the killers and even the killers themselves have to live next to the survivors …'.[5]

The argument is compelling and there is no doubt that the Rwandan experience demands an entirely different response to that adopted in South Africa. Whether the peculiarities of the Rwandan experience completely excludes a truth seeking exercise separate or complimentary to the justice model is another matter. This question perhaps warrants further consideration.

5.1 Falling short of the wider truth

The Rwandan transitional initiatives have been criticised for failing to advance the cause of national reconciliation for not exploring the wider truth behind the appalling atrocities of the early and mid 1990s. It has been pointed out that the 1994 genocide was a culmination of cyclical violence and mass killings that started as early 1959. Indeed some point to the roots of the violence starting in colonial times. The justice initiatives are unlikely to cover these periods in any detail. It does not appear that the international or domestic justice programme will deal with the waves of violence perpetrated by Tutsi led forces against Hutu targets.[6] It appears then that the facts of key

[5] A. Rutayisire, 'Achieving Justice: Truth and Reconciliation', Paper presented at the Seminar for Journalists organised by the United Nations Foundations and Quest Limited at the Intercontinental Hotel, Kigali, 26 June 2004.

[6] J.K. Sebarenzi, 'Rwanda: The Fundamental Obstacles to Reconciliation', 3 *GSC Quarterly* (Winter 2002).

aspects and periods of the wider story will not be interrogated and tested by a formally constituted inquiry. In short, it appears that the full story will not be told.

5.2 Falling short of reconciliation

Joseph K. Sebarenzi, a former speaker of the Rwandan Parliament, writes that each past regime, be it Hutu-dominated or Tutsi-dominated, established a system of structural violence against the other ethnic group that operated through physical violence, exclusion, humiliation, and inequality. He states further that a reconciliation process is needed to resolve the different contentions of the various parties, to provide a public accounting of the truth, to permit acknowledgment of harm suffered by all sides and ultimately to break the cycle of violence.[7]

Another critical concern regarding the *Gacaca* system revolves around the fact that the courts, in trying only crimes connected to the genocide, ignore the many documented war crimes attributed to the Rwandan Patriotic Army (RPA), responsible for bringing an end to the genocide. Observers note that the failure to broaden the jurisdiction of *Gacaca* courts to include other war crimes has resulted in the widespread impression in some quarters that the *Gacaca* courts represent little more than 'victor's justice,' and have thus led to demoralisation amongst those whose participation is fundamental to the courts.[8] Such perceptions have seriously eroded efforts to reach national reconciliation.

It is understandable that fear and suspicion pervades in Rwandan Society. These facts together with the nature of the *Gacaca* trials, where security, intimidation and fear of retaliation remain as issues, explain why some participants in the process are reluctant to speak out. Related to this is the failure to link the *Gacaca* process to a disarmament process of both civilians and ex-combatants within Rwanda, which is normally an essential ingredient of post-conflict peace building and reconstruction.[9]

---

[7] Ibid.

[8] N. Alusala, 'Disarmament and Reconciliation: Rwanda's Concerns', Institute of Security Studies, Occasional Paper 108, June 2005.

[9] Ibid.

5.3 **Practical considerations**

Finally there is the practical consideration of the sheer scale of the genocide. With approximately a million fatalities there is simply no prospect of bringing meaningful justice in the vast majority of cases. It has been estimated that some 32,000 prisoners who made confessions in 2002 incriminated approximately 250,000 other persons as accomplices. Attempting to diligently investigate a quarter of a million leads would overwhelm any system of justice.

6. CONCLUSION

There may very well be place for a truth and reconciliation commission, or perhaps expanding the role of the Unity and Reconciliation Commission, in the context of post genocide Rwanda. Such an exercise could be aimed at producing an impartial historical record not only of the genocide and its aftermath but also to trace the roots of conflict in Rwanda. In other words it would need to investigate the causes of conflict and genocide in Rwanda for purposes of making recommendations to ensure that such horrendous crimes never occur again. In this sense it not only deals with the past events but looks towards building a future in which the past is not repeated. It would need to be scrupulously independent and objective to ensure that its findings and recommendations are credible. While such a commission ought to strive to provide a platform where victims and perpetrators can feel free to come forward to tell their stories in a non-threatening environment, the thrust of the inquiries ought to be aimed at identifying trends and patterns and ultimately in providing the totality of the story. A truth commission could recommend a comprehensive package or reparations to redress the wrongs suffered by victims. Such a package could potentially be supported by the international community. A truth and reconciliation process should not be an alternative to the justice initiatives but should rather complement them. In so doing it may fill the lacunas in the current process and play a significant role in nation building and post conflict reconstruction.

